The TRUTH About
PUBLIC
SPEAKING

The **3** Keys to Great Presentations

ED BARKS

OGMIOS PUBLISHING

Praise for *The Truth About Public Speaking*

"I wish I had had the benefit of Ed Barks' advice when I was president of the National Press Club in 1973. Most journalists write better than they speak. As it was, I perfected public speaking the hard way before a tough audience, introducing prominent persons ranging from foreign heads of state and U.S. officials to entertainment personalities at some sixty luncheons. We were broadcast on public radio. Today, everything goes out on C-SPAN, and I would need the benefit of all those nonverbal skills that make a big difference as Ed so clearly demonstrates."

—DONALD R. LARRABEE
Former President, National Press Club

"For thirty years, my business success has been linked to effective presentations. If I had known Ed Barks when I started my business, I'd be on top today. Reading this book is like putting money in a savings account—it will pay dividends for years."

—COLBURN AKER
The Aker Partners

"The truth is that many public speakers think they are better than they really are. *The Truth About Public Speaking* gives the reader simple, real-life tips on how to successfully prepare for an effective presentation."

—PHIL SPARKS
Vice President, Communications Consortium Media Center

"As one who has given more than my share of public speeches, I can attest to the wisdom of Ed's book and its need to be part of your resource library to be used often. He focuses on the need to be prepared for any situation as best you can and to deliver on your mission. He also provides some very practical yet sometimes forgotten tips—like to be sure your portable microphone is turned off when you go to really private places!!"

—JAMES W. DYKE, JR.
Partner, McGuire Woods LLP, and former
Secretary of Education for the Commonwealth of Virginia

"Ed's book is a tremendously valuable and cost-effective resource for those engaged in any form of human communication."

—OFIELD DUKES, APR
Fellow Public Relations Society of America

"In today's business environment, three skills are necessary for survival and advancement: Public speaking, writing, and diplomacy. If you seek a competitive edge in public speaking and want to step into the winner's circle with confidence, *The Truth About Public Speaking* can help you get there. Learn from a master and position yourself for professional success."

—**DONNA VINCENT ROA**, PhD, ABC
Sr. Global Communication Officer, Water and Sanitation Program,
World Bank, and former president of the International Association of
Business Communicators, DC Chapter

"I've seen it time and again. Those who master their communications skills succeed. They get the promotions and the big raises, and their businesses grow more steadily. Yes, *The Truth About Public Speaking* helps put you in the winner's circle."

—**TOM ANTION**
http://www.Public-Speaking.org

"Hundreds of valuable ideas, and techniques for making better presentations leap off the pages of Ed Barks' new book: *The Truth About Public Speaking*. As one who has worked with many people charged with delivering important messages, I would recommend this book as an important tool that deserves a place on your desk—anyone from PTA president to corporate executive. It is loaded with useful counsel and good ideas. It will help in deciding your message, the selection of spokesperson and how to know if you have reached that audience successfully."

—**HARLAND W. WARNER**
Past President, Public Relations Society of America

"Ed Barks has taken his vast experience as a top-tier communications coach and turned it into a gift for anyone who speaks publicly. This clearly written book is loaded with good ideas, certainly. But its greatest value is its breadth. As Ed notes, the task of improving one's public speaking is a holistic endeavor. As such, it calls upon the whole person to take on a broad array of skills and abilities. Ed makes integrating all of the elements of high-performance public speaking look easy. Very simply, if you had time to read only one book on how to improve your public speaking skills, this would be the one to read."

—**THOMAS G. GODDARD**, JD, PhD
President & CEO, Integral Healthcare Solutions

"If you are looking for the unvarnished truth, a hard look at your fears, and a game plan to run with, you owe it to yourself to read *The Truth About Public Speaking.*"

—MIKE FANDEY
Training Director, Duron Paints and Wallcoverings

"Ed Barks knows that before you can win hearts and minds, you have to win eyes and ears. His book gives you a thorough grounding in the ways to do just that. You'll want to buy this book to polish your own presentation skills—and you may want to pass it along to your boss."

—HELEN L. MITTERNIGHT
President, Mitternight Communications

"Having done countless interviews and numerous presentations, I found myself nodding affirmation as I read each chapter. This is what you need to know to make that grand-slam presentation."

—MARK A. S. OSWELL
Chairman and Founder, Capital Communicators Group (DC)

"The text offers no-nonsense, straightforward and practical advice to speakers of every stripe and at every level."

—JANE CABOT
Executive Vice President, M Booth & Associates

"If you ever speak before groups of people, think that someday you might have to do so, of you have promised yourself that you will never, ever speak to more than two people at a time, you need to read this book—and then you need to read it again."

—WILLIAM H. MCCARTNEY, JD
Past President, National Association of Insurance Commissioners

"It's simple. The Three Keys to Great Presentations system works. Following these guidelines really heightens your public speaking abilities."

—KIMO KIPPEN
Vice President, Human Resources, Renaissance Hotels, North America

The Truth About Public Speaking
The Three Keys to Great Presentations
By Edward J. Barks

Published by:

Ogmios Publishing
P.O. Box 132
Berryville, Virginia 22611
ogmiospublishing@adelphia.net
www.ogmiospublishing.com

ISBN 0-9742538-5-5

Printed in the United States of America

This publication is designed to provide accurate and authoritative information in regard to the subject matter covered. It is sold with the understanding that the publisher is not engaged in rendering legal, accounting, or other professional service. If legal advice or other expert assistance is required, the services of a competent professional person should be sought.

> —From a Declaration of Principles jointly adopted
> by a committee of the American Bar Association
> and a Committee of Publishers and Associations

Library of Congress Control Number: 2004112149

Cover and book interior design | Lightbourne, Inc.
Cover photograph | Gettyimages.com

CONTENTS

FOREWORD

IT WAS 1981, AND I WAS SURPRISED TO ENCOUNTER the face of an unfamiliar Mainer in my Senate office. He turned out to be one of my new interns, a fellow named Ed Barks.

Ed had already experienced a career in radio broadcasting, but being a political animal, he now wanted a taste of policy. He got it, pitching in to help my legislative staff in areas from nuclear repositories to federal budget machinations.

Much water has passed under the bridge since then. I little suspected that I would have the opportunity to serve my country in such capacities as Senate Majority Leader and Chairman of the Negotiations that produced Northern Ireland's Good Friday Peace Agreement.

Similarly, I would wager that Ed didn't foresee he would end up owning his own public relations agency, using his expertise to train business, non-profit, and government leaders how to communicate with the public.

Back then, he may not have envisioned himself undertaking the seemingly daunting task of writing a book. But here we are, more than twenty years later, and Ed has indeed joined the ranks of authors.

Ed's style and his book are very much grounded in the real world. *The Truth About Public Speaking* offers advice that aids speakers whether they plan to address the local United Way chapter or the United Nations.

I have witnessed on the stage of world events time and again how crucial communications skills are. Whether your stage is global or local, I suggest you build your success on a solid speaking platform. The contents of these pages will help you achieve that success.

—SENATOR GEORGE MITCHELL
Washington, D.C.

FOREWORD

WHILE SURFING THE INTERNET A FEW YEARS AGO, I came across an offer from a public speaking trainer named Ed Barks. His web site looked professional and I was intrigued by his offer to put his money where his mouth was.

At that time, Ed offered to review a videotape and deliver a complimentary mini-critique to all comers. I know a good thing when I see it. I have been speaking in public for a long time, but realize the need to constantly sharpen my skills. (Naturally, I couldn't be happier to see that Ed includes a chapter on lifelong learning.) So, off went my videotape.

I had no idea if this guy would follow through on his promise. It did seem too good to be true. But just a few days later, Ed left a message on my voice mail indicating he had received my tape and had a few thoughts he wanted to pass along.

Ed and I soon connected and, true to his word, he had some ideas to share. He noticed right away that I had slipped into a bad habit. Oh, most audiences (and, I'm sure, most presentation skills trainers) would never have picked up on it. But Ed spotted the fact that I had not been using my eye contact to forge a bond with the entire audience. I had been ignoring nearly half the room! Since that conversation, I've put to use the technique Ed taught me whenever I speak. His advice works.

This book crammed full of Ed's knowledge can work for you. Professional victories come to those with gold-plated communications skills. In *The Truth About Public Speaking*, Ed maps out the path to speaking success.

You may be involved in professional sports, like I am, or any other endeavor. I am here to tell you this book can make a difference in your career and your life whether you are a business executive, athlete, philanthropic leader, even a politician.

You may not know Ed Barks yet. I didn't when I first took a flier on his expertise. After you read his book, you will learn as I did that he can help you and your livelihood.

Enjoy this step along the journey to lifelong learning.

—PAT WILLIAMS
Senior Vice President, Orlando Magic

PREFACE

I JUST GOT TIRED OF IT. BOOKS ABOUT public speaking that dwell only on nervousness or how to use acting techniques or personality tests.

To be sure, each is a valuable component of the polished presenter. But there is a larger truth about public speaking. The art of the presentation is a holistic endeavor. Every element must work in concert if you want to achieve success from the podium.

It is akin to the bodybuilder who concentrates strictly on his arms. If his chest and legs are unimpressive, he has no chance of winning the Mr. Universe title.

In my years as a presentation skills trainer, I have seen too many people who fear that there is too much to learn. The easy route is for them to give up.

They don't stop to think what they are sacrificing—opportunities for career advancement, new customers, leadership in community affairs, winning an election, even making more money from their speaking endeavors.

You have your own reasons for seeking to sharpen your communications edge. *The Truth About Public Speaking: The Three Keys to Great Presentations* is my humble attempt to bring everything together under one roof in an organized fashion.

Becoming a good presenter is hard work. I want to make it as straightforward as possible and allow you to attain your personal public speaking goals, however lofty or humble they may be.

I also admit to personal reasons for delving into authorship. Writing has been a lifelong pursuit of mine, normally undertaken with much joy and gusto. The 5:30 a.m. alarm has become a welcome friend, for it signals my special time to rise and write.

In my more than a quarter century as a radio broadcaster and public relations professional, I feel as though I have strung together enough words to reach the moon and back again. Broadcast news copy, magazine articles, speeches, training guides, news releases, Congressional testimony, and web site content are all old friends. So it seems the next logical step is to author a book. To put it bluntly, yes, there was a book inside me screaming to get out. That scream manifests itself in the form of *The Truth About Public Speaking: The Three Keys to Great Presentations*.

By no means was this a solo journey. The road has risen up to meet me thanks to the encouragement and tutelage of many to whom I owe deepest thanks.

Senator George Mitchell was the reason I first came to Washington, D.C., nearly a quarter of a century ago. Bob Rose was one of the first people to give me an opportunity to show what I could do in the nation's capital. Radio gurus from my early days—Mike Shalett and Jim Cameron among them— offered crucial guidance delivered with utmost patience.

Karen Lam's steadfast support and encouragement have played a large role in guiding this book toward reality. Who knew that a casual conversation in the back of a meeting room in Santa Barbara would lead to this?

The ride has been much smoother thanks to my wife, Celeste, who makes life so easy, so pleasurable, and so much worth living, and to our daughter, Polly, the absolute light of my life and a talented writer in her own right.

Thank you to all. May you enjoy.

INTRODUCTION

YOU SWEAT WHEN YOU ARE ASKED TO SPEAK IN PUBLIC. What's the big deal if your heart starts racing, your mouth goes dry, and your voice starts quivering?

After all, who cares about advancing your career, generating more sales for your business, carrying the day for your public policy issues, or earning esteem in the eyes of your peers?

Here is the truth about public speaking: If you aspire to anything beyond run-of-the-mill in either your professional or personal life, you need solid presentation skills.

A nervous CEO inspires little confidence on Wall Street. A fidgety business owner fails to win customers on Main Street. An edgy project manager proves unable to get the ball rolling. An ill-at-ease government official scores no points for her prime initiatives.

Yet public speaking involves much more than conquering a case of the jitters. Bookstore shelves groan under the weight of volumes that dwell on nerves. I want to make the positive case regarding the benefits of delivering presentations.

In fact, I believe the secret to great presentations entails stressing the positive. Tell your audience what you can do rather than what you refuse to do. Paint a picture of your accomplishments, not what your competition does.

It is how you perform in front of the room that counts. Note that I say it is what you do, not only what you say. Presentation skills—including your nonverbal abilities—are critical in opening up your audience to your message.

Sure, I will offer some tips on how to corral your nerves; that is part of evolving into a better speaker. But there is more. This book gives you the complete speaking package by zeroing in on the Three Keys to Great Presentations™.

Each chapter begins with its own set of Three Keys—specific objectives that tell you what you can expect to learn.

What you read on these pages will give you the same truth my clients gain when I lead them through a public speaking workshop. In teaching presentation skills to corporate, association, government, and non-profit leaders over the years, I have found the Three Keys to Great Presentations a remarkable—and fun—learning tool.

The ideas incorporated here are for you if you can see your reflection in these profiles:

- A highly technical mind that struggles to translate things into plain English
- A nervous individual who begins to quake at the mere thought of delivering a presentation
- A business leader who has just been promoted to a position of greater responsibility
- A middle manager who wants to climb the corporate ladder
- A CFO who needs to deliver complex quarterly results in an easy to understand manner
- A board member for a non-profit organization who needs to reach out to potential donors and volunteers
- A manager or team leader who must find a way to motivate team members
- A public relations professional who wants to be taken more seriously by senior management
- An expert charged with talking to the media
- A human resources officer seeking a seat at the executive committee table
- A salesperson in need of stronger interpersonal skills

I have often said that nervousness is the unchallenged number one killer of great public speakers. *The Truth About Public Speaking: The Three Keys to Great Presentations* shows you how to get beyond nervous.

But there is much more than that to your improvement when standing before an audience. I encourage you to develop a greater thirst for lifelong learning. That is why my goal here is to provide an organized method that you, as a speaker, can use to improve your craft on an ongoing basis.

This volume covers two often overlooked fundamentals—Preparation and Assessing Feedback—and offers strategies that put you on a path toward constant improvement.

Taken together, the Three Keys provide the comprehensive yet easy to grasp system you need to sharpen your communications edge.

Chapter One introduces the Three Keys, laying the groundwork and explaining their importance.

Chapter Two delves into the benefits—and there are many—of transforming yourself into an admired public speaker.

The first key—Preparation—is detailed in Chapter Three. Preparation is the equivalent of batting practice for a speaker. It requires your attention well in advance of your performance.

The essentials of the second key, Performance, are spelled out in Chapter Four. It covers everything from how to be introduced exactly the way you want to dealing with rude audience members.

Chapter Five is devoted to Winning the Communications Trifecta, outlining how you can benefit by using your Video Tools, Audio Tools, and Message Tools for maximum impact.

Nonverbal communication is the basis for Chapter Six, where we will delve into the research and then place things in context.

Chapter Seven answers the question, why are some speakers so bad? I analyze some case studies and offer a positive perspective that can help you grow your speaking talents.

Fielding questions from the audience is a big part of any presentation. Chapter Eight covers all the bases of Q&A, from handling challenging inquiries to shutting down the Agenda Hog who tries to steal your spotlight.

The third of the three keys—Assessing Feedback—is crucial in any field, including public speaking. Strangely, it is all too often ignored. Chapter Nine is dedicated to giving you concrete methods to gauge your performance. If you fail to measure your skills as a presenter, you might as well kiss goodbye your hope of sharpening your communications edge.

Chapter Ten helps you master the use of presentation software. Lots of speakers use slide shows; many of them use it quite badly. Here, you will gain an understanding of what a winning slide looks like, how you can brand each one, and more.

Chapter Eleven focuses on the vital step of developing a plan for lifelong learning. This aspect is too frequently ignored despite the fact that your future success depends on it.

The appendices are stocked with added resources, including:

- The form I use to gather information on upcoming presentations
- An exercise to help you sharpen your nonverbal skills
- A list of questions you should ask when searching for a communications trainer
- Recommended reading to enhance your lifelong learning
- A catalog of keyboard shortcuts designed to smooth your use of presentation software

If you are looking for a quick fix, you can stop reading now. I have no interest in explaining how you can get better by simply reading a book or participating in a lone workshop.

I am a firm believer in lifelong learning. In this volume, I want to show you how to set yourself up for a lifetime of ongoing enrichment as a presenter by using The Three Keys to Great Presentations: Preparation, Performance, and Assessing Feedback.

Here is the bottom line: You will *not* get better if you fail to prepare. And you certainly will not get better if you fail to learn the value of assessing feedback routinely.

The central question remains, what's in it for you? This volume can put you on the road to becoming a better speaker, whether you address the National Press Club or your local garden club.

If you take these lessons to heart, here is some of what you can expect:

- *Convey confidence* when speaking before any audience
- *Get rid of* annoying nonverbal habits
- *Utilize visual aids* and presentation software effectively
- *Refuse to be sidetracked* by off-point or hostile questions
- *Craft and deliver* a magnetic message
- *Find friendly faces* in any audience
- *Prevent nasty surprises* from your audio/visual equipment
- *Utilize your body language* for maximum impact
- *Reduce anxiety* when addressing a roomful of people
- *Develop* quotable quotes
- *Take charge* during the crucial question and answer period
- *Persuade, educate, or inform* your audience

I make no promises that you will become a great orator. You would be better served by investing in a pair of magical ruby slippers as in a book that guarantees to transform you into a star.

The only way to become a better speaker is to speak—a lot. You should leap at the chance to deliver a presentation whenever and wherever a sensible opportunity presents itself.

Here is my bargain with you: Use the methods and exercises contained within these pages; mix them with a healthy dose of dedication, hard work, and practice. Over time, you will improve no matter your current skill level.

An average speaker will become adept. An exciting speaker will become superb.

Finally, I shudder to think of a learning experience that does not contain an element of fun. I freely admit that I love my work—teaching today's leaders to become better communicators. I hope my passion shines through on these pages.

Engaging in lifelong learning to improve your public speaking skills is far from drudgery. It can lead to a better job, higher profits, more donations, and public policy objectives. That sounds like fun to me.

Enjoy the next steps contained on these pages. Let us now unlock the door to speaking success by helping you take possession of the Three Keys to Great Presentations.

So, start reading. As you glide through these pages, rehearse the techniques. That is the only assurance to improvement any reputable public speaking coach can offer.

—ED BARKS

WHAT ARE THE THREE KEYS TO GREAT PRESENTATIONS™?

THE THREE KEYS TO CHAPTER ONE

You can expect to learn the truth about the Three Keys to Great Presentations:

- The basics of the easy to remember yet effective Three Keys to Great Presentations and how they can sharpen your speaking abilities;

- Why leaders—from the Fortune 500 CEO to the non-profit volunteer—need solid public speaking skills to advance their careers and causes;

- The power of lifelong learning and why you need to view improvement as a constant endeavor.

THE WORLD IS COMING TO AN END. That is the mindset of many an individual who finds herself slated to speak in public.

She pictures herself striding haltingly to the front of the room, convinced the audience can see her heart leaping out of her chest with every rapid beat. Her knees knock together, keeping a rhythm that would be the pride of any flamenco dancer. Her voice? Forget it. It is as thick as if she just downed a mouthful of peanut butter. Her face is flushed to the shade of red used by fire engine designers.

Self-doubt not only creeps in, it kicks down the door brandishing a huge sign that reads, "LOSER!"

If most speakers were to ask the magic looking glass: "Mirror, mirror on the wall, who's the most nervous of them all?" they are convinced the magic looking glass would respond, "you, my pretty."

Well, it is time to separate perception from reality. I want to give you the power of a new truth about public speaking—one that provides you with a crisp reflection of a new you, the way you will look before every presentation from now on.

Let's look at the facts. Of the millions and millions of presentations delivered throughout history—from the days of Eve addressing the serpent—the earth has continued to spin.

After all, when is the last time you read the following headline?

SPEAKER PASSES OUT FROM STAGE FRIGHT; AUDIENCE ERUPTS INTO PEALS OF LAUGHTER OVER PRONE PRESENTER

It just doesn't happen. At the same time, I don't mean to belittle the panic that can strike in advance of a speaking engagement. Most of us—me included—have experienced the sweaty palms, trembling voice, knocking knees, and brain lock.

It doesn't have to be that way. Everyone has the potential to become a solid orator. All you need to do to unlock your "inner speaker" is take advantage of the Three Keys to Great Presentations. This straightforward method charts a course toward a sharper communications edge.

What are The Three Keys to Great Presentations? They are:
- **Preparation**
- **Performance**
- **Assessing Feedback**

Why the Three Keys? It is an easy to remember system that works. This ease of recall is important, especially in this day and age. We are inundated by more information in a single day's edition of *The New York Times* than a seventeenth century inhabitant of England was exposed to during his entire lifetime. Keeping track of our deadlines at work, our carpool schedule for the kids, and all the passwords we need to remember is a taxing endeavor. The last thing you need is a difficult to fathom speaking system that only adds to your overload.

The Three Keys are highly intuitive. Preparation covers what you need to take into account **before** your presentation. Performance deals with how you act **during** your remarks. Assessing Feedback puts you on the road to improvement **after** you speak.

Why Me?

You may think you can slide through life without top-notch presentation skills. Think again. More people than ever before need to deliver presentations today; opportunities range from a formal speech to a fifteen-second self-introduction at a chamber of commerce luncheon.

Here's the bottom line: Your goal may be to tune up for a speech to the National Press Club, present as part of a panel at a trade association annual meeting, deliver a sales pitch to a prospective customer, or network effectively at a cocktail reception. Look around you: Time after time, those individuals who have winning presentation skills are the ones who win more customers, gain more donations for their non-profit group, and persuade more people to agree with their point of view.

You are probably reading this book because you want to sharpen your communications edge. Allow me to clue you in to the single most powerful step toward improvement: *Practice! Practice! Practice!*

Practice is the key to success. There are no shortcuts. But you do have a wide array of choices when it comes time to practice. I will detail some of those in this chapter.

Emphasize the Practical

You will not find any mind-numbing charts or spaghetti-like mind-mapping diagrams here. This is practical information you can use right away to raise your level of performance. I will discuss a bit of theory to give you a quick peek behind the curtain. But the emphasis is on lots of insights from the front lines based upon my experience as a presentation skills coach.

I have seen communicators good and bad from both sides of the fence—as a radio broadcaster and as a public relations pro. These observations taught me about the need for an easy to remember system that could help anybody sharpen his presentation skills. The Three Keys evolved over the years and will no doubt continue to evolve in the future.

Under a Cloud of Anxiety

It is a well-known fact that most people are nervous before they speak. In fact, surveys find that public speaking ranks at or near the top on many people's list of greatest fears.

I freely admit that I still feel a few butterflies in the pit of my stomach when I step forward to deliver a presentation. I'm not ashamed in the least. Hey, I'm human, too.

This nervousness is nothing more than a signal that you are normal. Does it make you some kind of freak? Not at all.

I sometimes quiz participants in my presentation skills training workshops, asking for a show of hands if they get jumpy before speaking. The vast majority of hands shoot up in the air.

But there are always a few who think they are cooler than the rest of us. Here is what I ask them to do: Take the first two fingers of their right hand, place them on their left wrist, and feel if they have a pulse. Anyone who is living and breathing should feel a tad anxious. In fact, if you do not feel that extra shot of adrenaline, you will likely prove to be a lackluster speaker, one who will face difficulty persuading or inspiring your audience.

Here is what matters: You know how you feel when you prepare to speak—the trembling hands and tightened voice. You are the one that counts here. We are talking about you, not some theoretical automaton.

Also take into consideration that your audience normally wants to see you succeed. They are on your side in the vast majority of cases. If you appear a bit nervous, they understand. Many of them have probably been in exactly the same situation.

Anti-Nerve Pills

There is a variety of strategies that can help you calm your jagged nerves. It is up to you to consider them carefully and figure out which work best in your situation.

First, remember that you are the expert. Your host asked you to speak because you have a certain body of knowledge, a special point of view, or a unique ability to persuade. Take confidence in that fact.

In addition, it is important to breathe. Yes, we do this every moment of every day of our lives. But somehow that automatic switch gets knocked into the "off" position when we take to the podium. Breathe deeply—no shallow gasping allowed. This will help you overcome your nerves.

Some individuals find relaxation techniques of great use. I practice meditation daily and am convinced it helps me stay on an even keel. I also utilize simple visualization techniques immediately prior to my speech. I frame a mental picture of how the room will look and envision myself taking ownership of the room for the duration of my remarks. Other people use yoga or daily workouts as a stress release. Find the methods that work for you and use them religiously.

You will also settle down if you take some time to get accustomed to your new speaking environment. Take in the room and realize you have command of it for as long as you speak. At the risk of sounding too mystical about the whole thing, become one with the space. Familiarity breeds confidence.

Some presenters manifest nervousness by coming down with a severe case of cotton mouth. The best solution to combat that dry feeling is plain old water. Make sure you have a glass of the old H_2O at the ready when you speak. And I do mean water. Beverages like coffee, tea, and juice dry your mouth and will only make your cotton mouth worse.

What's more, be sure to hydrate yourself the day before you speak. Drinking plenty of water in advance of your appearance will lead to less thirst when you are on stage.

Once you are in the spotlight, use what I refer to as your Audio Tools—the way you sound. These tools include your vocal pitch, articulation, volume, emotion, and rate. If, for instance, you speak with a louder voice or with greater emotion, you will soon find those jitters dissipating.

Also make use of your Video Tools—the way you look. The basics here include action, facial expression, eye contact, wardrobe, and use of props. Bust those jangling nerves by increasing your hand gestures slightly or displaying a prop, for example.

Avoid the Confusion

All too often I have seen an individual walk into a presentation skills workshop clueless about how he can improve his public speaking skills and fearful of what appears to be a daunting task. The impression that there is too much to comprehend poses a real barrier to learning.

Worse yet, he may have received bad advice, confused by previous advisors who offered only a scattershot approach. You would be amazed at some of the whoppers I hear:

- Never use a podium
- Always use a podium
- Never use hand gestures
- Always use hand gestures
- Smile
- Don't smile

You get the picture. The Three Keys to Great Presentations system opens the door so that you can maximize your own speaking style. I am a firm believer that there is no single model for a good presenter. If someone tries to tell you there is, I strongly suggest you turn and run as fast as you can. Don't let anyone tie you up in a speaking straightjacket. Your personal style needs to fit you like a finely tailored suit.

Practice Makes Perfect

Let's talk about expectations for a moment. This volume will get you pointed in the right direction, giving you tools you need to improve. But it is up to you and you alone to assume ownership of those tools and use them wisely.

You see, great speakers are not born with natural speaking talent. That is a myth I would like to explode once and for all. Indeed, that is why many senior executives who ought to know better shy away from using a public speaking coach. They view their lack of innate talent as great orators as a character flaw. Baloney!

Want proof? Here I am. Just ask my high school classmates. I was the shy kid who wouldn't yell "fire!" even if my hair was set ablaze. Now I love getting up in front of a room to speak. In fact, I love it so much, it is how I make my living.

What transformed this bashful youngster into a ham extraordinaire? Although I didn't realize it at the time, looking back I can see that I was putting to use the Three Keys to Great Presentations.

I sharpened my public speaking talents thanks to a career in radio broadcasting. Sitting behind the microphone day after day sharpened my verbal and nonverbal skills to a fine point. It also gave me the confidence I needed to address groups large and small.

Your practice may not come behind a broadcast microphone. You may work to gain speaking opportunities before the local Rotary Club or chamber of commerce. Or you might join Toastmasters. No matter your choice of venue, find a setting where you can get lots of practice. As basic as it sounds, there is no substitute for speaking in public if you want to become a better public speaker.

Success comes to those who rehearse diligently, speak frequently, and pay attention to the Three Keys to Great Presentations.

The Essence of the Three Keys

In the following chapters, we will delve into the details of how this straight-forward system can help you. Let's review briefly the Three Keys—Preparation, Performance, and Assessing Feedback—and how each works to enhance your ability as a presenter.

Preparation involves thinking strategically about which speaking opportunities you will accept, and why. It takes solid research and a decision on what presentation format works best for your individual style. Preparation means adding punch to your remarks, heightening your confidence, and ensuring the room is set up to your liking. And, of course, practice is vital.

Performance demands both substance and style. It requires that you win the Communications Trifecta by mastering your Video Tools, Audio Tools, and Message Tools. Also keep in mind that you are putting on a show, so find a way to engage your audience both during your prepared remarks and the all-important Q&A session.

Assessing Feedback encompasses more than evaluation forms. Check your audience's pulse during your talk, mingle with them afterward, and touch base with your host organization to gain the feedback you need. Honest critique leads to improvement.

A Word about Leadership

The Three Keys to Great Presentations show today's leaders how to succeed when they deliver important presentations. I do not intend for the term "leaders" to refer to an exclusive club. Leaders are by no means limited to the CEO whose remarks are covered by CNBC or the national politico who delivers the keynote to the Democratic National Convention.

One of the secrets of successful people is that they know how to communicate in public. Few people rise to the top unless they have good communications skills. Those who sharpen the Three Keys win success in more than just speaking. They earn success when it comes to business, community involvements, friendships, politics, and more.

Anyone can be a leader in a given situation. Truth be told, public speaking is a great leveler. Taking the lead by delivering a presentation allows you to carve out your own profile as a leader. Individuals who use these Three Keys act like magnets for leadership responsibilities.

Your leadership role may occur at work when you pitch a new product to senior management. If Shirley leads the presentation, you can bet that people in that audience are going to see it as her project. She assumes the mantle of leadership.

It may occur in the community when you lead the charge against a development that would blotch the landscape with urban sprawl. Bob takes on the role of chief organizer when he is the one who agrees to speak before the city council.

It may occur on a personal level when you propose a wedding toast to a bride and groom. All of a sudden, relatives are coming to you for advice (and, hopefully, not for loans) because you are the one who had the nerve to stand up and celebrate the happy couple.

The Three Keys system delivers a means for you to create a magnetic message. Your audience is there to hear what you have to say—to be informed, persuaded, or entertained by your words. Your words are the essence of your performance.

The Three Keys approach strengthens your nonverbal tools as well. A bit later, I will discuss just how important these unspoken communication techniques are to your ability as a presenter. Suffice for now to say that your nonverbal cues count for well over half your ability to communicate.

As a speaker, you need a way to get your audience members involved and on your side. Heeding the Three Keys does exactly that.

Traveling the Road to Leadership

We talked earlier about the fact that speaking up is a sure-fire way to be perceived as a leader. How many leaders lack solid communications skills? Sure, there are some and always will be. But in today's heavily saturated communications environment, nearly everyone gets a star turn.

In the old days, leaders with sub par communications skills could indeed muddle by. There was no radio or TV, let alone streaming video on the Internet to capture their malaprops.

That is simply not a picture of today's world. Cameras, microphones, or at least a small crowd are guaranteed to be present nearly every time you speak.

That means you need to be "on" whenever you deliver an address. Engaging presentations pave the road to success in business, community projects, and politics. They also help you avoid failure and embarrassment.

A Lifetime of Scholarship

I would be remiss if I failed to address the notion of lifelong learning. Earlier, you were granted your mantra of *Practice! Practice! Practice!* Let me explain in a bit more detail what that means.

Larry has a big presentation next month for which he is 100 percent committed to practicing diligently. He knows it must be flawless if he is to win that new account. But Larry has a problem. Although he delivers presentations on a regular basis, it seems that he hasn't logged a serious rehearsal session in many a month.

So it takes him a good bit of time to get up to speed. He feels awkward during his rehearsals. That leads to frustration, which causes him to take his foot off the gas. His practice time dwindles to nearly nothing. The vicious circle has begun.

In one final panicked burst of activity, he pulls an all-nighter before his big show. On the appointed day, a bleary-eyed Larry is far from his best, turning in a lackluster performance. Kiss that big account goodbye. Larry might even wind up kissing his job goodbye.

If, like our friend Larry, you fail to commit to lifelong learning, you are nothing more than the student who crams for a test the night before. Oh, you might squeak by with a passing grade, but you certainly will not retain the information you will need later in life.

So it is with sharpening your presentation skills. Your audience will know, at least intuitively, when you try to slide by. It is disrespectful to them. Plus, you shortchange yourself.

That is why I am a strong proponent of lifelong learning. I want to instill in you that sense of professional curiosity.

Speakers who improve over time—those who become leaders in the workplace, in the community, and at home—share a commitment to ongoing education. It may come when they:

- Review a learning guide that keeps their knowledge refreshed
- Listen to an audio lesson that keeps their learning current
- Watch the videotape of their training to remind them of areas they need to sharpen
- Take advantage of a refresher course in six months or a year

Those who rehearse earnestly over time exude a presence lacking in those who try to slide by and cheat themselves and their audience.

The First Key: Preparation

We will delve into the specifics of each of the Three Keys in later chapters. For the moment, let's take a brief glimpse to set the baseline for your improvement as a presenter.

The first of the Three Keys to Great Presentations is Preparation. Without preparation, all is lost.

Legendary comedian W.C. Fields may have best summed up the need for preparation when he said, "always carry a flagon of whiskey in case of snakebite and furthermore always carry a small snake."

Many speakers fall flat because they forget how far in advance the preparation phase begins. Do you think it begins when you arrive at your venue to speak? When you first set pen to paper or fingers to keyboard? When you get that e-mail asking you to speak at your company's employee development day?

You need to go back even further than that if you want to think strategically. Chart a course that guides you toward speaking opportunities you want. Even before that phone rings asking you to present, decide which types of speaking invitations you will accept.

Your guidelines should take into account whether this is an audience you need or want to reach. Let me give you a personal example. I know in advance that if I receive an invitation to speak before a group of senior public relations executives, I will quickly accept. Why? I partner with many public relations agencies; that is an audience I long ago made a conscious decision to target. On the other hand, even an engraved, personalized invitation from the local knitting society will not get me before that organization. That is not part of my target audience (unless my research tells me that a senior public relations executive loves to knit and is a member of the group).

Later on, I will deliver plenty of ideas detailing how you can gain the advance information you need so that you can target your remarks to the audience at hand. I will also talk about how you can get someone else to brag about you in front of your audience.

Are you confused about how to structure your speech? You have many choices, with each appropriate in different circumstances.

Once you have decided upon your main message for each individual performance, I will show you how to punch up your wording and avoid dry, sleep-inducing language.

When you speak, do you use gear such as microphones, laptops, or LCD projectors? There is a bucketful of strategies in Chapter Three that will help you stay away from any technical snafus. And if they should arise unexpectedly, I will show you how to work around them.

In addition, you will receive pointers on how you can diplomatically assume control of your speaking venue—everything from planning your seating arrangement to what you need to check when you arrive onsite.

And if you are curious about the best methods for fielding questions from audience members, this volume spans the range of issues from the friendliest softball to the zinger posed by a heckler.

The Second Key: Performance

The second of the Three Keys, Performance, offers you a chance to blend substance and style into a convincing speaking combination. Performance is much more than a matter of simply reciting a speech.

To cultivate a receptive audience, you must be interesting to watch and listen to. Think of the speakers you have seen who had Grade A content but put people to sleep because they droned on in monotone or stood stiffly behind a podium.

Perhaps the vice president who heads your division at work fits this description. Or maybe the president of the non-profit board on which you serve comes to mind. I can even think of a few college professors who had stimulating ideas but spoke in voices so disinteresting they became famous for putting students to sleep.

Throughout this volume, I will discuss lots of seemingly small points about your performance that add up to a positive setting designed to boost audience attention.

The Third Key: Assessing Feedback

Let's move on to the third of the Three Keys to Great Presentations, Assessing Feedback. This is the one that most presenters ignore. Do so at your own peril.

It is difficult if not impossible to succeed if you do not evaluate how you perform. Better speakers get better results, whether the goal is to climb the corporate ladder, win a grant for a non-profit group, or champion an environmental cause.

It is my observation that most speakers pay so much attention to drafting their remarks and delivering them, they fail to find ways to gauge how they did. The tendency is to spend a disproportionate share of time drafting their remarks. Practice comes in a distant second. Often, assessing feedback is not even on the radar screen. It needs to be, for assessing feedback is a key to lifelong improvement.

The most basic instrument most speakers use to assess their performance is an evaluation form. By all means, use one, but don't make it the only measurement you take.

Accomplished presenters employ a bounty of methods for measuring feedback that go well beyond the evaluation form.

Three Keys Work in Harmony

Preparation, Performance, and Assessing Feedback—the Three Keys to Great Presentations. Is one more important than the others?

Each of these keys is vital to your success as a speaker. In addition, they must work in combination, harmonizing with one another if you are to gain maximum advantage.

Think of it this way: Your car needs gas, oil, and water to run. Forget to fill up the gas tank and you will soon hear the sputter of your engine choking to a stop. Neglect to change your oil and you will lurch to a halt when your engine seizes up. Fail to add water and it won't be long until the billows of white smoke pour out from under your hood. If you neglect to use any of those necessities, your car won't be going anywhere.

Similarly, if you do not heed each of the Three Keys to Great Presentations, you are sure to encounter a roadblock on the path to speaking success.

This straightforward speaking system shows you how to succeed when you deliver your next presentation. You will sharpen not only what you say, but of equal importance, how you say it. The Three Keys give you a way to get your audience involved and on your side.

Now you have the baseline of information you need to begin to systematically improve your public speaking skills. Let's move on to examine why becoming a good communicator matters.

WHY DO I NEED TO SPEAK?

THE THREE KEYS TO CHAPTER TWO

You can expect to learn the truth about the benefits you gain from speaking in public:

- The roots of nervousness, and strategies you can use to combat your personal public speaking demons;
- Why it makes sense to sharpen your existing skills before you undertake the struggle to improve your weaknesses;
- How to come to the aid of a boss with poor communications skills.

SOME INDIVIDUALS ARE CONTENT TO MUDDLE ALONG. Their fear of public speaking can be positively paralyzing. Is it really worth the time and effort to shake that image of being a sub par speaker?

Let me reframe that question: Does it matter to you if your co-workers are getting promotions ahead of you? Could it affect your career if your competitors succeed at your expense? Is it really that big a deal if the charity you serve misses out on key funding sources?

Speaking Success Equals Professional Success

The answer to all of these questions is simple: Yes! The truth is accomplished speakers are the ones who climb the corporate ladder, serve as leaders in their professional societies, earn bigger donations for their non-profit organizations, and win elections in the political arena.

If you do not care about getting a better job, gaining a reputation as a leader in your field, or shining as a leading public policy light, fine. Feel free to continue to stumble along. In fact, you might as well close this book right now and pass it along to someone with the burning desire to be a leader.

You decided to consult these pages for a reason. You are already motivated by goals like earning a better living for your family and winning the public recognition you deserve. That is what the Three Keys to Great Presentations can do for you.

Starting from Scratch

Don't panic if you are not yet a solid presenter. No one begins the game as an expert speaker. Rest assured that you can, with hard work and dedication, improve your skills.

The first thing to realize is that there are no naturally gifted speakers. Your executives did not roll out of bed one day with all the expertise needed to run an enterprise. Similarly, none of us emerge from the womb with flawless speaking abilities. The key to success involves lots of practice.

Did you ever wonder how the best speakers got to be the best? How does that presenter who looks so natural and at ease in front of an audience do it? I can guarantee you in almost every case they take their rehearsal time seriously. They make it look effortless because they put so much effort into their preparation.

Baseball slugger Barry Bonds has a hitting coach. Robert DeNiro has learned from acting coaches. Your leader, even if he is a speaking superstar, needs a trusted coach who can continue to advance his learning. This applies to your improvement, too.

Do First What You Do Well

The path to quickest improvement treads familiar ground. That is, you get better faster by sharpening to perfection skills that are already sharp. If, for instance, your ability to express emotion is a particularly strong suit, you will benefit most from emphasizing that quality and working to hone it to a razor sharp edge as you practice.

Similarly, your ability to vary the rate and volume of your speech may come more naturally. Leverage those qualities when you address a crowd, using them to full effect.

If, by contrast, using presentation software befuddles you, it is best to stay away from it. Or if you find reading a full text speech scary, stay away from that format. Why call attention to your defects?

It is true that you can improve your weaknesses in the long run. But it takes a lot of effort, a lot of concentration, a lot of dedication, and a lot of time.

My recommendation is to knock off the easy stuff first. Aim for improvement where you are likely to see the most dramatic results in the shortest span of time. Later, as your schedule allows, work to sharpen the tools that are rustier.

While I go to great pains to point out that none of us is born with the talent to be a great speaker, it is beyond dispute that each of us has qualities that are inherently stronger or weaker. It is simply not possible to master every earthly skill. Both time and talent are working against you. Apply your energies to the qualities that will give you the most bang for your buck.

Trying to build up your shortfalls by yourself is quite a tall order. You will find a smoother road to improvement when you work with a skilled coach to improve your weaknesses.

Here is a tip for finding a coach who is a good match for you: During your rehearsal sessions, he should zero in on answering the question, "what did you do right?" instead of accentuating, "here is what you did wrong" (see Appendix C for a list of questions that can help you find the coach who is right for you).

This is not to say he should neglect to point out habits that interfere with the delivery of your message. If, for instance, you tend to turn your back to the audience or talk at too rapid a clip, you need to correct that quickly for those behaviors will indeed detract from your performance by steering your listeners away from your message.

If, however, you should find yourself working with a trainer who is bound and determined to force you to use props when you find dealing with them distracting, you need to question whether you are getting the value you deserve from that relationship.

To be sure, a coach should stay on the lookout for weaknesses. But reinforcing strengths paves the quickest road to progress.

Practice with a Purpose

While attending a business meeting in San Francisco, I met a human resources executive who told me she still gets nervous when the time comes for her to deliver a presentation. It wasn't debilitating in her case. But it still bothered her and she was in search of a strategy to conquer it.

The first thing I tell people is to get plenty of practice, and walk into a venue with a positive attitude and a healthy dose of confidence. Remember, the audience decides to attend because of you and your reputation, expertise, or provocative viewpoint.

She took the question one step further, saying she practices quite a bit. Yet those nerves still rear their ugly head.

I suggested she analyze her practice habits by considering a few questions:

- Do you rehearse often enough?
- Are you paying attention to practicing your opening and conclusion?
- What about getting comfortable with any props or slides you intend to use?
- Do you take your practice time seriously enough?
- Are you rehearsing in front of others who can help critique you?
- Have you taken advantage of an organized training program with an experienced coach?
- Do you record your sessions on video or audio tape?
- Do you dedicate the time to reviewing details on the tape? (Hint: If you fail to pause and rewind the tape frequently, you will miss many of the subtle nuances that are key to improvement.)
- Do you maintain a positive frame of mind throughout your rehearsals?

These questions will vary depending on your individual circumstances. The important point is to define the issues that matter to you.

Personal Roadblocks

Beyond plain old nervous tension, there is a bounty of reasons why some people just cannot seem to get the hang of public speaking. Let us lift the veil and examine why even some individuals in positions of high responsibility are hesitant, and talk about some strategies for dealing with these presentation worries.

People manifest anxiety in different ways. Those of us who are internalizers may display a poker face on the outside, but the heart rate races and the sweat glands (what the academics refer to as electrodermal responses) work overtime. Alternatively, externalizers who wear their emotions on their sleeve evidence few physiological indicators.

As your presentation skills gain a sharper edge, you want to get to a place where these concerns melt away. As in medicine, I much prefer to treat the disease as opposed to the symptoms. Step into the examination room so we can diagnose your particular malady:

Stage fright. Most commonly associated with actors, some speakers also suffer from stage fright. As the curtain goes up, so does your pulse rate and your level of adrenaline. The body is harkening back to the "fight or flight" mechanism vital to our ancestors. This manifestation does not mean you lack intelligence or emotional stability. There are many methods for addressing stage fright. Studies show that the single biggest repellant is our old friend practice. The more you speak, the better you become at harnessing this wayward energy. Releasing that nervous energy through your Audio Tools—more varied pitch or greater volume, for instance—and your Video Tools—such as more gestures and facial expression—can serve as an escape valve. Just be sure not to go overboard and allow your voice to take on the character of an announcer at a wrestling match or let your arms resemble a windmill.

Shyness. This affects a lot of us, me included. Let me give you a personal insight. I am not Mr. Outgoing. In fact, if you look in the dictionary for "life of the party," you will see me listed as an antonym. My personal experience is that hard work and conscious effort are the recipe for conquering shyness. No, it may never feel natural to me to eagerly plunge headlong into a crowd like a presidential candidate. But I have learned, over much time, to adjust my mind to seeing it not as a fearful event, but as an opportunity to grow both personally and professionally.

Uncertainty about your topic. You need to be an expert who happens to speak, not someone who thinks it would be a great idea to speak but has no idea on what theme. Become an expert in your subject matter. Read everything you can get your hands on. Keep up with the latest news in your field. Network with experts who can give you insights into the latest trends and research. Write articles, columns, op-eds, and books to demonstrate your expertise. Good old-fashioned learning is the only way to overcome this fear of uncertainty.

Arrogance. This is the flip side of uncertainty. Do not come across as a know-it-all. There may well be someone in the crowd who knows more than you about certain areas of your speech. Leave the haughty attitude at home if you want your audience to embrace you.

Foolish pride. Foolish pride is the cousin of arrogance. No matter how long you have been speaking, there are always things to learn. It may be a mannerism you pick up from observing another presenter. Or it may be a piece of strategic advice you gain from a new trusted advisor. Swallow your pride and acknowledge that you need to continually sharpen your communications edge.

Being a bore. This fear of leading the audience into a state of ennui is the mirror image of arrogance. Your audience wants to benefit from what you have to say. Assuming you deliver a magnetic message with solid Audio and Video Tools, boredom will not be a cause for concern.

Judgement day. Will the audience hate me? Will they rise up in revolt? Will they storm out because they disagree with me? The odds of your audience judging you this harshly are pretty slim (unless you understand in advance that you are walking into a hornet's nest). Your listeners will generally be on your side unless you give them reason to turn against you.

Ill-prepared. You have no excuse for not being equipped for an engagement. Practice is the basic solution to a shortage of preparation.

Lack of passion. You have to care about your subject matter. Your dearth of enthusiasm will be evident to your audience, resulting in a flat speech. Do not speak unless you have a personal or professional stake in the outcome.

Wasting time. Some presenters, particularly early in their careers, get the idea that they are wasting the audience's time. Not true. You have been invited to speak for a reason. If you offer an engaging performance, your advice can help your audience save time in the future.

Reluctance. We all have our individual likes and dislikes. Me? There is nowhere I would rather be than watching a pitcher's duel under a cloudless sky behind the home team's dugout on a sunny, 80-degree day. So it goes with speaking. Some people cannot wait to bound up those steps to the stage, smile to the crowd, and unleash their energy; others simply don't take to it. A low level of enthusiasm doesn't make you a weirdo. But it does mean you need to recognize your natural proclivities and make some extra effort to buck yourself up before an engagement. Ask a friend to offer some encouraging words. Read a passage that inspires you. Find a way to psych yourself up as an athlete would before the big game. Whatever you do, do not bring that reluctance on stage with you. Your audience will see your absence of enthusiasm and fail to warm to you.

Never been taught. None of us are born with the skill to speak in public. It is a matter of lifelong learning. If you have not taken advantage of any formal training, that is the first place to start. A word of advice: Be cautious about who you listen to. There are far too many people in this world who think they are presentation experts when, in reality, their advice can backfire and prove dangerous to your career.

Bad advice about how to present. Beware! There is a lot of bad advice out there and plenty of hacks more than happy to sell it to you just to make a buck. Carefully check the credentials of anyone who tries to offer counsel to you. Are they experienced as a coach or did they speak to the local garden club once and suddenly turn into an "expert"? Do they believe in lifelong learning and keep their own knowledge up to date? Is he or she a good public speaker?

Physical problem. If you were born with a stutter or poor eyesight or a physical disability, I commend you for taking the plunge and speaking in public. If you want to work to overcome your challenge, consult with a professional such as a speech pathologist, ophthalmologist, or your personal physician.

Poor facilities. This nerve-inducer will not hit you until the day of your presentation, but at that stage it can add to speaker anxiety. You may arrive at your room to find the projector you ordered is nowhere in sight. Or there are no markers in the white board tray. Those problems you can deal with; find someone from the site's facilities team right away and get him on the case. Other discoveries can be a bit more problematic. You may, for instance, be shoehorned into a room that is too small or too big for your anticipated crowd. Or you may encounter an oddly shaped room with support pillars blocking lines of sight. Your first option should be an attempt to switch rooms. If that is not possible, by arriving early to prepare, you will at least be able to determine the most advantageous approach and minimize the negative.

Organizational Roadblocks

Individuals can certainly erect roadblocks. So can many organizations. Speaking frankly, some groups are dinosaurs. They don't adapt well to change and they certainly don't encourage any underlings to outshine the brass. You have probably worked for an organization like this. I know I have.

Your leaders may not give you license to soar. They may deny you speaking opportunities for which you are perfectly suited. The boss may be jealous of your abilities, both in your presentation skills and your knowledge of the subject matter. There may be corporate infighting involving your department. You could be denied access to information you need to make your presentation meaningful for your audience.

You face many difficulties when your own outfit puts obstacles in your path. Short of a management shakeup, the best advice in many instances is to get out. But that is not always practical, especially when job markets are tight.

There are volumes galore about teamwork and how to approach your managers written by individuals far more versed than I in that area. What I can tell you is you need to find a means of overcoming these barriers to the best of your abilities.

For instance, if one department denies you critical information (and assuming this information is not subject to privacy concerns), seek out help from another department. Perhaps someone is purposely keeping your boss out of the loop because of an internal squabble. Create your own loop. Or try searching the office intranet. Such networks are often rich with unimagined tidbits.

If your manager refuses to let you speak for whatever reason—such as jealousy or insecurity—generate your own opportunities outside of the workplace. Speak before groups to which you belong such as professional associations and service clubs. Ask friends and associates to keep you in mind for speaking opportunities that come across their radar screens. Find a Toastmasters chapter that matches your abilities and get involved. Special hint: Advertising your availability as a last-minute substitute for a no-show presenter makes you a true hero in the eyes of an event's organizers.

Be as assertive and creative as you can. Solutions may not be easy. But you can often find a workaround for seemingly impossible organizational hurdles.

Telling It Straight

While we are on the subject of challenging bosses, let's talk about how you can shine when you help him sharpen his communications edge.

The fact is the boss is sometimes his own worst enemy. Part of the role of a trusted advisor sometimes involves delivering frank advice to an organization's leaders. If you need someone to lay the cards on the table in your workplace, hire some outside help.

Your issues could range from your CEO's favorite lime green leisure suit to a bad hairdo to a penchant to talk about the negative rather than the positive. A skilled communications trainer understands the value of working with you to diplomatically move the boss to a higher level.

Someone needs to be open and frank if your leader is to attain communications success. That could be someone in your organization. Or, it could be the coach you select to guide your leader's improvement. In fact, some matters are so sensitive that staffers dare not raise them with the boss (perhaps because they want to keep their job!).

Take the example of the Inc. 500 CEO I coached. He admitted to absolutely no confidence when delivering presentations. One reason for this was his inattention to organizing his thoughts. He had no comprehensive message to guide him. Further, as an engineer, he had little practice speaking to crowds. He became nervous and felt as though he had no control of the situation.

When starting his business, being a great engineer was sufficient. As the firm grew, however, his responsibilities shifted to those of an executive. It doesn't take long for a true business leader to recognize the need for superb communications skills.

After his first workshop, our CEO gained a solid understanding that he did indeed have the power to assume control. With a tight message and sharper presentation skills, he felt more prepared for addressing his key audience—his employees. Yes, this business leader who had built an enterprise from the ground up and given jobs to these people had shied away from speaking to them as a group, allowing his uneasiness to control him.

This story has a happy ending. He went on to ace a series of presentations to his workers, opening up lines of communication that had previously not existed.

What to Do When the Boss Says "No"

Not every leader is as receptive as our Inc. 500 CEO. He understood that he needed to improve. I have seen too many business executives, medical thought leaders, celebrities, and others deny their need for lifelong learning in the area of public speaking. It is a fact of life that some CEOs refuse to acknowledge their communications skills could use a tune-up.

This section is dedicated to those who work in public relations, public affairs, and communications.

With some it is a matter of vanity. They fear they will be viewed as weak if they reach out for assistance. I do not understand this thought process, but it is very real in some organizations.

If you encounter this road block in your organization, turn things around by appealing to your leader's vanity. Let's face it, she did not achieve her current lofty post without a healthy ego. Use it to your advantage.

Position the need for coaching by telling your boss that he is nurturing an increasingly high public profile. What was good enough for him as a manager is no longer good enough for his new, more visible role. His prestige merits some individual coaching.

Communications pros often find they break down barriers when they talk about the personal benefits executives stand to gain when they become better communicators.

What specific personal benefits will the boss earn by honing her speaking abilities?

- *Boost career opportunities*
- *Inspire employees*, customers, members, and investors
- *Demonstrate confidence* when speaking in public
- *Get rid of* trembling voice and knocking knees
- *Enhance opportunities* for professional advancement
- *Take charge* when dealing with any audience
- *Avoid tricks and traps* posed by questioners
- *Sharpen nonverbal tools* for maximum advantage
- *Steer clear* of being misunderstood or "misquoted"
- *Dodge the embarrassment* of poor performance during a high-stakes speech
- *Assume control* when question and answer time arrives
- *Keep from wandering* aimlessly when delivering presentations
- *Conquer distracting* nonverbal tendencies
- *Leapfrog others* on the career ladder

Climbing those Golden Stairs

Responsibility for improvement rests not only with our friends in public relations. Executives are also personally accountable to their organizations. When they signed on to the job, they took a vow to make it a better place.

The focus may be on improving things financially, cleaning up from a previous leadership that left a horrible workplace environment, integrating recent acquisitions, increasing community involvement, or any number of other objectives.

Your arguments prove more persuasive in the executive suite when you make it clear that your organization also reaps rewards from a more polished leadership. Sell that improvement by stressing these organizational advantages:

- *Block rivals* from stealing your customers
- *Position your organization* front and center in the minds of your public
- *Develop and reinforce* magnetic organizational messages
- *Prepare for* a crisis situation

- *Save time* by hammering out messages and preparing in advance
- *Gain an edge* on the competition
- *Decrease the odds* that your next product launch will be a dud
- *Instill organizational discipline* among those charged with delivering your messages
- *Offer ongoing education* to senior members of the executive team who deal with the public or press
- *Inspire greater confidence* in the public and in your markets during media interviews

I speak on the subject of motivating the boss to groups of communicators. I emphasize the leader's obligation to his organization to become a better communicator. Highlighting the above benefits drives that point home.

Get the Ball Rolling

Someone in your organization—quite possibly you—needs to assume that tough task of sharpening your CEO's communications skills. Your organization and your CEO personally stand to benefit from improved proficiency. If she neglects this part of her leadership toolkit, she is failing to fully maximize her leadership responsibilities. Your organization will pay the price in lower revenues and lost prestige.

It is part and parcel of a leader's job to connect with many publics—delivering speeches, talking to the media, and testifying before lawmakers, to name a few.

Responsibility for improving a leader's communications skills rests squarely on the shoulders of an organization's communications staff. When it comes to learning the ropes of speaking in public, it is your job to persuade your boss to sharpen his communications edge.

Not many of us have the good fortune to work with experts or bosses who have the oratory skills of former Texas Governor Anne Richards, the mass appeal of Tiger Woods, and the intelligence of Albert Einstein. All too often, our principals' presentations bring to mind all the flair and brainpower of Homer Simpson.

Your leaders need both message and style if your organization is to succeed in the public arena. For a business, a communications-challenged executive means lost revenues and fewer customers. In the public sector, it leads to decreased public confidence and a failure to achieve public policy goals. For non-profits, lower membership and declining donations are the results.

It is important to engage your executives and get them involved with their self-improvement campaign. Get them talking about their message. Toss some questions at them:

- What do they want to say about the issue at hand?
- What is the problem?
- How do you see us solving it?
- What steps do you want employees, customers, and vendors to take?
- How can I put things into context for the audience?

In today's hyper-competitive environment, you cannot afford a CEO who does not know how to get a message across, for there are some real costs when your boss fails to measure up as a communicator. Among them are lower revenues, lost sales, and, for non-profits, lower membership levels and fewer donations.

It is your job to turn your boss' "no" into an enthusiastic "yes!"

Your boss may not be Anne Richards, Tiger Woods, and Albert Einstein rolled into one. But as a communications professional, you need to work with what you have. It is up to you to educate the boss and provide the solutions that will sharpen her communications edge.

Learning from a Master

One of the best speakers I know is Pat Williams. In fact, Pat does many things very well. In addition to his presentation talents, he is a prolific writer, a voracious reader, and a devoted father to nineteen children (most of them adopted). In his spare time, he manages to serve as Senior Vice President for the NBA's Orlando Magic basketball team.

In his book *The Paradox of Power*, Williams mentions two quotes that go to the heart of why you need to become a better presenter. He first cites Winston Churchill, who said, "Of all the talents bestowed upon men, none is so precious as the gift of oratory. He who enjoys it wields a power more durable than that of a great king."

Williams also quotes Colin Powell saying, "Great leaders are almost always great simplifiers."

These two passages serve to highlight the differences between the run-of-the-mill presenter and the great one. If you are a good speaker with a simple yet powerful message, you win far more frequently. Similarly, if you use your nonverbal talents to convey emotion, you also emerge a winner.

Teaching Solid Skills

Most people tend to think that presentation skills are important only when they watch someone deliver a speech. But this aptitude is crucial to success in any walk of life. Take teaching, for example. My daughter's school featured a back-to-school night, where parents got to rotate through all of their children's classrooms and hear from all the teachers.

After listening to some of the "educators" for a scant ten minutes, it amazes me how the kids stay awake for an hour or more while being subjected to some of these zombie-like drones.

It so happens that one of my daughter's favorites in middle school was an English instructor. It was easy to see why. She had told me that this teacher kept things fun. Boy, was she right.

In a short seven-minute talk, he had the parents eating out of his hand. He challenged them to begin thinking about college for their middle schoolers, explained what the youngsters would be learning during the course of the year, and did it all with a marvelous sense of humor and terrific delivery within his allotted time frame. His Video and Audio Tools were working in high gear.

When you think about it, sharp presentation skills put you ahead of the pack no matter your endeavor. You may not stand in front of the room every day like a teacher. But you interact constantly in the workplace, delivering mini-presentations to co-workers. Have you ever noticed that the ones who get those fat raises and promotions year after year tend to be the stellar communicators?

Your executive may be one of those who is hesitant to firm up his communications abilities. You can help both him and your organization by serving as a catalyst for improvement. The benefits are many. Get to work to turn the boss' "no" into an enthusiastic "yes!"

Integrity Counts

I do not want to leave you with the impression that an ace presentation involves little more than a strong voice and appealing manner.

Your personal integrity is at stake every time you address a crowd. You must believe in what you say. If you just go through the motions, your audience will sense your lack of commitment. People can intuitively sniff out a fake.

Word spreads quickly when it involves your reputation. One phony move and your integrity will lie in tatters. Once damaged, it is next to impossible to stitch together that pile of rags into a gown for the ball.

Truthfulness, credibility, and passion are hallmarks of top-flight presenters. Be sure to pack these qualities in your briefcase as you prepare to speak before any audience.

THE FIRST KEY: PREPARATION

THE THREE KEYS TO CHAPTER THREE

You can expect to learn the truth about the first of the Three Keys to Great Presentations—Preparation:

- How preparation helps you avoid the failure and embarrassment that leads to a stalled career, lost customers, and a tarnished public image;

- Concrete steps that pave your way to thorough preparation, no matter what type of presentation you deliver;

- How to organize and write your remarks using the style that best suits your personal strengths.

DON'T LET ANYONE TELL YOU GREAT SPEAKERS are born with the gift of gab. It is true that some people have a bit more innate speaking talent. But the fact is presenting is an acquired capability.

Just as we can learn nearly any skill—from driving to typing to gardening—we can also learn to speak in public more effectively. Do I have a magic wand that transforms mediocre speakers into polished pros? Unfortunately, no. It takes a strong commitment to lifelong learning. But speakers can go from below average to reliable, or from decent to accomplished.

No matter your skill level right now, people like you are speaking in public every day. Your presentations may not be formal speeches. Maybe you need to offer an informal assessment of your department's performance at work. Or you are asked to deliver a few words at a friend's going away party.

What is the truth about your improvement as a presenter? Let us begin to answer that question by zeroing in on the first of the Three Keys to Great Presentations: Preparation.

The First Key to Great Presentations

How vital is preparation? Let me give it to you straight. I can guarantee that your presentation will fall apart if you do not prepare. That means lost customers if you operate a business; fewer votes if you are a public servant; and embarrassment, no matter who you are, if you perform like a clown in front of a roomful of important people.

Business executives, government officials, non-profit executives, sales managers, and other leaders understand the need to keep their presentation skills honed to a fine point. There is one simple way to stay sharp.

The critical factor is preparation. If you take away nothing else from this chapter, drill into your mind the fact that preparation is the key to success. It leads to success in business, community projects, politics, and more. What's more, it also helps you sidestep failure and embarrassment.

I am an unyielding advocate for preparation prior to a presentation. There is too much at stake to leave your speech to chance. If you give a sloppy performance filled with mistakes, your audience will see you as a huckster trying to pull a fast one. That is why you need to knock all those errors out by practicing diligently.

You deserve specifics, not pie-in-the-sky theory. Here are a few examples of how people can prepare before they take to the podium.

An Expert Who Speaks

I am working on the assumption that you know the topic of your presentation and have some expertise and legitimacy in your chosen field. It may be anything from financial planning to floral arrangement to bobsledding. The intent of this book is not to help you pick a speech topic. That should come naturally as a result of your expertise and passion.

You need to have something to say before you can say it. You need to be an expert who speaks, not a speaker who will talk about anything.

You may be surprised how many speakers will take any invitation that comes along. Indeed, there are some wannabes who claim a desire to make their living speaking. Yet it is almost comical that some of them have no idea what they want to talk about.

Far be it from me to dissuade anyone from becoming a presenter. But you must have something to say—some special expertise, a comedic delivery, or an insider's viewpoint.

I occasionally attend meetings of my local chapter of the National Speakers

Association. This is a group dedicated to serving individuals who make their living, at least partially, speaking to groups around the country and the world. I stopped counting how many times I have asked new members about their areas of proficiency only to be met with hemming and hawing. They respond that they want to speak, but they are not certain what subject to choose.

This is akin to putting the roof on the house before you lay the foundation. The rewards go to the expert who speaks, not the speaker with no expertise. The clueless speaker deserves to be hooted out of the auditorium.

A Yes or No Decision

There is a step you must take before you ever start organizing your presentation. It is one that all too many people ignore: Deciding whether or not to accept a speaking invitation.

More presenters should think about this instead of agreeing to any engagement that comes over the transom. You do not need to accept out of a sense of politeness or duty. Saying yes should be a conscious decision you make after you fully assess the pros and cons of whether the invitation will advance your cause or career.

What is the best way to gauge which speaking invitations to accept? Start with one simple question: Will it allow me to reach an audience that has some value for me?

As noted earlier, I partner with public relations and medical education agencies, so any engagement that puts me in front of agency principals is a no-brainer.

If you are a beginning or inexperienced speaker, I suggest that you relax these guidelines a bit. You need practice in front of a live audience, so you should accept most invitations that come along. One caution: Do not tackle any high profile engagements if you are not ready for them. Build your skills in the minor leagues before you try to star in the World Series. It is tough to rehabilitate a tarnished reputation.

You need to know all you can about the profile of your prospective audience. For instance:

- Who are they?
- How many are expected?
- Where do they come from?
- What is the age range?
- Is it predominantly female or male?

- Do they already know each other or are they meeting for the first time?
- Is attendance mandatory?
- How much do they know about your topic?
- Is there likely to be someone in attendance who may know more than you about certain aspects?

Also ask your meeting planner what type of presentation the organization is seeking. Like the rest of us, there are times when they are rushed and fail to do their homework. An organizer may contact you because a mutual acquaintance referred you. But if their meeting calls for a comedian and your subject is nuclear physics, the mismatch will make for a most uncomfortable presentation.

Next, dig a bit deeper into some of the personalities expected to attend:

- Who is the most senior person in the room?
- Who is the star of the organization?
- Who are the people no one can stand?
- Who is the veteran of the group?
- Are there any new members or employees?
- Is there someone who is known as a joker?
- Who has a reputation for causing trouble or being difficult?
- Has anyone captured a major award lately?

This gives you a better sense of your audience. When you mention these individuals during your presentation, you prove once again how much you know and value them.

Measure Twice, Speak Once

How do you measure a good opportunity? I start with a presentation information form that collects the info I need to make a judgment (see the form I use in Appendix A). The basics include:

- What are the logistics—when and where will the event take place? Be specific. Get the exact date and time. Also get the precise room where you will appear; the name of the hotel or office building alone will not get you where you need to go.
- Who is the contact person that will supply you with the background information you need and serve as the liaison prior to your presentation? (Note that in some cases this may be two separate people.)
- What topic do they want you to talk about? Here, too, get specific. If an organization asks me to talk about public speaking, for example, that does not give me much of an idea of their needs. If, however, they

tell me they need to hear how their vice presidents can successfully manage interviews with reporters, I can focus my presentation much more precisely on their needs.

- How long are you expected to speak? Are they expecting a ten-minute warm up for the main speaker or a sixty-minute keynote?
- How many people are expected to attend? Is this a cozy group of 10 or a crowd of 10,000? Don't forget to request the attendance list, and get an updated roster periodically, right up to the day before your presentation.
- Do they expect you to field questions from audience members?
- If there are other panelists involved, who are they? This is particularly critical when you will be on the dais with others. Does everyone else support your viewpoint, or are you being set up as a sacrificial lamb? (Hint: Think twice—then think two more times—before you accept this type of engagement.) And be sure to request the biographical sketches of your fellow panelists.
- Who precedes and follows you? Do they support or oppose your point of view?
- Does your audience already have great familiarity with your topic or will you be starting from scratch?
- What is their level of sophistication? Are you expected to talk to a group of C-level executives or should you gear your remarks to front-line supervisors?
- Did this group hear a similar presentation at its last meeting? If so, how can you set yourself apart by providing new information?
- Will your presentation be open to the media? I always assume when I speak in public that my remarks are liable to show up anywhere and speak accordingly. Save the sarcastic witticisms about your last boss, for instance, for the privacy of your own home.
- Will the organization e-mail or fax you an agenda for the entire meeting? You need to know if there is another speaker on the program you want to hear or make contact with. Are there other sessions running concurrently? If so, get a bead on the competition. You may decide to do more advance marketing than normal to get fannies in the seats in your room.
- Can the organization handle your technical needs for items like a projector, microphone, or flip chart? Will they copy handouts or do you need to bring them yourself?

Remember that you need to ask these questions just to make a decision on whether or not to accept a speaking invitation. Your purpose in speaking is to convince, inform, or entertain. In order to attain your goal, it is mandatory that you raise these issues so you can define whether or not this is an invitation that meets your criteria.

You may wonder about the value of some of the questions on my presentation information form. For example, why does the percentage of male vs. female attendees matter? I like to know this because women tend to laugh more readily. Plus, rarely will you find a woman heckler.

Why do I need to know how many people I will be addressing? That total will have a big impact on room set up. You will likely need a stage or a riser once your audience approaches fifty individuals.

In addition, a bigger crowd means a slower reaction time. It is like the difference between tossing a pebble into a small pool and a large lake. It takes no time for the ripples in the pool to reach the edge and bounce back. So it is with the reactions of a small audience. But larger groups react like the lake where the ripples go on and on, taking time to play off one another.

And Your Name Is...?

What is a speaker's top priority? I argue it is the audience. Your goal should be to learn all you can about those coming to see you.

Begin the process by conducting some due diligence. You need to learn who they are and what they need to hear from you. Stop and ask yourself, "Am I speaking to a group that favors clean air or clean hair?"

Get to the bottom of such issues as:

- What do they need to hear from me? How can I best deliver value to them?
- What is their viewpoint on my topic? Are they hostile? Supportive? Totally ambivalent?
- What specific problems do they face relative to this issue?
- How can I press their hot buttons if, indeed, they have any?
- Do they have expertise in this area or is this a new way of thinking for them?
- Do they have a stake in what I have to say, or are they forced by their management to attend?

From a substantive point of view, your presentation revolves around your expertise. But from the critical people perspective, it is your audience that is paramount, not you.

Do Your Homework

Although you are an expert in your subject, you need to layer that knowledge with additional research. This is absolutely vital to your preparation. Ready yourself like the Bolshoi Ballet prima ballerina who watches her videotape after every performance.

Think of all the research tools you have at your fingertips. Here are but a few:

- Your personal knowledge of the situation;
- Knowledge from co-workers, networking contacts, friends, and family;
- Industry sources and professional associations;
- Public libraries. Make friends with your local research librarian and you stand to unearth a treasure trove of information you never guessed existed;
- Books, magazines, newspapers, and white papers;
- Legislative and regulatory testimony filings;
- Web sites. Don't rely exclusively on your host organization's official web site. Do some digging and find out what their competitors and critics are saying about them;
- Web logs that may offer a more unvarnished perspective.

If you really want to get the lowdown on the challenges the organization faces, pick up the phone and call a few audience members in advance. Ask them for their insights, and be sure to probe so you can determine what they want to learn.

This gives you two important benefits. By telling you what they hope to gain, they will help outline your presentation for you. Second, it gives you some familiar names you can connect with the day of your presentation.

How Much Can I Say?

With your research in hand, it is almost time to write your remarks. However, you still have a few decisions to make.

Prime among them is the need to decide how much of your story you can tell in the given time frame. You could no doubt speak for hours about your area of expertise. The fact is, your host organization only has a twenty-minute window.

What to do? Cram in as much dense information as you can? Talk faster? Don't laugh. I have witnessed both of these futile methods, and you probably have, too—the presenter who sounds like a Top 40 deejay on speed when she realizes time is running short. No, that is not the way.

I recommend that you make a conscious decision about what to include. We will get into much more depth in Chapter Five about your message. Suffice for now to say that you need to decide on the three to four main points you want or need to stress, select some vivid proof points to buttress those messages, then shape your talk to the time you have been granted.

There is no physical way to stuff two dozen eggs into a carton designed to hold twelve. Similarly, you cannot wedge two hours worth of ideas into a twenty-minute talk. Don't even try.

This part of the preparation phase will save you a lot of energy as you practice and, more importantly, a lot of headaches during your actual presentation.

A Matter of Style

I am a firm believer in redundant systems. If something goes wrong—and it will if you speak with any frequency—a backup plan will keep your stress level from going off the charts.

Part of that redundancy involves carrying a spare copy of your remarks in the event your primary text is lost or scattered or someone spills coffee on it. I make it a point to carry two copies with me. My primary copy is held together with a paper clip so that I can avoid the need to noisily turn over the pages of a stapled copy. The backup set is stapled together. That ensures they stay in the right order, which becomes important if my primary sheets scatter to the floor in a disorganized heap.

Here is a related question I frequently hear: How should speakers organize their remarks? Should they write out the entire presentation or just jot down some talking points?

Some advisors will sternly tell you that you should write out every word. Others rebuke you if you don't memorize everything. But this is not a matter of black and white.

It revolves around your personal preference. Often, the people urging you to write out your speeches verbatim are speechwriters. These people get paid by the word. Of course they want you to deliver a prepared script.

Regardless of your choice of style, it is vital that you internalize your material. If it sounds like you are mechanically reciting a script, your audience will quickly tune you out. Don't let those written words interfere with your ability to make a solid connection with your audience.

If you want to avoid the appearance of using notes, prompt yourself with an index card containing only key words. For example, the word "daughter" might remind you about an anecdote concerning your daughter. Or the number "500" might prompt you to tell about an event that occurred during your presentation before 500 doctors.

Using key words jogs your memory, allowing you to easily recall each portion of your presentation while at the same time streamlining your talk.

Speaker, Promote Thyself

Now that you have decided to accept that speaking invitation, you need to make it easy for your host organization to promote your program.

Send them a short biographical sketch they can include in the event's program. And include your photo. A head shot (a formal photo of you from the shoulders up) is normally preferred. A word to the wise: When you pose for your photo, do not let anyone talk you into one of those goofy looking shots where your hand is draped at your chin. Those poses make you look thoroughly unprofessional.

While some groups are terrific when it comes to promoting their meetings, others haven't a clue. When it comes to publicizing your event, do not rely on the sponsoring organization. It may not be as high a priority for them as it is for you. They may fail to follow through or forget about their commitment. Or they may simply stink at marketing.

Take it upon yourself to let the world know you will be the featured speaker. Send a news advisory to the appropriate media. Include word in your company's newsletter. Send an e-mail to contacts in the area. Mention your upcoming appearance at networking events. Post flyers at strategic locations. Do whatever it takes to ensure a full house.

If the organization fails to do any advance publicity, you have done them a big favor. If they have done a responsible job, you have just bought yourself a double shot of public relations benefits, not to mention the gratitude of your host.

Practice! Practice! Practice!

Whether you take advantage of a formal public speaking workshop or not, don't ever neglect the need for practice. This does not mean simply giving your presentation a cursory once-over. You need plenty of rehearsal time before you are ready for the big show. An earnest practice regimen is the single biggest key to successful presentations.

The more you practice, the more comfortable you become with your subject matter and your delivery style. The more you internalize your material, the less you have to worry about the day of your performance.

In other words, "Internalize to Verbalize." The more your speech becomes a part of you, the easier time you have conveying your message. Internalize to Verbalize.

It is essential that you practice your presentation aloud. What looks great on paper may not sound as good to the ear. It is the same difference a writer experiences when he writes a magazine article as compared to copy for broadcast news. One form is targeted toward the eye, the other toward the ear.

Most people who have not studied public speaking in depth have little real idea what to look for without the steady guidance of a communications coach. Your success depends on gaining counsel from a professional who can properly interpret the research and lead you to a higher communications performance. (The questions in Appendix C will help you locate the individual who can chart a course for your continued improvement.)

Learning Methods

What practice format works best? I strongly recommend the videotape route. Arm yourself with a video camera. You do not necessarily need a professional set up complete with bright lights and wireless microphones, or a broadcast quality product. You simply need to be able to see yourself. Your personal camcorder will do the job.

And don't let that video sit there once you shoot it. Rewind it and play it back immediately—multiple times. As you review the tape, assess each player in the Communications Trifecta by weighing your Message Tools, Video Tools, and Audio Tools.

What if you lack access to a video recorder? At least record your voice on an audio tape recorder and play it back. Again, nothing fancy is needed. A simple portable audio cassette recorder will suffice.

If all else fails and you cannot find a way to record yourself, rehearse in front of a mirror. Just be alert to the fact that everything you observe will be a reverse image, the exact opposite of what your audience will see. This arrangement is not optimal, but it will offer at least a minimal gauge of your abilities.

If you want to rehearse alone during your first few run-throughs, that's fine. That can allow you to work on your rate of speech, gestures, and the like. But as you get closer to the day of your presentation, arrange to practice in front of real, live human beings. When the big day arrives, you will be speaking before a crowd of people. So enlist co-workers, friends, or family as your test audience.

Make it a point to ask them for feedback. Tell them you need honesty, not flattery. If an anecdote runs too long, you need to know in order to correct it. If your eye contact is spotty, they will perform a great service by informing you.

As you transition into your final practice sessions, be sure you are working with your final remarks, or at least a final draft. Whether you opt to work from an outline, notes, full text, or slides, rehearse using the finished product so that you know where to insert a pause, when to display your props, and the like.

I sometimes hear from companies with a group of four or five senior managers who could really use some help with their presentation skills. But the organization doesn't know how to go about teaching them.

My suggestion? Interactive, experiential training. People learn by doing. Practicing and reviewing your performance on videotape is the most powerful learning tool I can recommend.

Of course, much depends on the specific situation. Your group may benefit most from:

- One session that includes everyone
- Two separate sessions divided by areas of expertise, seniority, or some other logical grouping
- An executive training for your CEO and separate seminars for your vice presidents, managers, and supervisors
- Breakout groups using multiple trainers

The key is flexibility, honoring each individual's needs by giving them what they need.

Everyone Is a Speaker

More people are speaking in public more frequently than ever before. Think of your own situation. It is altogether likely that you find yourself speaking before inter-office meetings or fellow volunteers at community service organizations more frequently than five or ten years ago.

There are many different types of forums open to you these days. I want to review some examples of the types of opportunities you may confront and offer some practical ideas for improvement:

- Panelist in a discussion vital to the interests of your organization.
  - *Practice hint*: Draft the people in your office who are known for interrupting when conversing and use them as practice panelists.
- Sales or marketing pitches to prospective clients.
  - *Practice hint*: Become intimately familiar with your props before using them in front of a potential customer. This ranges from how you will demonstrate your product to when you will transition from slide to slide. Also, know your material inside out; the show must go on even if your presentation software is deep-sixed by a frozen laptop.
- Extemporaneous presentation to co-workers.
  - *Practice hint:* Prepare in advance. Don't try to wing it just because you know these people well. For all you know, your boss may be sizing you up for a promotion or deciding whether your merit increase should be two percent or ten percent. Know what you are going to say, then practice it beforehand.
- Wedding toast.
  - *Practice hint*: Do not try off-color humor at someone else's expense. Even if you find yourself a little too happy from drinking the bubbly, tell yourself that this is not the time to broadcast the groom's adventures at last night's bachelor party. Always respect your audience and, above all else, the guest of honor when one is present.

Once you get a bit more accomplished as a presenter, even more opportunities will present themselves. For instance:

- Brief analysts with regard to your company's quarterly performance. Many such briefings are now delivered online via webcast. It is important to recognize that this medium has its own rules of etiquette. Decades ago, radio and television changed the rules for effective communications. Webcasts have done the same thing. You owe it to your organization to get up to speed on this new tool.
  - *Practice hint*: Observe webcasts other businesses have produced as part of their analyst briefing efforts. Use techniques that work; discard those that fail.
- Speak before the National Press Club. Your presence must fill up the room when you speak in a large hall or ballroom. This means you must make full and effective use of your Video Tools (action, facial

expression, eye contact, wardrobe, and props) and your Audio Tools (pitch, articulation, volume, emotion, and rate). And, by the way, you also need a first-rate speech.

    □ *Practice hint*: In large halls, you cannot make eye contact with everyone individually. Overcome that by dividing the room into six parts—front and back; left, right, and center—and commit to making contact regularly with each of those six areas.

- Become a professional speaker. There is a small band of intrepid souls who make their living speaking in front of corporate, association, government, and non-profit organizations. Their specialties vary from keynote speeches to seminars to breakout sessions. The topics range from the doctor who has a unique practice to the financial services expert who offers a new twist on retirement planning. Each is an expert in her given field. But all are not expert presenters. What's more, even the most accomplished speakers need the occasional tune up.

    □ *Practice hint*: Contact a sampling of your audience members before each speech. Ask what they want to hear, and then deliver what they want.

If you speak long enough and commit to ongoing improvement, you will experience a wide range of opportunities. You will meet with more success if you work to get a grip on the differences among them.

What Time Do You Have?

Another choice you must face is what time of day you will deliver your presentation. Generally speaking, some times are better than others because your audience will be more alert. My preferred times are mid to late morning and early evening. During these time slots, people are normally awake and not looking forward to a nap.

There are other options best left on the table. Here is why these time slots normally prove deadly dull:

- *Early morning*. The early bird may catch the worm, but the early speaker rarely catches an attentive audience. They are still wiping the sleep from their eyes and thinking more about that first cup of coffee and how to plan their day than about your topic.
- *Post-lunch*. The siesta became tradition for a reason. It is normal to experience an after-lunch lull.

- *Late afternoon.* Not only are individuals suffering from another energy shortage, many are distracted, thinking about how they can wrap up the day's affairs or finish one more task before the end of the workday.
- *Late evening (after 8 p.m.).* You are competing with the urge to call it a day. If your audience is not bone tired, they are at least mentally checked out until tomorrow. Worse yet, at many functions you may find certain people imbibing their favorite spirits.

Have I accepted engagements during these less than preferable time slots? Sure, if that is my only option and it involves an audience I want to reach. But if I am part of a larger program, I will ask if it is possible to switch times.

If you find yourself slotted in one of these challenging time periods, you need to be extra vigilant with regard to your nonverbal talents. Your Video Tools and Audio Tools must be super sharp, and you will need to mix things up frequently to keep audience members on their toes.

Also be aware if your audience is traveling through many time zones to hear you speak. For instance, if you are addressing a sales convention in Hawaii, it is a safe bet that, at least during the first few days, many of the participants will get tired earlier than usual due to the time change. That might make an early morning presentation more desirable. Just remember to gauge your audience's body clock as well as your own.

A Plethora of Options

Your next decision is how to structure your talk. Do you prefer to work from notes? Does this occasion call for the use of presentation software to better drive home your message? Is it a formal speech that requires you to work from a prepared text?

The thing to recognize is that you have choices in how you structure your speech. Don't let anyone tell you there is one proper method for every circumstance.

The appropriate choice is what works best for your style and suits your comfort level. If you hate reading from a full text, your audience will sense it. Or, if you are uncomfortable without at least a few notes, your listeners will see your trembling. So choose what you are comfortable with, provided it fits the situation.

This means you must combine your personal criteria with the format of the meeting and the meeting space. For instance, you do not want to stand behind a lectern to read a speech to a half-dozen listeners. Nor do you want to come prepared with a dazzling slide show in a space not equipped to handle a projector.

You do have a wide range of options when it comes to your chosen format. You can work from a prepared text, talking points, an outline, presentation software, 35 mm slides, or speak extemporaneously. Let's talk about the advantages and disadvantages of each method:

- Full text.
  - PRO: When you write out every word and read your speech, you have a ready-made handout (or handup, as I like to call it) for your audience. It is also nearly impossible to go off message. Plus, full text is a good option when you need to deliver specific language for legal reasons.
  - CON: It is a challenge to read a speech and sound natural. You must be ready to commit to a great deal of rehearsal time when delivering a full text speech.
- Outline or talking points.
  - PRO: Avoids the canned sound of a full text speech, particularly for those who find it difficult to master reading a script while sounding natural.
  - CON: Speakers sometimes lose their train of thought. It is more difficult to get that train chugging again when using only a bare bones tactic.
- Presentation software, 35 mm slides, or overhead transparencies.
  - PRO: Allows you to demonstrate visual concepts and gives you a ready-made handup to distribute to your audience.
  - CON: It is a mind-numbing experience when a presenter talks to the screen instead of the audience or when the room goes dark (see Chapter Ten for a full treatment of presentation software).
- Extemporaneous (remarks are prepared but not written out).
  - PRO: Avoids reinventing the wheel if you speak about the same topic to the same type of audience frequently.
  - CON: Strong temptation to veer off into uncharted waters, straying off message.
- Impromptu.
  - PRO: None. I vehemently discourage this "winging it" method.
  - CON: You will lose your train of thought, fail to deliver your message, and look like an unprepared amateur. Mark Twain summed

up the impromptu speech best when he said, "It usually takes more than three weeks to prepare a good impromptu speech."

- Stump speech.
  - □ PRO: This style, in which 90 percent of your material is the same every time you speak, maintains your consistency of message in every situation while allowing you to tailor matters to your specific audience. The remaining 10 percent—the "donut"—speaks to that day's audience.
  - □ CON: Since this is a variation of the full text speech, you must work hard not to sound canned.

Which format do I use? It depends. If I want something "for the record" to distribute to audience members or reporters, I normally work from full text. If it is a short presentation, I might deliver using a few notes. And I have worked with everything in between. I cannot say that I have a favorite. It depends on what is best for the audience at hand.

Regardless which of the above formats you decide to utilize, make it easy for your eyes to scan your copy. If you work with full text, increase the font size, bring in the margins (left and right, top and bottom), and make each sentence its own paragraph. Do not use all capital letters; contrary to popular belief, it is harder to scan text printed in all caps. Jot down cues to yourself in the margins that remind you when to bring a prop into play or when you want to remind yourself to pause for effect, for example. You can also insert dashes, commas, or ellipses as signals to pause for a beat. If there are some key points you really want to hammer home, underline the text or put it in bold face to make it stand out.

When presentation software is your medium of choice, do not make your printout so small that you cannot easily read each slide along with your notes.

Punch It Up

As you craft your remarks, keep in mind the need to add some punch. One sure way to put your audience to sleep is to bore them with dry language. There are lots of ways to pump up your presentation. Consider:

- Stories
- Numbers
- Extremes
- Case studies
- Jiu jitsu

- Quotations from famous individuals
- Anecdotes
- Analogies
- Topics du jour
- Clichés
- Personal experience
- Humor

Most of these techniques are intuitive and straightforward. Still, it is worth taking a few moments to review how you can put them to work for you.

Stories. As children, we all craved bedtime stories. As members of an audience, we still find, "let me tell you a story," to be one of the most intriguing phrases a speaker can utter.

Numbers. Millions, dozens, percentages, fractions, and other numerical measurements lend credence to your arguments. Just don't overwhelm listeners with statistics. You are leading a presentation, not a math course.

Extremes. Trumpet the fact that your product was the *first* to function as both a floor polish and a dessert topping. Explain that your company is the *only* one that offers flights to the moon. Don't shy away from talking about the *best*, the *worst*, the *first*, the *latest*, the *hottest*, or the *coolest*.

Case studies. It is your job to bring your story to life. Everyone can leverage the power of case studies, from CEOs to accountants to doctors. Even communications trainers. I could talk to you until I am blue in the face about the necessity of media training for anyone who deals with reporters. On a rational level, you probably believe me.

Yet the point gains added punch when I tell you about the time I helped a physician ace a crucial TV interview. His media training workshop taught him that he needed to be concise and get to the point right away. His time slot amounted to a scant three minutes.

In that limited window, he succeeded in getting across his main message, complete with anecdotes, numbers, and personal experiences that made his story real for the viewer at home. Notice how the case study builds a much stronger claim for the benefits of media training.

Jiu jitsu. This ancient martial art, used verbally, turns your adversary's words against him.

Here is an example: I once worked for an association of state regulators that had a devil of a time convincing federal officials about the value of the role played by the states. The General Accounting Office (GAO), the watchdog arm of Congress, issued periodic reports largely critical of our positions.

After years of diligent attempts at persuasion, the GAO issued a conclusion that included a positive mention of our key endeavors. It was only a few sentences buried in the conclusion. But you can bet we inserted that passage into our officers' speeches and our conversations with reporters at every opportunity. Employing jiu jitsu helped us soften some of the blows from critics we otherwise would have endured.

Quotations from famous individuals. Borrow a few words from an expert in your field or a well-known personality to bolster your case. There are volumes upon volumes of books containing quotations, and the Internet is replete with such sources. Remember to attribute the quotation to its original author.

Anecdotes. Some people are natural storytellers. If you fall into that category, use your talent to spin a yarn that engages your audience while reinforcing your message.

Analogies. Comparing one thing to another—using an analogy—can drive your point home. You might tell your listeners that delivering a presentation used to be like slogging through the desert sands, but now it is like the feeling an Olympic swimmer gets slicing through the water.

Topics du jour. Examine newspapers, magazines, current films, television shows, advertisements, and books for ideas that relate to your topic. It is particularly useful to scan the local newspaper for local color when your speech takes you out of town.

Clichés. These are the old saws that everyone knows by heart. They can be effective when used judiciously; just be sure not to overuse them. Too many clichés make your speech sound trite. Or, to borrow a cliché, "too many cooks spoil the broth."

Personal experience. Each of us brings a distinct perspective and a unique set of feelings. Give your audience a peek into the real you by sharing personal experiences that relate to your topic.

Humor. There are many ways to get a laugh. Find one that works for you. I will caution you that there are few among us who can tell a joke successfully. Unless you are trained as a stand-up comedian, it is best to forgo the Chris Rock approach.

However, you may be skilled at ad libbing or poking fun at yourself. Visual humor such as photos and cartoons can elicit laughs in nearly any culture (if you use such visuals, be sure you have the rights to do so; determine if you need to pay royalties). Bringing a bit of humor to your presentation helps to enliven it. But don't try to force a laugh if that is not your style.

The Jargon-Free Zone

While we are talking about spicing up your remarks, I should mention one technique that is certain to instigate boredom. Using jargon will do it every time.

Leaders involved in such technical professions as medicine, engineering, law, and high tech really know how to load up on the jargon. To the rest of us, they might as well be speaking in tongues.

Here is the problem: Their education has taught them that there is a right answer for nearly everything. Mathematical equations and scientific formulas make for a nice, orderly world. If only it were so in the world of the communicator.

When speaking in public, plain English is a virtue. It is important to be understood. You may be the smartest person in the room, but if no one can comprehend what you are saying, you will come across as nothing more than a pompous know-it-all who lacks a clear message.

Some technicians consciously use their industry's language as a barrier or to impress listeners with their insider's knowledge. Over the years, I have worked with my share of doctors who certainly don't believe they spent all that time in medical school so they could talk like the rest of us. Most often, however, they have simply lapsed into the practice of speaking in their own brand of gibberish out of sheer habit. In their world, day in and day out, their colleagues actually understand them. But get them beyond the confines of their workplaces, and you and I can make neither heads nor tails of what they are trying to tell us.

I hereby apologize in advance if you hear laughter from the audience when you utter words like, "end-to-end solutions" or "marketplace synergies." The chuckling will be mine. This type of shopworn jargon has no place in a professional presentation.

Your audience research comes into play when you decide how many buzzwords you can get away with. Take a good hard look at your audience as you prepare and figure out how technical you can go.

Let us take the example of a doctor—a specialist speaking before a group of general practitioners. Even though they all have medical degrees, they may not have the same baseline of knowledge as the presenter and may not speak the same lingo. So go easy on the technical terms.

If that same doctor presents before a group of patients, it becomes even more critical to dial down the jargon meter.

In the final analysis, I always recommend starting with the basics in plain

English. It is always easier to build in an appropriate level of detail once you get a sense of what a particular audience can handle.

It is important to be understood. Leave the techno-babble within the four walls of your office.

Allow Me to Introduce Myself

Some speakers encounter difficulty in figuring out how to introduce them-selves. They think it sounds boastful to cite all their accomplishments.

And they are right. Enumerating all your credentials will act like warm milk with a baby, putting your audience to sleep in no time. They need to know enough to understand that you are the expert, but they do not need to know where you went to grade school (unless your topic is ushering your children through grade school) or how many alphabet soup designations you have after your name (unless you are speaking before an industry group whose members have similar credentials).

At the same time, you do need to work your bona fides into your speech. Research by UCLA professor Albert Mehrabian, PhD, shows that, when a speaker is introduced in a hurried or sketchy fashion, the audience assumes a lack of respect for her and for her work.

You can script your own introduction in a very casual sounding, yet con-sciously planned manner. When I speak, to cite an example, I could tell lis-teners that I am the greatest communications trainer ever to wander the face of the earth. But such braggadocio is vain. As a result, the audience would dismiss it as so much puffery. Instead, I will mention a client I worked with last week or an experience I had as a radio broadcaster. That gets my point across without being heavy-handed.

A Few Words About Our Speaker

Of course, there is an obvious solution to singing your own praises. Have someone else sing the lyrics you write.

When you arrange the logistics for your presentation, ask in advance who is going to introduce you. If the organizer has not thought of this, you have just done her a favor by reminding her.

Have at the ready a one paragraph biographical sketch that you can give to your introducer. This spares someone who may not know you well from the pressure of having to make something up.

More importantly, when you write it you get to choose how you are introduced. You can be as florid as you like. After all, this is an objective person saying how great you are. As Will Rogers said, "If you done it, it ain't bragging."

Include a line or two about why you were selected to speak. Is it due to your outstanding expertise? Did the program chair hear you at another event and realize immediately that you were the expert she needed at her meeting? Have you worked with the organization in the past and, since you received such rave reviews, the organizers just had to invite you back?

Your introducer can also run a humor test for you. If your subject is cheery and you prefer to make use of humor as part of your presentation, sprinkle the introduction you write with a bit of levity. If the audience chuckles during the introduction, you will know it is safe for you to proceed accordingly. If the lightheartedness falls flat, however, it is time to consider Plan B, the approach that maps a more serious course.

Pay particular attention to this if you are speaking in an early morning time slot. People's laugh reflexes just aren't awake yet. Also keep it in mind when addressing a heavily male audience. Generally speaking, they are less inclined to laugh than are women.

If you are strict about how you prefer to be introduced, you can jot a note at the top of your script explaining why it is important to read it verbatim. You can even suggest your introducer lead the applause as you trot onstage.

No matter the style of your opening, send your introducer a copy in advance AND bring one with you to your presentation. As often as not, he will forget to bring it or will misplace it in the hubbub leading up to your big day. If that turns out to be the case, you can pull your copy from your back pocket and hand it to him. Presto. You have proved once again what a problem-solver you are.

Hand the backup to your introducer, telling her you brought an extra. Don't ask if she needs it. If indeed she has forgotten it, that question could prove embarrassing. Just hand it over as a spare copy.

Flying Solo

If yours is a small and informal gathering, there may be no one charged with introducing you. In that case, you need to present your own credentials to the audience. A brief rundown of your experience is fine, but how do you work in those items that border on boastfulness? It is easy when someone else is citing your accomplishments (even though you have written it your-self). Immodesty is not seen as a virtue in most people's eyes.

After citing your experience, plan to work in some highlights from your past as you speak. You could very seamlessly during your talk include credentials like:

- "When I covered the Republican National Convention as a radio reporter…"
- "When I spoke before the International Association of Business Communicators…"
- "As I told the executive team of the XYZ company last week…"

This approach raises your profile while avoiding charges of conceit.

A well-planned introduction plays another critical role: It helps to establish trust with audience members. Trust is, after all, a quality that is earned with time and familiarity. There may not be much you can do about the time factor, but your introduction can help remove unfamiliarity and suspicions.

To Podium or Not to Podium?

One choice you are likely to face sooner or later is whether or not to use a lectern or podium. This is particularly true as your speaking efforts mature and you find yourself invited to address larger gatherings where podium use is almost mandatory.

Technically, I realize that the two words define slightly different items. For the record, the podium is the platform from which you speak; the lectern is the stand upon which you put your notes. Now you know. That made your day, didn't it?

Some people get all bent out of shape if the proper term is not used. Count me out of that debate. It is more important you learn how to use one rather than quibble over definitions. But custom and usage has made the terms largely interchangeable.

Some "experts" recommend that you always use a podium. Others tell speakers to avoid it like the plague. What is my counsel? I return to a guiding principle: There is no one-size-fits-all answer.

It depends on factors like personal preference, the size and layout of the room, and whether you plan to use visual aids such as slides or presentation software. Only you can make the call that is right for your individual circumstances.

A word of caution if you opt for a lectern: Keep reminding yourself that it is nothing more than a place to put your stuff—your notes, laptop, or any props you plan to utilize.

Pay attention to the positioning of your lectern. If you are using presentation software or overhead slides, place the lectern to the left of the screen as viewed by the audience. Since we read left to right, this will return their attention to you more readily. Place it at a slight angle, no more than 45 degrees. This allows you to gesture to the screen more readily.

Nail Down the Details

Clarity is a good thing during the preparation phase. Spell out your expectations with regard to matters like audio/visual equipment, microphones, flip chart, seating patterns, stage set up, lighting, room temperature, and placement of refreshments.

Be as specific as possible. For instance, what type of seating plan do you normally prefer—classroom? Theater? Round tables? Another example: What type of microphone suits you best? I make it clear that my first choice is a wireless lavaliere (the small clip-on model that comes with a battery pack that hooks to my belt). Also, do you need floor microphones to capture questions from the audience?

It is important to remember that you are the star of the show. There are fannies in the seats because of you. You own that room for the duration of your presentation. This means that you have some say in the layout of your room.

Be polite. But be firm and insistent on ensuring that the set up is to your liking. An unfriendly environment makes for an unpleasant experience for speaker and audience alike. Tighten up as many of those details as you can before the day of your presentation. Still, no matter how diligent your efforts, something is guaranteed to slip through the cracks. That is why you need to arrive at least an hour before your scheduled start.

The bottom line here is to make it easy for organizations that ask you to speak to do business with you. Have routine items like your biographical sketch, photographs, and your preferred introduction ready for distribution. Better yet, place them on your web site where the meeting organizers can grab them at their convenience.

I even clue them in to the fact that I am a vegetarian and request a veggie entrée if my presentation occurs during a meal. This saves last-minute scrambling on the part of the kitchen staff and spares the organizers of any possible embarrassment.

Get the Right Gear

It is a good idea to maintain a checklist of your preferred room requirements. Some organizations may not be able to fulfill all of your wishes, but I recommend you be as clear as you possibly can with your logistical expectations.

One of the areas you need to clarify is the equipment you need:

- Do you prefer a wireless lavaliere microphone (the small clip-on units) or do you want a hand-held microphone? Or, if you are speaking in a small room, do you need to be amplified at all?
- If you are showing slides, do you need a projector or do your travel with your own? If you carry yours, don't forget to pack the cables you need. You will likely bring your own laptop but, if not, specify that you will need one. And remember to request a screen.
- Do you need a flip chart or a white board with markers to jot down notes and record audience thoughts?
- When conducting training workshops, I always make it a point to ensure there is a television and VCR available to play back the sessions I videotape.
- I also specify whether I supply the camera crew or I expect my hosts to do that.

Also, spell out how you want your room set up:

- Do you want theater style seating? My preference in this format is to have all the chairs facing me. This means each row is curved and every chair is angled, as opposed to arranged in straight rows as most facilities normally do. You may find that you need to educate the set up team on how to do this. They will be amazed to learn that they can actually squeeze more seats into the room by angling them toward the speaker. Plus, it is more comfortable for audience members who now have no need to crane their necks throughout your presentation.
- If attendees will be eating, how many do you want seated at each table? Most banquet facilities routinely set up tables of eight or ten. But if you are planning any small group activities, that may not suit your needs. Do not hesitate to ask for tables of four or five people.
- If you plan to speak from a lectern, remember to request one and indicate where you want it positioned.
- Has your audio/visual crew taped all wires and cords to the floor? Insist that they do so. You do not want anyone—you included—injured or embarrassed by tripping over a loose electrical cord.

- Is a stage necessary? In a large room, the answer is yes. You can dispense with the stage before gatherings of fifty or fewer people.

There are also a number of items you should request for your personal needs:

- I like to have a small table near the front of the room where I can lay some notes.
- You will also need a good supply of bottled water and a drinking glass. Keep the water at room temperature or only slightly chilled as cold water tends to tighten up the vocal chords.

Show Time

You have decided on your topic, researched it thoroughly, and written and practiced your remarks. The day of your presentation arrives. Are there additional preparation steps? You bet.

You need to locate the room where you will speak. It sounds basic. But if you have trouble finding your room, so will your audience. Post some directional signs at key points if necessary. You want as big a crowd as possible.

This means you must arrive early. How early? I recommend at least one hour ahead of your scheduled start time. Some executives look at me askance when I suggest this. But the ones who have been victimized by electrical outlets that don't work, incorrect seating arrangements, and missing flip charts know exactly what I mean.

Upon your arrival, check to be sure your microphone, flip chart, markers, projector, and other items you may have requested are in the room. Check to confirm that each one works.

Is the room set up to the specifications you provided to your meeting planner? Are there any seats obstructed by pillars or electrical equipment?

Introduce yourself to the audio/visual crew. Get a business card from at least one member and know how to reach them either on a house phone or by using your cell phone. If an A/V crisis should crop up, it is vital that you know their names and how to contact them.

Your early arrival expands your comfort zone and gives you time to debug any glitches. Projectors have a way of not talking to laptops. The most carefully prepared equipment list has a way of being ignored by the set up crew. The markers for your flip chart have a way of disappearing. Microphones tend to feedback at certain spots.

Allow yourself ample time to troubleshoot anything that could go wrong.

This final preparation step provides the best blood pressure medication I know. Arriving early is a real stress reducer.

Once you are satisfied with your technical run-through, it is time to meet and greet your audience. Your goal here is twofold. First, create a few additional friendly faces you can connect with during your remarks. Second, get the audience on your side by letting them know you will be talking about topics that matter to them.

Ex-baseball home run king Roger Maris summed up the value of doing your homework when he said, "You hit home runs not by chance but by preparation."

I Can Make You Look Real Bad

A few more words about introducing yourself to the audio/visual technicians. Not only is it common courtesy to do so, your tech team can make you look very good—or very bad.

If you act like a pompous jerk and talk down to them, guess what is going to happen if your microphone cuts out? Probably not much, since you will have succeeded in alienating the only experts who could help you. If, on the other hand, you treat them as the valuable partners they are, your technicians will often make suggestions that add to the professionalism of your presentation.

Conduct a complete tech check. Here is a useful checklist to get you started:

- Confirm your microphone works.
- Discuss any cues your tech crew needs to watch for if you want the lighting changed at some point or need to switch from slides to videotape.
- Review your cues if someone else will be physically changing slides for you. Avoid at all costs uttering the all too common and ultra-annoying, "next slide, please."
- Walk around the room and listen for any feedback hot spots.
- Make sure the projector and any attendant equipment works.
- Ask if your technician has a spare bulb available.

Be sure you meet the individual responsible for running your A/V. In some cases, this will not be the same person who performs the set up. You need to get your signals straight with the individual taking the hands-on role.

I was once assigned a camera operator during a presentation skills training in Dallas who was a very friendly fellow. But he seemed a bit behind the curve during the set up process. I made it a point to ask a few gentle yet probing questions.

It turns out that he normally ran audio and freely admitted he did not do much camera work. That clued me in to the fact that I needed to explain more in advance and provide more detailed direction during the workshop. Some of his shots still left something to be desired, but I was able to steer clear of a disaster thanks to that advance preparation.

Check Your Logistics

Now for specifics about preparing your venue. Take a quick but thorough scan of the room as you enter. Here are some keys to heed:

- Is your flip chart there, complete with markers that work?
- Is there at least one blue marker (the easiest color for most audiences to read)? Or are they all yellow or pink, which will be visible to no one?
- Is the microphone present? Does it work? Do you know how to turn it off and on, if need arises?
- Is the projector set up?
- Do you have the cables needed to connect the projector to your laptop?
- Is the seating pattern arranged to your specifications?
- Are there any obstructed views you will need to deal with?
- If you need to change the seating arrangement, can you do it yourself or, if it is a union facility, does someone there have to do it for you? (You never want to run afoul of union workers; they can make your day very unpleasant if you violate the terms of their contract.)
- If you plan to use a podium or lectern, is it the proper height?

Now let's deal with a few environmental matters you need to consider when conducting the final check of your room:

- The room temperature should stay cool, ideally between 68 and 70 degrees. A warm room makes audiences drowsy. A hot room makes them uncomfortable. A cold room proves terribly distracting. If you have a few people suggesting that they are a bit chilly, you have the setting about right.
- Keep the lighting bright. This, too, avoids audience drowsiness. The only exception is near the front of the room when you work with slides.
- Run an audio check to be sure all the speakers are in working order. If one is blown, get it fixed or cordon off that section of the room, if feasible.

Your scan of this new environment needs to include a few additional matters for your audience's benefit. Determine the location of the nearest restrooms and know how to direct people there; this is especially important if you are delivering a longer presentation with a scheduled break. So, too, is the site of refreshments if those are available.

Also, be prepared to inform audience members where they will go after your presentation. Remember, you are their host, so know where to guide them.

Finally, always make a point to search out the nearest fire exits in advance. On the slim chance something goes wrong—smoke starts coming through the vents or the lights go out—your audience will be looking to you for leadership. When I speak in a hotel, I prowl the service corridors until I find the fire door.

It is also a good idea to carry a flashlight with your gear. I never travel without a small pen-size flashlight. It may be small, but the beam is powerful enough to be a life saver should the need ever arise.

A World Built on Punctuality

By the time you have completed your initial inspection, there may be someone there from the sponsoring organization. But maybe not. I often finish my preparation checklist before any representatives from the sponsoring group arrive.

They are surprised to see me there early despite the fact I have ensured ahead of time I will be able to get into the room an hour before my remarks are slated to begin. I suppose their astonishment tells us all something about the poor preparation habits of many speakers. Taking your preparation seriously is another means to distance yourself from the pack.

Now that you are comfortable with your room arrangements and you have touched base with your host, tend to your personal needs. Set aside a few moments to touch up your makeup, brush or comb your hair one last time, and get a glass of water.

And don't neglect a visit to the restroom. Hey, people sometimes laugh when I remind them of this, but your comfort is vital if you are to succeed at the podium. The last thing you want to experience is the panic the juror in the TV commercial for an incontinence product experiences—"gotta go, gotta go, gotta go right now!" When finished with your business, remember to zip up. I have seen it and you probably have, too—the open-fly presenter. There are few more embarrassing sights than a speaker who suddenly realizes he is revealing more to his audience than intended.

Center yourself by using any techniques that work for you, whether your preference is a quiet moment or two alone or warming up by having a colleague fire some questions at you.

As you prepare to take charge of your room, your mindset becomes critical. Picture the meeting planner handing over the keys to the room. Assume ownership of that space for the duration of your presentation.

To put yourself in the proper frame of mind, make at least one change to your speaking environment, no matter how small. Reposition a chair, change the angle of a table, write some advance notes on the flip chart, or slightly move the lectern. Such actions reinforce your sense of control and confidence.

With the right amount of preparation and a shot of confidence, it must be showtime, right? Not quite. About fifteen minutes before I am scheduled to hit the spotlight, I take up a position at the door to meet and greet audience members as they enter. This final preparation step wins me some friendly faces and turns me into a flesh and blood person, not an amorphous stage presence, in their eyes.

Any gracious homeowner knows enough to make his guests feel welcome. Do the same thing with this room you now own. Greet audience members as they arrive. Shake some hands and flash a smile. This is company coming to call. Put out your own personal welcome mat.

A Sense of Place

The site of your speech also matters. If you are booked to speak in a hotel meeting room, learn what is going on in the rooms near you. A neighboring religious revival or high-octane sales seminar is not likely to be a tame affair. Ask to be moved if you sense the noise may interfere with your audience's ability to concentrate. A cheerleading convention or Aerosmith fan club meeting may be fun if you are in the midst of it. But they hardly make friendly next door neighbors for a speaker.

If conditions do not allow you to relocate, you will have to ensure your program contains a bit more pep than usual. Increase the level of interactivity, for example, to raise the odds of your audience listening to you instead of humming that gospel tune from the next room.

In addition, acknowledge the disturbance. It will be impossible for your listeners to ignore the elephant next door, so be up front. Tell them conditions may not be optimal, and that you need their help. Ask them to concentrate a bit harder today. Most people will understand this is out of your control and will work to help you succeed.

Try your best to ensure the size of your room is appropriate. There are few things that deaden a presentation more effectively than having the dozen people you anticipate scattered about a room suited for 100. It makes it look like no one had any interest in coming to see you. It is far preferable to have a smaller jam-packed space with standing room only. That gets across the notion that you draw huge crowds.

If your program necessitates lots of bells and whistles—perhaps a projector to beam your presentation software slides or the ability to view video clips—investigate whether your room has the technical capability to perform to your standards. If you are booked into an older facility, it may, for example, not have the electrical capacity your set up demands.

Speaking outdoors is even trickier. You may need to deal with wind, rain, and the sun in your eyes. One gust of wind and there goes your script. One squall drives your audience away. Sunshine in your eyes transforms your audience into a blur. On top of all that, props are very difficult to manage in an outdoor environment. Charts may topple over in the breeze and slide shows will be washed out by the sun. This argues for keeping props to an absolute minimum when presenting outside. The bottom line here: If it is an audience you want to reach and this is your only opportunity, go for it. But if you have other chances to touch that same audience indoors, take a pass on Mother Nature's living room.

Seating Chart

We used to see it all the time in school. Students that sat in the front row tended to get good grades. Why? It was easier for them to pay attention.

You may not be planning to give your audience members a test at the end of your session, but you do want them taking heed of your message. They will tend to be more attentive if you find a way to funnel them into the first few rows. Here's how.

Before they begin to arrive, tape or rope off the last few rows of chairs. Very few people will violate this system. Cordoning them off serves your purpose of channeling them into the front rows.

Remove the tape only when the front rows are nearly full. It will be easier for you if you ask an assistant or the event organizer to take care of this for you. You will have enough to think about without tending to such details.

Even better, set up fewer seats than you expect you will need. You can always have your helpers pull in more chairs if needed. It is to your benefit if it looks like an overflow crowd is clamoring to hear what you have to say.

Broadway producers love "SRO," or standing room only. If it is good for their image, it is good for yours.

Shapes of Things

Every now and then, you may be confronted with a meeting room that is peculiar in shape. Odd-shaped rooms are the bane of a meeting planner's existence. Facilities with nooks, crannies, pillars, and funny angles pose a real challenge.

The worst experience along these lines I can recall occurred at a meeting room in a venerable Washington, D.C., hotel where I led a media training workshop. This was, and still is, one of the grand dame hotels in the city. But the layout of this particular meeting room was clearly an afterthought. It had angles everywhere. Not only that, it had so many pillars that getting even a single good camera angle posed a challenge. Fortunately, I was working with one of the best audio/visual pros in the city (yes, I use him a lot), and he was able to overcome that obstacle to a large extent.

You can overcome such obstacles, though it does take some diligent planning. Here is how you can negate the odd size meeting room:

- Sketch out a floor plan indicating where you want the stage and podium, and how you want the seats arranged.
- Arrive even earlier than usual the day of your event.
- Sit in the seats before the audience arrives to check for obstructed views.
- Decide what extra effort you need to make to connect with anyone sitting in an obstructed view seat.
- Make your concerns known to the facilities management staff and seek assurances they will be responsive to your needs.

Remodeling may be out of the question, but with enough preparation you can neutralize a quirky room.

Don't be shy about explaining exactly what you need and expect to the facilities management staff. While they cannot change the shape of the room, they should bend over backward to make a less than suitable venue work for you.

A Moderating Influence

Serving on a panel raises additional dynamics. You are no longer flying solo, no longer in total command of your speaking environment. At times, you have to compromise and may need to give up some of your preferred methods. You should still feel free to request your ideal set up, but be prepared for a bit of give and take.

I recommend talking with your fellow panelists ahead of time. They may not grasp the need for preparation, so you can help them in this regard. If a face-to-face meeting is impractical, arrange a conference call. And be sure to include your moderator in this pre-planning endeavor.

If no moderator has been appointed, place the choice of that individual at the very top of the meeting's agenda. He or she will be crucial to the success of your panel. An experienced moderator understands how to:

- Get the session started on time
- Introduce the panel
- Involve all panelists in the discussion
- Stick to agreed-upon time limits
- Direct question and answers
- Advocate for your needs
- Handle unruly audience members
- End the presentation at the appointed hour

What should the agenda of your pre-session include? Start with these issues, at a minimum:

- Who talks about what subjects
- The order of speakers
- If and when you will take audience questions
- The need to reinforce time limits

Although these "iron out the kinks" meetings are invaluable, there is the exception that proves every rule. If you anticipate a panel that has been designed to spark verbal fireworks a la CNN's *Crossfire* program, skip the advance meeting. There is no point in locking horns ahead of time with someone vehemently opposed to your viewpoint. If you want to sort through the logistics in a case like this, assign that task to a trusted aide.

Lovely Parting Gifts

Allow me to follow through on the concept of a handup by first addressing a point of semantics. I prefer to call them handups. The term handout implies I am giving audience members a worthless scrap for which they need to beg like a dog. That is not at all the case. I am giving them rich information, offering a hand up in their professional and personal lives.

Make it a point to check with the sponsoring organization to confirm they have no objections. Such a reaction is exceedingly rare since they realize most attendees love getting free stuff. Ask if it is permissible to distribute the text of your remarks to the audience. This is particularly effective if you deliver a full text speech or want to leave them a copy of your slide presentation.

Your handups should be rich in content. Your audience took time from their busy day to hear your thoughts. Sure, in some cases they were compelled to be there by the boss. In any event, you must honor them with a resource-filled handup they can use to further their lifelong learning.

That said, your handups also represent a terrific way to market yourself. If your goal is to speak on a regular basis to a variety of organizations, you need to take every opportunity to broadcast your availability and talents. Now, I am not suggesting that your turn your handup into a marketing blitz. That is over the top and disrespectful to the organization that hired you.

But do be sure to include at a minimum your contact information: Name, address, telephone number, e-mail address, and web site. And don't be shy about tossing in the subjects of your top presentations. You never know who among those present may be in search of a speaker for their next event.

You say you don't have anything to use as handups? Look around you and think again. Consider that article you wrote earlier this year for your association's newsletter, that special report your organization just issued, or a page or two from your web site that speaks to the heart of your subject.

If it turns out you have absolutely nothing in your back pocket, write a "Top 10 Tip Sheet" or "Delightful Dozen Ideas You Can Use Today." These are quick and easy to put together, and people love walking away with a reference that is concise and easy to implement.

You can make your handups as short or as long as you wish. Of course, their content is likely to differ from audience to audience. If you are offering only brief remarks, a list of ten tips may suffice. If it is an all-day seminar, a workbook may be more appropriate. And there may be cases where you will want to staple together a series of articles, tip sheets, and checklists.

No matter the format of your handup, include a heavy dose of useful content with a dash of promotion on each page. That gives audience members loads of value while discouraging them from keeping only the pages with content and trashing your marketing information.

Adding Special Value

In certain circumstances, you can consider taking the handup to the next level by giving away something of more value to select audience members.

Perhaps you have written a book or produced an audio CD that parallels your talk. Such items make great door prizes.

If you plan to donate a door prize, script out in advance how you will conduct the drawing. Who will draw the winner? Will that duty fall to you, the organization's president, or another honored guest at the meeting? What system will you use? Selecting a business card from a bowl? Placing a star under one plate at a luncheon function? Announcing a lucky number in the event's program? You want the drawing to run smoothly so that all thoughts are on your product, not on how you fumbled in the front of the room.

Why give away something for nothing? Think of the potential returns. First of all, you have gained more goodwill in the eyes of your listeners by giving them a chance to win a valuable prize. Second, you have just created instant demand for your products if you offer them for sale after your presentation.

You could have your winner come forward to claim her reward once her name is called. Or you could pass the prize through the audience to your winner. That tactile maneuver provides a subtle way to help you create more demand for your products. Once people touch something and examine it for a moment, they are more likely to want to own it.

Clear your giveaway with your host first. You do not want to alienate them by springing an unwanted surprise. Send a complimentary copy to the program chair or meeting planner. They not only get to check it out, they get a free gift for all the assistance they have provided you.

A note of caution about product sales: Some organizations are highly sensitive about this and may not allow you to offer your wares following your presentation. You must gain their explicit approval to do so. Ask whether you are allowed to distribute promotional materials. Some groups frown upon what they view as "commercialism." Be sure to ask before you find yourself in an embarrassing pickle.

I suggest you write the provision into your contract. Position it as extending the attendees' lifelong learning. You are allowing them to take away a resource they can use to reinforce the seeds you planted during your talk.

But, in the end, if the organizer says no sales, it's no sales. It is not worth going to the mat over this issue if I want someone to do business with me in the future. I will take a long-term relationship over a quick buck any day.

Save It for Posterity

You also need to consider whether you want to record the session. There are two reasons for taping yourself. First, it gives you the ability to perform an immediate self-critique. There is much to be said for reviewing the tape while the performance is still fresh in your mind. It allows you to compare the impressions you had as you spoke with what you see or hear on the tape.

Second, you can keep the tape on file to add to your lifelong learning collection. Your personal tape archives provide a barometer of performance over time.

If you come equipped with your own digital recorder and microphone to record only the audio, no problem. Just be sure you conduct a trial run immediately before you speak to ensure everything is functioning properly.

What if you are videotaping the session? It is critical to test the video and audio. If you plan to play back the videotape immediately as I do with the exercises in my media and presentation skills training workshops, make sure your playback unit works. Sometimes the A/V crew shows up with a format other than VHS. If you do not give yourself time to rig up a way to play back, you're toast.

Under no circumstances are you to allow your technician to talk you out of this real time test. It's your show. If something goes wrong, you are the one who looks like the fool, not him.

If you plan to field questions from the audience, make sure there is a microphone they can use. And insist that they use it, explaining that everyone needs to hear and that you are recording the session. If you are stuck without a microphone, restate the question so everyone understands the topic at hand.

On occasion, the organizers may decide it is a good idea to tape your presentation for their records. From your point of view, this could be either a good or bad deal. Here is why: Your speech is valuable intellectual property. If you give another group the okay to record you, make sure they sign a specific agreement that preserves your rights to all the material.

You can turn this situation to your advantage, however. Assuming a professional crew is doing the video shoot, ask for a finished copy of the tape. Presto! You now have an instant product you can sell through your web site's e-commerce capabilities. Plus, you can use it for promotional purposes. This product clearly has a value. It may be wise for you to factor what amounts to an added payment into your rates. Be sure your contract spells out the fact that you retain the rights.

In addition, you may decide to allow the organization to use it as an in-house training vehicle for an added fee; but, again, you should retain control of your priceless intellectual property.

I suggest you try to short circuit this request to record your presentation by notifying clients in advance that there will be an extra fee if they want the right to do so. But surprises do happen the day of your talk. Be prepared to stand firm on this point and pull out a copy of your contract if need be. Better yet, if you have an associate with you, let her or him handle this piece of business.

Get It in Writing

A few words about contracts. Use them. The time to begin the initial research for a speech occurs when you have a signed contract and deposit check in hand.

A contract is a sign of commitment. It is also a great clarifier. It helps avoid confusion about when and where you will speak. And it spells out the obligations and responsibilities both you and your host have agreed to. Any reputable organization will understand the need to set forth the specifics of what is expected of each party. If they balk when you tell them you will send along the necessary paperwork for their signature, think twice about whether this is the type of group you need to reach.

There is no need to call in the lawyers and rack up expensive legal bills every time you send out a contract. I have a simple template that suffices for most occasions. It is less than two pages and is written in plain English. Yes, I had to practically sit on my lawyer to get her to see the value of this when she reviewed it (and no, she is no longer my lawyer!). But I care about protecting my rights, not confusing and inconveniencing clients with a twelve-page legalese-infested document printed in 8-point type.

Sure, I sometimes feel comfortable working without a contract. Long-time clients with which I do a heavy volume of work fit in this category as do some pro bono presentations. Even in those cases, I am careful to send a letter of understanding outlining what I view as our mutual rights and responsibilities.

Whether you choose to use a contract or letter of understanding, I urge you to put something in writing for those rare cases when confusion reigns or disputes arise.

The Essence of Preparation

Let me restate my single best insider's tip for communicating more effective-ly with any audience: Practice! Practice! Practice! That simple step unlocks the door to winning presentations.

Preparation, the first of the Three Keys to Great Presentations, leads to success in business, in community projects, in politics, and more. Preparation also helps you stay away from failure and embarrassment. Let us recap the benefits noted earlier:

- *Reduce anxiety*, the unchallenged number one killer of good public speakers.
- *Channel your nervousness* and make it your ally.
- *Deliver memorable presentations.*
- *Discover how to "work the room"* and find friends in any audience, even among a crowd of strangers.
- *Convey confidence* when speaking before any audience.
- *Gain an edge* on your competition.
- *Stop being distracted* by off-point or antagonistic questions.
- *Create and communicate* a magnetic message.
- *Utilize props and slides* effectively.
- *Develop quotable quotes* that create a positive buzz at your meeting.
- *Persuade* undecided audience members.
- *Rid yourself of* annoying nonverbal habits.
- *Eliminate that quiver* in your voice and the wringing of your hands.
- *Assume control* when fielding questions.
- *Prevent your competitors* from carrying the day.

Now it's show time—and it really is a show. All your groundwork pays off. It is time for you to move from the Preparation phase into the Performance segment of your presentation.

CHAPTER FOUR

THE SECOND KEY: PERFORMANCE

THE THREE KEYS TO CHAPTER FOUR

You can expect to learn the truth about the second of the Three Keys to Great Presentations—Performance:

- How to grab your audience with an awesome opening and a killer close;
- Why paying attention to your audience pays dividends;
- How to deal with distractions like slamming doors and ringing cell phones.

LITTLE JOHNNY'S BIRTHDAY HAS ARRIVED and you need to assemble his shiny, new bicycle. If you forget one step in those instructions and neglect to tighten one nut, his wheels will fall off and Johnny will wind up with skinned knees. He'll look up at you with those big, doleful eyes wondering why he couldn't trust you.

The same truth holds with your presentations. Fail to take note of even the tiniest aspect of your performance and you will end up with broken dreams just like Johnny. Plus, doubt will begin to creep in, leading you to question whether you can trust your speaking abilities. This chapter will help you tighten up those details.

There are many aspects to performance—nonverbal signals, handling audience questions, and using presentation software, to name a few. Separate chapters are dedicated to each of these vital areas. For now, let us begin at the beginning.

Grab Your Audience by the Ears

There is a classic 1970s television comedy sketch performed by Bob Newhart in which he plays psychiatrist Robert Hartley. The good doctor is interviewed on a morning TV show in Chicago by a sweet-sounding interviewer who turns out to be a pit bull. During the lead in to the interview, she accuses him of quackery and overcharging patients. Shocked, he leans over during the break and seeks her assurances such an attack will not happen again.

She responds that she was just using a grabber to get the audience's attention. Newhart rejoins, "Well, we won't be doing any more grabbing, will we?"

The answer for your purposes as a speaker is, yes! You want to issue that grabber to begin your remarks. Seize your audience by the eyes and ears and let them know they have a special treat in store.

The old saw about not getting a second chance to make a first impression rings true in the world of presentations. You have a very narrow window for connecting with the audience before they make a snap decision to tune you out. If you blow the first thirty seconds, you can forget the next thirty minutes. Your audience certainly will.

Here is one deadly dull trap many presenters fall into: "Good morning." There is nothing more boring than a speaker who steps forward with a big grin and a, "Good morning. How is everybody today?" Zzzzz.

Launch your presentation with a gem of a quote, a surprising statistic, a news headline, a question, or a provocative idea. The possibilities are endless. Find the techniques that work for you. Keep it positive. No complaints or apologies allowed. Get off on the good foot.

To do this, you must use all the verbal and nonverbal tools at your beck and call to establish a tight connection.

I am not an advocate of memorizing your entire talk. But there are two exceptions when you do want to memorize important sections of your presentation. The two times you should not use notes are during your opening and your conclusion.

Learn your grabber by heart. Practice your articulation, eye contact, and other Video and Audio Tools until your grabber is razor sharp. Magnetize that audience to ensure they are strongly attracted to you and your message, particularly during those first crucial seconds you hit the stage.

Icebreaking Techniques

Fortunately, you have a lot of options for structuring your opening remarks. Here is a partial list of your choices:

- Pose an intriguing question.
- Tell a brief story or recount a meaningful anecdote. This could be a personal experience or one you have observed or heard about.
- Cite a quotation by a famous individual. Try not to make this trite. Everyone has heard, "A penny saved is a penny earned." Dig deeper for a relevant but less shopworn line.
- Link your topic to something that occurred today in history. Just make sure your case in point is relevant to your topic.
- Promise your audience that they will learn something intriguing or valuable to them either professionally or personally.
- Personalize your talk to the profession your audience members belong to. If you are presenting to a group of allergists, as one example, identify with the fact that allergy season is just about to begin.
- Discuss a historical event specific to your audience. If you are speaking to a Stanford University alumni association, for instance, you could recount an interesting fact that occurred when Leland Stanford founded the institution in 1891.
- Say something surprising or seemingly contradictory.
- Offer an "inside baseball" glimpse that relates to their organization.
- Tell an inspiring and emotional personal story of how you overcame a challenge or snatched victory from the jaws of defeat.
- Stimulate your audience's curiosity with an unusual or provocative thought.
- Present them with a puzzler that fits the subject of your presentation (just be sure it is not too much of a mind-bender or they may focus on it instead of your talk).
- Describe a problem you intend to solve.
- Recount an item in the news that relates to your presentation.
- Tell about a character, either real or fictitious. This could include anyone from the CEO of your company to a noted political figure to Oliver Twist.
- Tease them by hinting at the important news you plan to deliver. Don't spill everything at once. Let the air out of the balloon gradually; do not pop it right at the start.
- Tell your audience something seemingly obvious that they may not

have thought about in the context of your remarks.

- Take off on a topic du jour. Popular movies, televisions shows, and commercials create good fodder here.
- Tell them something interesting about the venue in which you are speaking. Perhaps you discovered that President John F. Kennedy once spoke in this very room.
- Present a historical perspective. Years ago, speakers were limited to flip charts and blackboards. Now we have presentation software and projectors. How has this changed what you need to learn as a speaker?
- Cite a trend that fits into your topic. From politics to pop culture, trends are all around us.

You may have refined additional techniques to spice up your opening. No matter how you do it, make it a point to work hard on your opener for every presentation. This really helps get the audience on your side.

Have You Heard the One About...?

Note the above list does not suggest you begin with a joke or insert humor into your opening. Don't do it! It requires split second timing most of us have not mastered.

If your joke falls flat, you have just succeeded in getting off on the wrong foot. You will have to spend so much time rescuing your presentation you will never succeed at delivering a memorable message.

Run the other way when someone advises you to begin with a joke. Very few of us are skilled joke tellers. Unless you have the comedic skills of Jay Leno, avoid the stand up routine.

If you choose to aim for the funny bone during your presentation, there is more than one form of comedy to consider. Rather than aim for a Rodney Dangerfield-like stand up act, you can use situational or ad libbed humor. Or you could use visual humor by flashing a cartoon or a funny photo or video clip. Legal note: If you are using material created by someone else, be sure you have the rights to use it as part of your talk.

Another option is to borrow someone else's humor by citing a witty quotation. If the audience laughs, you still get the credit.

Also, make sure your levity fits the situation. Yukking it up may not be appropriate if you are discussing a dread disease or heavy political issue, for instance.

Good taste rules when it comes to humor. You are only licensed to make a crack about an audience member if you have cleared it with that individual in advance. Even then, be ultra-careful with your jesting. Everything in your remarks must be in good taste. Your listeners may not realize that you have planned this and that the other person is in on the joke. They might view it as a slap at one of their fellows.

Winning the Communications Trifecta

Let me introduce you to the notion of Winning the Communications Trifecta (see Chapter Five for a full treatment). This Trifecta consists of the three sets of communications tools you have at your beck and call. It empowers you with a common sense way to gain a better grasp of how you can sharpen your communications edge.

The three sets of tools are:
- Video Tools—the way you look
- Audio Tools—the way you sound
- Message Tools—the words you speak

Considering your message tools first, it is important to understand that your story must be made up of more than merely a collection of facts.

You must aim for what I call a magnetic message, one that attracts listeners to your point of view and makes it easy for you to stick to your message when delivering your presentation.

A magnetic message is built upon four strong legs—central ideas that can withstand rigorous questioning. Think of your message as a strong four-legged chair. If one of the legs of your chair is weak, the chair will collapse and send you tumbling to the floor. So it is with your message.

Just one weak link in your story will cause your message to crumble to the ground. That is not a position you want to assume when addressing an important audience.

What about your Video Tools? You have five basic Video weapons in your arsenal:
- Action
- Facial expression
- Eye contact
- Wardrobe
- Props

Your Audio Tools contain five major compartments:
- Pitch

- Articulation
- Volume
- Emotion
- Rate

We will dig into this concept more fully in chapters to come.

Never Assume Anything

Your advance research has given you some insights into the sophistication of your audience. Still, I suggest you play it safe by openly setting the baseline early in your presentation.

Assuming everyone is on the same page is a dangerous supposition. So take a few moments to paint the landscape. Give your listeners a road map to let them know about the journey ahead. You don't need to go into great depth unless your research tells you that is necessary.

But you do need to establish a common understanding. This is particularly important when you speak before a diverse crowd with differing levels of sophistication regarding your topic. If you neglect to provide the needed directional signs, the message you intend to send will not be the one they will receive.

Indeed, the whole notion of sending vs. receiving merits some discussion. There is simply no way to ensure that the message you transmit is received by your audience in exactly the way you intend. We all travel with our own personal filters, experiences, and biases. The more common ground you establish—in terms of language, culture, experiences, examples, stories, and visuals—the higher the odds your listeners will gain the meaning you want them to gain.

If you plan to speak in another nation, get a sense of the culture before you hit the stage. Conduct your research well in advance of boarding the plane. Below are some methods for gathering intelligence:

- Visit the U.S. State Department's web site for details on the country.
- While you are surfing the Internet, check out that nation's official site.
- Seek out a few travel sites.
- Talk with a native; if you don't know anyone, put your network into high gear.
- Pose questions of friends and business associates who have traveled there.
- Interview an official from that country's embassy.

With all of these tools at your disposal, there is no excuse for total ignorance when you travel abroad.

Expect the Unexpected

There is simply no way to prepare for every contingency. To be sure, you can search out the fire exits and prepare yourself to guide attendees if evacuation should become necessary.

But out of the ordinary distractions, while rare, can spring up at any time. Let me share a story with you. I was part of a media training team working in New York with an entertainment conglomerate the day anthrax was found at NBC's Rockefeller Center headquarters. NBC *Nightly News* anchor Tom Brokaw's office had been the target of the anthrax attack, with one of his assistants exposed to the toxin.

During a break for lunch, some of us heard the reports by chance when we happened to glance at the television news. Everyone's face paled as we exchanged shocked glances. All was uncertain. My New York colleagues were not sure they would be able to get home. I was unsure if I would be able to get to the airport and, if so, would my flight be cancelled?

I called my office to get a more informed perspective on the situation. After a brief consultation, we decided to acknowledge the problem rather than have rumors spread among our trainees, and continue with the workshop.

As it turned out, all of us got home that night. The hugs were a bit longer and tighter and, I will admit, my exhalation was greater than normal upon landing back home at Washington's Dulles International Airport.

There is absolutely no way to plan for events like this, other than to understand that you need to keep your wits about you and make the best decisions possible with the best information you can obtain at the time.

Caucus with your hosts and map out a plan of action. And remember, people will be looking to you for guidance and reassurance. You may need to work hard to maintain that calm exterior. Just remember that is part of your job.

Lectern Etiquette

You may be surprised by the number of presenters who don't know how to use a lectern properly. I see it often, even among experienced speakers. If you do opt for a lectern, understand its function.

A lectern (or podium, for our purposes) is simply this: A place to put the materials you will need during your presentation. That's it. No more, no less. It is not a barrier, not a crutch. It is simply a tool to better organize yourself. Arrange the podium to suit your individual needs and preferences, then leave everything alone until you need it. Don't fiddle nervously with your index cards or the microphone cord.

Do not follow the example of George W. Bush and lean sideways on the lectern. You evoke a far more open and professional image when you stand straight and tall. Plus, your voice will be stronger thanks to your improved posture.

Once you approach the lectern, take ownership of it since it will be your home for the duration of your speech. How do you make it feel like home? Here are some podium protocols:

- Commit to standing behind it. Resist the urge to wander. If you bounce back and forth, you will seem indecisive.
- Ensure it is the right height for you. Do you need a riser to elevate yourself a few extra inches? Under no circumstances do you want to seem like a little kid barely able to peer over the top. If you are tall, your chief problem may be that the microphone attached to the lectern is too low. Adjust your microphone accordingly and avoid bending over to speak into it. Stooping plays havoc with your non-verbal abilities, weakening your wind power and interfering with your eye contact.
- Adjust the microphone so that it captures your voice. If you need to turn your head in one direction to reference a slide on the screen, for example, be sure the microphone is on the side to which you will turn so that your voice carries across it. If you need to reposition it, don't be shy about asking your technician to do so.
- Check the lighting at the lectern. If the room is dim and your podium is not equipped with a reading light, you may not be able to see your notes or your laptop's keyboard.
- Determine if it has a light and a clock. Play around with them to gain an understanding of how they work. Be alert to the fact that podium clocks are notorious for displaying the wrong time.
- Do not lean on the lectern. This is not a bus stop. Get a good night's sleep and stand up straight like your mom taught you.
- Do not hug it for dear life. It is not a life preserver. Your personal flotation device comes in the form of preparation and practice.
- Do not grab the lectern. White-knuckle speakers wear their anxiety on their sleeves or, more precisely, at the joints of their fingers. You would be amazed at the number of lecterns that have fingernail marks embedded in them from past speakers.

- Leave your hands free to gesture or in a neutral position, not locked to the lectern. It is fine to gently rest them on the surface or on the sides. When you do bring your hands into play, raise them above the level of the lectern so the audience can see them.
- Do not hide behind it. Your audience knows you are there. It is too late to escape.
- The one time you should absolutely consider coming out from behind the podium is when you field audience questions. Unless the audio requirements or physical set up demands that you stay behind the podium 100 percent of the time, make an effort to get closer to your listeners during this segment of your presentation.

If you arrive early to set up and notice a lectern you did not request, remove it. You do not want anything in the room that makes the audience wonder why it is there or when you will get around to using it. Nothing should distract their attention from you. Whether you see a stray lectern, projector, flip chart, extra chair, anything—get it out of there beforehand.

One final point: A lectern is not mandatory, and don't let anyone tell you otherwise. It makes sense in some situations and for some speakers, and not in others. The decision is yours.

Vote with Your Feet

When coaching, I make it a point to watch my clients' feet. I am not checking out their cool shoes, admiring their calves, or making them victims of a foot fetish. I need to see their foot position.

Why? Your feet are a vital part of your speaking repertoire. No, this is not an advertisement for a podiatrist.

Here is how to position yourself: Stand with your feet shoulder width apart, one foot slightly forward of the other. This gives you the ability to move when you desire, but keeps you away from the side-to-side swaying that turns your audience green with seasickness.

If you stand before your audience with no podium, the feet also matter. Find a comfortable stance and settle in for a bit. Resist the temptation to pace constantly just because you are standing. You will betray your nervousness. Do not run back and forth like you're in a track meet or lumber about like the mad professor who incessantly strolls back and forth in front of his less than captivated students.

We have all, as audience members, been distracted to no end by the speaker who wanders. Be alert so that you are not carried away with the urge to ramble. You do not want to look like a duck in a shooting gallery.

Tales from the Foot Locker

Two stories demonstrate the importance of good foot position. The first is a positive story of a doctor. I worked with this key opinion leader in the field of gynecology twice in the span of one month. The first time we worked together, I demonstrated the advantageous stance outlined above. The next time we met, she made it a point to tell me that, during her most recent presentations, she set her foot position as I recommended. That one technique allowed her to hold her position and raised her confidence level. She was ecstatic. Sometimes all it takes is that one seemingly small but important detail to transform a decent speaker into a star.

The second tale, unfortunately, does not possess that positive quality. It involves an experienced presenter for whom I have a lot of respect.

During a slide presentation, he kept shuffling his feet and moving about aimlessly behind the lectern. That was distracting enough. But coupled with the fact that he incessantly crossed in front of the projector beam, obstructing his slides on the screen, he did not inspire confidence.

The lesson here: If you use a lectern, find your shoulder-width stance and hold it. This is not to say you should lock your knees, prop yourself with a stick running up your spine, and stand stock still. Action, as we learned, is a good thing even when you are locked behind a podium. Keep your actions judicious.

While we are playing speaker's podiatrist, avoid any toe tapping while speaking. Whether you are truly impatient or not, your audience will think you are.

On a related note, be wary of turning your back to the audience. You will see speakers do this to reference a slide. Wrong, wrong, wrong!

Get acclimated to your room the day of your remarks. Take note of any potential obstacles and practice how to walk backward without crashing into something and taking a tumble.

Rehearse how to walk sideways. This crabwalk lets you maintain eye contact with the crowd while you move from side to side.

Quiet Down

Every now and then, presenters encounter unruly audience members. I need to stress disruptions occur in only a tiny minority of situations. But should this happen to you at some point, I want to be sure to provide some suggestions for handling them.

Let's divide interruptions into the unintentional and the intentional. Unintentional disturbances include:

- Loudly slamming door
- Ringing cell phone
- Wait staff dropping a tray of dishes
- Sudden burst of noise from the room next door

Intentional disruptions include:

- Side conversations
- Cell phone conversations
- People reading the newspaper
- People who refuse to hold questions until the end, if you have made clear that is your preference

Deal with accidental interruptions in advance as much as possible. Ringing cell phones, for instance, can be minimized if your introduction includes a reminder to turn off phones and pagers.

If you are speaking at a breakfast, luncheon, or dinner function, disruptions from the wait staff can be controlled if you place a clause in your contract prohibiting the busing of tables until the conclusion of your remarks. You can also request that dessert be placed on the table before you take to the stage. That leaves one less round of clattering dishes.

When unintentional events occur—and they will at some point—treat them with grace and diplomacy. If an audience member drops a load of books on the floor or forgets to turn off his cell phone ringer, that is an honest mistake.

Nonetheless, cell phones are the bane of many a presenter in today's world. The best way to deal with them is to stop the ringing before it happens. Have the person introducing you remind audience members to turn off their phones.

If someone neglects to do so and you are plagued by a ring tone during your presentation, take advantage of the situation. Tell your audience, "Right on time. There's the call reminding all of us to turn off our cell phones."

When confronted with a relatively minor inadvertent distraction, try to stop it without calling attention to it. If most of the audience hasn't picked up on the episode yet, try to keep it that way.

If the occurrence is unintentional but a bit more obvious—a waiter dropping a tray of dishes, a loud cell phone, or a riotous outburst from an adjoining room—acknowledge the disturbance and move on. Have a few lines at the ready that recognize the disruption and, importantly, assure the audience that the problem will be dealt with quickly:

- "I see that idea really brought the house down. I'm sure the crackerjack staff will have things cleaned up in no time."
- "Look at that. We're even having people call in with questions. That's a good reminder to all of us to turn off our cell phones and pagers."
- "Boy, those people next door are sure enjoying their presentation. The speaker must be one of the people I taught last week."

When the Going Gets Tough

Intentional incidents are a bit different. Someone who noisily turns the page of their newspaper or a group that believes its conversation is more interesting than your presentation needs to be treated with a firmer hand.

I will deal more thoroughly with interruptions in Chapter Eight. For now, let us cover some basics.

If the level of background chatter becomes obvious and distracting, however, it is audience participation time. Give them a chance to burn off some of that energy by moving to an interactive exercise, asking them a question, requesting a show of hands, or asking for yeas and nays. Get them moving and give them a moment to vocalize.

Whenever possible, I try to have an assistant in the room and instruct her in advance to nip any interruptions in the bud. You can also entrust a colleague in attendance with this duty. Of course, hosts should also step in to play Miss Manners at times like this, but the reality is they often fail to do so.

It is important that you stamp out any potential disruptions right at the beginning. Be up front with your audience. Ask for their attention in advance. Make a deal with them. No newspapers, e-mails, or office paperwork.

Get everyone's buy off at the very start, especially if your advance research tells you there may be some problem children in the crowd. Set forth the ground rules of no cell phone ringers, no side chatter, and the like, then ask anyone who does not agree to raise his hand. The wise guys in the room might shoot up their hands once in a while in good fun. But if someone has a serious problem with your ground rules, you are well within the bounds of civility to suggest he might want to take it outside.

Now, if a disruption occurs, everyone has agreed to play by your rules. Remind them of what you as a group agreed to. Peer pressure can be an effective enforcer.

The Heat Is On

Another potential distraction is everyone's physical comfort. A hot room is no friend of the speaker. A tropical-like climate is one of the best ways to lull your audience to sleep.

When you arrive at your venue, adjust the thermostat so that the environment is comfortably cool. At larger facilities, such as a hotel or convention center, you will need to find someone from the maintenance staff to lower the temperature for you. If a few people complain about feeling chilly, you probably have it about right. The coolness will keep them awake.

Put that assistant or trusted colleague in charge of monitoring the temperature. Some facilities seem to have two options for their HVAC systems: On or off. If the heat pumps out relentlessly, it will soon feel like an oven. If the air conditioning blows too cold for too long, you could soon find yourself speaking in an ice box. Either extreme is distracting for you and your audience.

Take steps in advance to ensure your listeners remain comfortable throughout your presentation. Learn where the thermostat is located or, if you are speaking in a large conference facility, know how to contact the facilities staff who can regulate the temperature.

While you do want cool, you do not want arctic conditions. That can be as uncomfortable as a greenhouse-like atmosphere. In fact, a big chill could chase people from the room. Late night host David Letterman is notorious for keeping his theater ice cold, with temperatures hovering in the 50s. That's why, when the cameras pan to the crowd, you frequently see audience members with coats and jackets on. You are not likely to have those millions of watts of lighting that heat the stage, making it easier for you to settle on a temperature at which most people will feel content.

To maximize your audience's attention, aim for a room that is comfortably cool, not brutally cold.

Engage the Crowd

Your confidence level, as well as your level of performance, takes a noticeable jump when you are able to pick out friendly faces in the crowd. You will note those who nod their head, smile, and maintain friendly eye contact.

Reference ideas that you discussed with your audience during your pre-presentation research. It is natural for people to be curious about what they are going to hear when they talk with you beforehand. If you tell them you are going to discuss a topic, be sure to deliver on your promise.

During your presentation, you can reference people in the audience, mentioning ideas you discussed with them earlier. Calling people by name is beautiful music to their ears. You will already know some names thanks to the networking you did before your speech. If the group is small enough, you can learn everyone's name by going around the room for a round of self-introductions as you begin.

You also hit a grace note when you thank the individuals who made it possible for you to speak—the meeting planner or program chair. In addition, the big cheese always loves to hear his name mentioned. Obviously, you want to reference people in a very positive manner. Do not make denigrating remarks or jokes at someone's expense unless you have cleared it with them in advance. Even then, think twice. You must always remain 100 percent respectful of your audience.

Above all, bear in mind that your presentation is all about them, not you. News commentators, in noting the success of Sen. John Edwards (D–N.C.) in the early stages of the 2004 Democratic presidential race, noted his ability to connect with voters by using the word "you" to maximum effect. This tactic allowed the candidate to connect. He succeeded at getting crowds to believe that he was thinking about them, not his own odds for capturing the nomination.

You can also engage the crowd by slightly varying how you use your Video Tools and Audio Tools. Think of all the possibilities. You can change your rate of speech, vary the volume, shift your position as it relates to the audience by walking among them, or use your presentation software for only part of your speech. Come up with the variations that work best for your individual style and make the most of them.

If you choose to use humor as part of your presentation, your friendly faces will prove invaluable. Aim your punch lines at audience members who will laugh. Make eye contact with them as you punch it out. Once they begin, the laughter will ripple throughout the crowd.

Give Yourself a Break

Public speaking is hard physical labor. When I finish a presentation, all I want to do is relax and recover. A friendly chat, a mindless book, or a ballgame on TV is all I ask.

That is why I make it a point to lessen the demands on my physical being at various points throughout a talk. How? By turning the spotlight to the audience for brief bursts.

This strategy accomplishes two purposes. First, it gives me a short but vital time out. Second, it engages audience members by permitting them to focus on something else momentarily.

Here are some favorite methods for getting the crowd involved while still maintaining control:

- Ask them a question.
- Instruct them to break into small group discussions.
- Begin a small group exercise.
- Report the results of their discussions.
- Give them a quiz. You can do this verbally, in writing, or on a slide.
- Use a prop.
- Dole out a short yet thought-provoking reading assignment.
- Distribute a quick written assignment.
- Enlist an audience member to act as a scribe to write down audience ideas on a flip chart.

Tuck a few of these techniques in your back pocket. They help keep your energy level up by granting you short physical and mental breaks during your presentations.

Respect Your Audience

It is difficult to pick out friendly faces if you fail to pay attention to your audience. I once witnessed a rare public speaking feat—a discussion in which all three panelists managed to offend the audience in their own unique ways.

Panelist number one got off to a positive start with his prepared remarks. He kept the crowd's attention with a well-prepared argument and solid if not spectacular use of his Video and Audio Tools. But he pulled a real no-no when the time came for questions. He vaporized his earlier goodwill by hogging the Q&A session. Even if you think your comments are the most fascinating words on earth, give your fellow panelists some breathing room.

Audience members detest a stage hog. *Lesson: Don't insist on answering every question. Leave space for your fellow panelists to respond, too.*

Speaker number two then stepped to the podium. His woes started with his prepared remarks. He made use of a full text speech which, as I noted earlier, takes some practice in order to sound natural. He raced through his written text in a monotone while making little effort to gain eye contact with his audience. The result was the predictable noise of the audience shifting in its seats. *Lesson: Your Video Tools, such as eye contact, and your Audio Tools, such as pitch, are vital in forging a bond with your audience.*

The third panelist, similar to the first, served up his prepared remarks serviceably. Then, inexplicably, he checked out. Oh, his physical being was still on stage. But he made it clear that his mind was elsewhere and he was done with this audience. When time came for Q&A, everyone could see him sitting on the dais doing paperwork! *Lesson: Never insult your audience members by ignoring them. Pay them the respect they deserve.*

Remember, an organization honors you when it asks you to speak. Act like you would if you were a dinner guest in someone's home. Let others talk, engage them, and show them the respect they warrant.

End with the End in Mind

As noted earlier, a strong beginning is important. Similarly, a plan is imperative when the time comes to wrap up your remarks. End with a bang.

Restate your message clearly and powerfully. You want the audience walking out that door singing from your hymnal. You have achieved victory from the podium if you turn your listeners into disciples who spread the buzz about your message in the hallways at the conclusion of your speech.

When you finish speaking, pause and hold eye contact with your audience for a couple of beats. Then walk off with a purpose. Don't amble off lazily.

Make sure your final words drive home your point in no uncertain terms. Refuse to taper off to nothingness like the presenter who weakly mumbles, "Okay, it looks like that's all I have. We're done."

Your audience will walk out of the room with the final image of you emblazoned on their brains. Leave them with a strong impression.

Know When to Say When

Finally, you must know when to say when. Long-winded speakers rarely impress people with their vast knowledge. Rather, they frequently induce resentment or the instinct to take a nap.

If you have been invited to speak for a half-hour, tailor your remarks for twenty-five minutes. Most speakers run longer than they anticipate. Plus, ending early has been known to delight many an audience. As it is written in Job 16:3, "Will your long-winded speeches never end? What ails you that you keep on arguing?"

To end on time, you need to keep track of the clock on the wall. Resist the temptation to glance at your wristwatch every so often. It looks like you are waiting for a bus and tells your audience that you can't wait to get away from them.

Remember the damage this wristwatch glance did to George H.W. Bush during one of his 1992 debates with Bill Clinton? Clinton was speaking and there was Bush in the background, gazing at his watch to see when this waste of time was going to end. It did not add up to a positive image for the Republican candidate. Message? Can I please leave now?

To avoid running over your allotted time, you can arrange a set of signals with an assistant in the audience. Two cautions here. One, agree on what the signals are. Does a wink mean you are out of time or you have five minutes left? Is she scratching her left ear because she is trying to signal you, or does she simply have an itch? Two, be sure you know where your assistant will be sitting or standing. You have enough to do without having to think about locating your designated signal-caller.

Why is it important to keep track of time? If you wear out your welcome, people will begin stealing glances at the clock, shifting in their seats, and mentally checking out.

The best method for monitoring your time is to have a clock on the wall facing you. But this is not available in many rooms. If you use a lectern, some come equipped with a digital clock although the time is, more often than not, incorrect. I advise against using your wristwatch as your main timepiece; the numbers are usually too small to read from a distance, causing you to squint in a vain and obvious attempt to discern the time.

The easiest solution is to carry a small portable clock you can unobtrusively set on the table you are using for your notes, one with a digital readout that you can quickly scan at a glance. Face it toward you and away from your audience. Most people will not even realize it is there.

Mom Always Told You

As the curtain lowers following your performance, there are a few personal details to consider. At the risk of turning this into a treatise on good grooming, hygiene is an important part of your aura.

Before I take to the stage, I always try to find time to brush my teeth or, if that is not possible, pop some sugarless gum into my mouth. It not only freshens your breath, the chewing action helps clean food from between your teeth (just don't forget to take the gum out of your mouth before beginning your presentation).

Try to find a moment to refresh your breath after your speech, too. The air from your stomach does not exactly smell like flowers, and it will find its way into your mouth while you speak. The result? When you are done, you may find yourself with a case of dragon breath. I used to find it cumbersome to pop a breath mint. They do not dissolve quickly enough, meaning you needed to talk with audience members while rolling a mint around in your mouth. Now there is a convenient solution: Quick dissolving breath strips. They melt away quickly and give your breath that temporary ounce of fresh air you—and especially your audience—will appreciate.

Like Riding a Bike

There are parallels between little Johnny learning how to ride his bicycle and you sharpening your speaking skills. You may take an occasional verbal spill from the podium. But, like the little tyke, you need to get back up on that bike and practice it one more time.

Over time, Johnny's skinned knees will heal. So, too, will your bruised ego. Keep performing and you will come out a champion.

CHAPTER FIVE

WINNING THE COMMUNICATIONS TRIFECTA

THE THREE KEYS TO CHAPTER FIVE

You can expect to learn the truth about Winning the Communications Trifecta:

- How Winning the Communications Trifecta helps you pack a punch both verbally and nonverbally;
- How to use your Video Tools and Audio Tools to maximize the power of your presentations;
- How a simple equation can help you develop a magnetic message sure to attract any audience.

THE TRUTH IS IT IS YOUR JOB TO MAKE YOUR audience care about your topic.

Listeners can only be as enthusiastic and emotional as your delivery gives them license to be. This means you need to use your nonverbal skills to snatch your audience's attention and hold it throughout your speech.

This chapter delves into what you need to do to sharpen your communications edge. Let's start with a few tips to help get you energized.

First, be yourself. Be true to your own style. To be sure, you can learn from studying other speakers. But don't copy anyone.

Second, remember that your success as a speaker will come as you learn to maximize your strengths and improve those areas you find challenging. Stick with those tools and talents that are your most powerful. You can work to correct your weaknesses; but remember, that is an effort for the long haul.

Third, maintain your confidence. You are the expert. The people in the seats came to hear what you have to say.

Successful presenters need a system that enhances presentations, makes for more effective dealings with the media, and helps achieve public policy goals when testifying before lawmakers and regulators. That is precisely the strength of the Communications Trifecta.

Introducing the Communications Trifecta

I developed the Communications Trifecta as a means of helping my clients communicate in public with greater impact.

It is an intuitive, easy to remember system that allows you to communicate effectively before any audience. Plus, the Trifecta works to sharpen the communications edge of any speaker—novice or pro.

Here are the three areas that come into play in Winning The Communications Trifecta. Betting on these tools transforms you into a winner when you communicate with the public:

- Video Tools
- Audio Tools
- Message Tools

Your Video Tools, in particular your facial expression, help your audience judge how pleasant or positive you are. Your Audio Tools communicate your level of authority or influence.

It is vital that you appear both interesting and interested when using your Video Tools. This dictates how you look in your audience's eyes. Your Video Tools consist of A FEW Pointers (in anagram fashion, think of them as A FEW P):

- **A**ction
- **F**acial expression
- **E**ye contact
- **W**ardrobe
- **P**rops

Your Audio Tools determine how effective you are as your audience listens to you. Think of this set of tools as the PAVER formula that can help pave your way to a sound voice:

- **P**itch
- **A**rticulation
- **V**olume
- **E**motion
- **R**ate

Your Message Tools consist of the words you use. This is, in the end, why you decided to speak in the first place—to convince others of your point of view.

Your goal may be to ace a presentation before a national political convention, at the local chapter of your professional society, as a sales pitch, or while networking at a chamber of commerce reception. This chapter will show you how to be the star of your show.

Some Surprising Numbers

How do we impart our messages when we communicate? The numbers are surprising to most people. As noted earlier, the typical audience member receives more than half of her signals—55 percent—based on how you as a speaker use your Video Tools. Meanwhile, your Audio Tools transmit just over one-third of your story—38 percent. Bringing up the rear is the all-important Message with 7 percent.

These oft-quoted findings are based on research conducted in the 1960s and 70s by UCLA professor Albert Mehrabian. His groundbreaking work found that 7 percent of feeling and liking was communicated verbally (Message), 38 percent through the tone of voice (Audio Tools), and 55 percent via facial expression (Video Tools).

These findings must be interpreted with care. I do not for one moment suggest that your message is unimportant. That is why you accepted the speaking engagement: To persuade or educate people about the value of your position.

The point is this: You must make full use of your nonverbal tools—both Video and Audio—to make people receptive to what you have to say and to drive your message home with maximum impact.

Your Video Tools

It is time to talk about specifics related to the Video group. Remember, you need to look like an individual who is both interesting and interested in the eyes of your audience.

How can a speaker sharpen her or his Video abilities? Let us examine in depth *A FEW Pointers* that can sharpen your communications edge when it comes to your Video performance. Again, they are:

- Action
- Facial expression

- **E**ye contact
- **W**ardrobe
- **P**rops

Let's deal with each of these factors in depth. First, we will zero in on why action is important.

Become an Action Figure

The film director yells, "Action," and the scene comes to life. Public speaking is not all that different. Speakers are performers attempting to get across a point of view or to entertain.

What is it that makes action so attractive to us? It signals confidence, commitment, and passion, or a lack thereof. A speaker who turns his back to the audience, slumps his shoulders, and stays in the dark during his slide show does nothing to inspire confidence in his knowledge. What's more, this shortage of action serves as a human sleeping pill, putting his audience down for a catnap. So, too, the up tight individual who stands ramrod straight or paces ceaselessly detracts from his own message.

On the other hand, the presenter with fluid, natural action who stands up straight and faces the audience radiates self-assurance and wisdom. Audiences tend to accept the message of the speaker who conveys energy, stamina, and strength. The confident speaker also earns a higher degree of trust.

From head to toe, you have a lot of options that can make you more interesting to watch. A tilt of the head does wonders. Continuing down the body, a shrug of the shoulders shows more meaning than many words ever could.

People also tend to like us when we gesture. Studies show that teachers who gesture get better results from their students and that their pupils like them more (share this with your children's teachers and see if they respond with a gesture or two). When you deliver a presentation you are, to one degree or another, a teacher. Gesture as you speak and feel the love.

Give Me a Hand

Your hands represent a mother lode of possibilities. Outstretched palms connote openness while a quick jab in the air can help to drive your point home.

Some speakers, even experienced ones, have difficulty determining what to do with their hands when they deliver presentations. Even though we have been operating them twenty-four hours a day, seven days a week, all of our lives, we suddenly become conscious of them when the time to speak draws near.

Find a comfortable neutral position for your hands. Leave them at your sides or occasionally clasp one hand inside the other in front of you. Just be sure not to hinder your gestures by interlocking your fingers, thereby locking up any action you might want to display.

Whatever you do, do not stuff them in your pockets and fiddle with coins or keys. Do not fidget or wring your hands. Steer clear of revealing any anger with a white-knuckled look. Also, avoid the fig leaf (covering the genital area) and the "at ease" position (arms clasped behind your back).

And never cross your arms (unless you are doing so for effect when telling a story, for instance). There is no better way to erect a barrier between you and your audience than to fold your arms across your chest.

A few notes of caution about using your hands. Number one, if you don't normally use hand gestures during conversation, don't make them up and force your hands into motion in front of an audience. You will appear stilted and uncomfortable, and your audience will view you as phony and unnatural. Not everyone needs to use their hands.

In addition, keep your gestures close to your body. You do not want to give the impression that you are flailing about on stage.

Finally, make your gestures purposeful. Avoid scratching your chin, wiping your eyes, tugging on your ear, and rubbing your hands together. These distractions (academics call them self-touching or self-manipulation) sharply reduce your credibility.

The spacing between you and your audience also matters. In general, the shorter the distance, the more you enhance your persuasiveness. But beware of getting too close to them and invading their sense of public space. This could cause them to feel uncomfortable, perhaps without their even knowing why.

Research published by Donn Byrne and Jeffrey Fisher in the *Journal of Personality and Social Psychology* (1975) found that, when it comes to territorialism, men tend to feel more threatened when approached from the front. Women, conversely, become more stressed when you draw near from the side.

Stand Up, Sit Down

Your position when facing an audience is also an important part of your action. Do you stand? Roam the room? Use a podium? Sit behind a table?

The key here is to find a position that feels natural to you and one that fits the situation. Perhaps it is walking among your audience. This is especially effective if you are delivering a persuasive pitch, for the smaller the distance between you and your audience, the more convincing they perceive you to be. Or you may present a slight forward lean toward your listeners. There are many ways action can enhance your presentation abilities.

Regardless of your choice, stake out a firm position when you speak. This is not to say that you should strap yourself into place, lock your knees, and stand rigid until your feet go numb. Rather, assume a comfortable posture of authority and avoid shuffling your feet.

Face your audience as you address them. No sideways glances or turning away from them. Studies show that audiences favor the presenter who positions his upper body toward them.

No matter if you are addressing an auditorium full of people or a handful of individuals in a small conference room, move only when it makes sense for you to do so, and move with a purpose when you do shift positions.

If there is no need to move, stand still. Don't constantly shift your weight from foot to foot. Don't nervously fold and unfold your hands. Don't fidget with a pen. Stand there and look important. Allow your impressive body language to back up your impressive words.

Movin' On

When is a good time to move? Action can signal a change in your topic or tone as you transition from one part of your message to another, or segue from telling a narrative story back to the subject matter of your talk. Action is also useful when you sense the audience needs a bit of a wake-up call. If you stride to another position, you shift your audience's visual focus. This will help to keep their interest level higher. Another good time to add some action occurs when you perceive the need to create a closer bond with your audience. Perhaps a listener is having a hard time understanding one of your concepts. Demonstrate your empathy by reaching your hand toward him or moving in his direction as you take a moment to explain further.

If you are presenting behind a podium, find a comfortable foot position and maintain it for the duration of your performance. If you are seated, posture counts, so sit forward in your chair. No slouching allowed. If you prefer to walk in the front of the room or among the audience, that's fine. Just be sure to make your actions deliberate and understated. You do not want to pace skittishly in the front of the room or sprint from the front to the back in one fell swoop.

While we are on the subject of your stance, I will mention one more tool. Leaning forward provides you with a powerful means to establish a closer connection with your audience. Whether you are standing or sitting, this represents a real positive in terms of your ability to bond with a group.

The forward lean also applies if you are seated. While leading a large group presentation skills training, I observed one of the presenters lean forward in his seat during the Q&A session. I pointed out in the critique immediately following that this is a good way to demonstrate excitement. Talk about a learning moment. A number of the other presenters who followed also adopted this forward lean. It not only made them seem more engaged, it also raised their energy level.

Tension Headache #101

Your audience will perceive, intuitively if not knowingly, when you are tense. If you look like you have a rod running up your back, you will come across as stiff and unpersuasive. Be sure to monitor your body for any tension as you perform. Your back should be straight but not ramrod stiff, your shoulders relaxed and not hunched around your neck, and your knees bent ever so slightly.

This is not only important in how you are viewed, it will also keep tension from building in your head, neck, shoulders, and back. That tightness leads to aches and pains all over your body. A hurting speaker is neither happy nor effective.

Also, beware not to swivel your upper body from the hips. This move can negate any other positive nonverbal cues you may be sending. We innately view the torso twist as a sign of discomfort or, worse, reluctance to interact.

I need to add one note of caution: Don't force anything. Unnatural action at best makes an audience uncomfortable. At worst, it makes them laugh out loud at your expense. We have all seen the clumsy-looking politicians whose hand gestures look totally unnatural. Unfortunately, they have been overcoached and told they need to use their hands. That is bogus advice. Don't ever let anyone try to squeeze you into someone else's skin.

The trick is to maximize existing strengths. If it doesn't come naturally, leave it. If you are not one to gesture with your hands when you speak in normal conversation, for heaven's sake, don't start using your hands when you deliver a presentation. You will succeed only in looking like Pinocchio—wooden, stiff, and as if someone is pulling your strings.

The significance of action is to make it natural for you. Your strengths are different from the speaker who precedes you on stage. Leverage your own assets to their fullest advantage.

Facial Feelings

Your facial expressions—such as the raise of an eyebrow or a frown—send subtle messages. Indeed, researchers over the years have determined that facial expression in and of itself can communicate a whole host of feelings from fear to happiness and surprise to confusion.

Perhaps the most powerful facial feeling of all is the smile. Remember the lyrics of the old James Taylor song, "Whenever I see your smiling face, I have to smile myself."

Just keep a watchful eye so as not to overdo it. Smiling too much actually works to your detriment; we think someone with an overly eager grin is trying to pull a fast one on us. On another level, it would be inappropriate to smile if you are discussing a grimly serious topic.

An unnaturally active rate of overall facial movement also connotes high anxiety. In fact, affected expressions used repeatedly—biting your lip, puffing out your cheeks, narrowing your eyes—distract your audience.

Fundamentals of Eye Contact

Solid eye contact denotes honesty, confidence, and credibility. That is why you always direct your focus to the audience. Paying attention to eye contact, the second of your Video Tools, helps you achieve integrity.

Your audience has come to have an exchange with you, not to watch you read a speech. Just think back to the last time you were bored to tears by a lecturer who read his prepared text without glancing up once, or the speaker who read her slides from the screen verbatim, all but ignoring the audience.

In a normal conversation, our rate of eye contact is approximately 70 percent when we talk. When addressing a roomful of people, aim for 100 percent. In real life, we have a term for this: Staring.

It is important to realize that your level of eye contact during a presentation is an altogether different animal than a normal conversation. Your goal is not to lock in on one person, but to distribute your gaze, visually touching different audience members continually. This negates the impression of staring.

If you are using slides, you can shift your gaze to a particular graphic to draw attention to it. And you will need to reference your notes on occasion.

But the most important spot in the room is your audience. Do not stare at your shoes. Do not use the actor's "fourth wall" technique and peer above your audience's heads. Do not mumble into your notes. Look out to the people who honor you by deciding to hear you speak.

I recall being in the audience for a panel discussion at the National Press Club. Most of the politicos on the dais were old hands and were able to maintain solid eye contact with those of us in the cheap seats. But one of the speakers insisted on staring at that fourth wall, ignoring the audience. My guess is that someone once upon a time gave him some stupid advice and he listened. What a shame. His arguments may have been persuasive, but he blew it by never giving himself the chance to forge a connection.

Also, take note of your blink rate. For most people, this is something that is second nature. Not for me. I tend to have a slow blink rate. It shows up when I review the videotapes of myself. Even in still photographs, I am usually the one who looks like he has fallen asleep because I am caught with my eyes closed. This is one of the challenges I need to work on constantly.

Another thought about blinking: Frequent blinking connotes submissiveness or weakness. It is almost as if someone is saying, "Please don't hurt my feelings," or, in a more base fashion, "Please don't hit me." So be sure you don't look like you are trying to send a message in Morse Code with your eyes while on the dais.

For some individuals, this is a physical reaction. If you are prone to allergies or if your eyes water when you visit a smoke-choked restroom, pack a bottle of eye drops in your speaker's kit. Your audience will never see you blink.

Plotting Your Eye Contact

You know by now that preparation is key to the success of any presentation. That applies to eye contact as well. When you connect via eye contact, you send a signal to your audience that the communications channel is wide open.

You need to plan ahead of time how you will make that visual connection when speaking. In a small group—no more than ten to fifteen people, depending on the length of your talk—you are able to make eye contact with everyone numerous times during the course of your presentation.

That is not possible with a large group. Large audiences tend to flummox less experienced speakers for that very reason. Here is how to work a bigger hall: Divide the room into sections. Visually separate it into front and rear; and left, center, and right. As you speak, spread your eye contact around each of those six sections periodically—right front, center rear, and so forth.

Practice this technique. It is not as easy as it sounds. Some presenters tend to look like automatons, robotically scanning the room. Your challenge is to make it appear natural. Don't scan the front three sections, move on to the rear sections, then do it all over again robotically. Change the order of your eye contact patterns. Just be sure to aim for a roughly equal distribution by the time you complete your speech.

It doesn't matter whether you are speaking in a huge auditorium, a small conference room, or a classroom. Include everyone. No matter the forum, remember to distribute your eye contact throughout your audience. Don't leave anyone out. Avoid focusing on only one area of the room or omitting one or two individuals. Be inclusive so no one feels ignored.

Speak to one individual for one to two sentences at a time. In the case of a large hall, you are speaking to one section of the room instead of a single person.

Once again, remember to avoid the actor's "fourth wall" technique. Looking over the heads of your audience is a bad idea. Crowd members will rightly sense that you are speaking at them rather than with them. Eye contact is vital to your success.

Here is one more eye contact tip that will really help you drive your story home: Maintain eye contact as you deliver the end of each sentence. When you need to steal a glance at your notes, do so at the beginning of a thought. Your crescendo should be delivered with solid eye contact.

Wardrobe Words of Advice

The next portion of the Video group is wardrobe. This term applies to more than clothing. Wardrobe also includes jewelry, accessories, hair style, and grooming. In other words, anything visual about you as a person factors into your image.

You want your wardrobe to support your desired image. My focus is primarily on producing a professional persona, but if you speak before other types of audiences, you will find some useful advice here, too.

Unless you have attained supermodel status, your wardrobe is not what your audience comes to see. You need a look that is neutral, one that your audience members won't talk about one way or the other. It does you no good to have the crowd leaving your speech chattering about the sharp suit you wore. And you certainly do not want them walking out the door ridiculing that outmoded 1980s bouffant hair style. You want them discussing the message you came to deliver.

Take your suits to the dry cleaners regularly and make sure your clothing shows no wrinkles. When you travel and need to stuff your garb in a suitcase for a few hours, take a good look at it when you arrive at your destination. Most hotels have irons and ironing boards. Use them.

In general, check yourself out from head to toe. Is your hair trim and neat? Do you need a shave? (Men, this means your face; women, look at your legs.) Do your nails need a trim? What about your shoes—could they stand polishing?

The research explains why your wardrobe is so critical. When given a list of ten characteristics they take note of when meeting people, women chose clothing first when encountering both other women and men. It turns out that men are much the same; clothing is the first thing they notice about other men while women's wardrobe is the third factor they heed (behind their figure and face).

Here is my bottom line: Save the fashion statements for your personal time. When you are presenting, you must exhibit a professional appearance. You want the audience to focus on you and your message. You do not want their prime takeaway to be that overpowering cologne or loud tie you decided to wear.

I am not about to launch into a discussion of what colors look best on you or how to apply just the right amount of mascara. There are people who do this for a living, though I tend to avoid them. Why? Many of them wear makeup that makes the Bride of Frankenstein look like an ingénue. Plus, the loud scarves, choking perfume, clanking bracelets, and huge brooches fail to connote a professional, authoritative image.

If your goal is to sell cosmetics or you are not aiming for a professional look—perhaps you speak before children or take on the character of a clown—go wild with the pancake makeup. In every other case, I strongly urge you to assemble an image that enhances your professional standing. An appropriate amount of lipstick, eye shadow, and hair product can enhance your look.

And do pay attention to your hair. Remember to check your look in a mirror immediately before you go onstage. An unruly cowlick or one wayward strand can distract an audience and make them lose track of your message. For those wearing wigs or hairpieces, take one last glance in a mirror before going onstage to ensure it is not askew.

One note on your wardrobe for those who wear eyeglasses: If you speak frequently, especially in larger halls with bright lights or on television, consider springing for some non-reflective lenses. That way you lessen worries of looking like a monster from a B-grade outer space flick shooting light rays at your audience.

Business Pro or Beach Bum?

Your audience develops a stereotype of you based in part on how you accessorize. That flashy jewelry, wild tie, or loud scarf plants an image in their minds that could prove tough to shake no matter how skillfully you deliver your words.

If you present yourself with day-old stubble dressed in a t-shirt with no socks, they will likely be expecting a talk about the finer points of surfing. Similarly, if you walk in with a beat up briefcase or a purse filled to the bursting point, that, too, detracts from your professional image.

Lots of people these days opt for tattoos. Every so often I try to picture what they will look like once the population ages and we are faced with a bunch of older folks with sagging skin laden with distorted images. It is not a pretty picture. But I digress. The point I want to make is that, similar to your wardrobe, an audience will judge you a certain way if they see your tattoo. Long sleeves and slacks will cover most body art. Unless your tattoo is integral to your presentation, see to it that yours is covered by your clothing so as not to distract anyone in the crowd. You do not want them trying to guess what your tattoo signifies at the expense of listening to your message.

Treat body piercings similarly. While a navel ring should not be visible when you are onstage (I hope!), think twice about that stud in your nose, ring through your eyebrow, or bevy of hoops that make your ears look like a strand of holiday lights. Such accoutrements may be very meaningful to you, but to your audience they are distractions, reducing your ability to drive home your message.

This paragraph may sound indelicate, but a few additional items need to be mentioned. Remember the deodorant. You will at some point be up close and personal with the audience. Don't make them regret it. It is also a good idea to make sure your deodorant contains an antiperspirant. How many times have we witnessed a speaker raise his arms to make a point, only to be treated to the sight of ugly perspiration stains on his underarms? Such a scene hardly shouts out the word, "professional."

Men vs. Women

It is time to go clothes shopping. The best choice is a neutral wardrobe, one that doesn't detract from your message. For men, this means a dark suit, light blue shirt, and a traditional tie. I am partial to red-based ties because they offer a nice contrast with the rest of my wardrobe. I view that as my "uniform" and nearly always deliver presentations dressed accordingly.

There are exceptions to every rule, including this one. As you will recall, part of your preparation phase involved a questionnaire for the organization that invited you to speak, with one of the questions centering on the dress code for the meeting. If you gain assurances that the gathering is business casual, you may be able to forgo the tie and jacket.

But at the very least, I bring them along. It is all part of my image: The Ed Barks brand, if you will. I never want to be seen as the worst dressed person in the room. As a matter of fact, I always aim for the top 10 percent. There is a psychological factor at play here that says the person who dresses best is the smartest. When in doubt, I opt for the suit and tie every time.

Leave the loud, comical tie your kids gave you for your birthday and the narrow-striped shirt that will drive your audience's eyes crazy in the dresser drawer. They have no role in your professional attire.

Women face similar wardrobe choices. The best bets are subdued colors, skirts and dresses of appropriate length, and no plunging necklines. This may sound indelicate, but if you wear a short skirt, it is a sure bet that most of the men in the audience will be sorely distracted from your message, particularly if you are seated on a stage. The same applies to a low-cut neckline.

It is all-important that you stick with the subdued wardrobe if your presentation is delivered via closed circuit television or is videotaped. Stay away from the herringbone or seersucker suits or any patterns on your tie or scarf that include tight checks, small pictures or graphics, or wavy lines. They will break up on the video and distract the viewer. People will spend more time wondering why you decided to wear that garish outfit than they will listening to the important words you have to say.

Pointers for Props

The final part of the Video group consists of any props you decide to use. I define props as anything physical you must deal with during your presentation that helps bring your message to life for your audience.

And I do mean anything—photos, your company's products, books, maps, balloons, charts, toys, magic tricks, magazine articles, and hats, just to list a few possibilities.

Slides, graphs, photos, handups, and flip charts also fall into the props category. Why? They are things you need to deal with physically. You need to acknowledge slides on the screen, advance your slide presentation, and distribute handups, for example. This is why slides prove tricky for many speakers.

We have all seen presentations in which the speaker doesn't know how to advance or reverse his slides, finds his overhead transparencies out of order, or fumbles with a visual aid. The focus shifts immediately from the substance of his talk to his technical shortcomings.

Your props need to fit the situation. Never force the use of a visual aid. You will force your audience to waste time thinking about how this fits into your presentation, distracting them from your message.

Once you have settled on a prop, ensure that it is large enough to be seen by all. You may find the perfect photo to prove your point. But if it is too tiny for people to see, it adds nothing to your performance.

Work your props into your practice routine. The front of the room is not a place to get creative, so plot ahead of time how and when you will bring your prop into play. If, during your rehearsals, you find the prop is not working or is too difficult to manage, ditch it.

Out of sight, out of mind is a good rule of thumb for your props. Unless it is too bulky to be hidden, keep your visual aid out of the audience's view until you plan to use it. They may spend time trying to figure out what that toy is doing on the front table rather than listening to you deliver your message.

Distribute larger props in different areas in the front of the room. For example, center your screen and place your flip chart to the right of that. On its left you can position the TV/VCR that will play your videos. This causes the audience to shift in its seats as you reference each tool. Even though this shift is ever so slight, it serves to keep them more alert. Moving their gaze from time to time helps them avoid the tedium of a single perspective for a long and boring period.

As another example, I sometimes quote from one of my publications. That means I need to make up my mind ahead of time not only what pages I will read from, but how and when I will physically display it to the audience. I need to decide whether I will pass it among them (a good way to build desire if you have resources you sell when you speak), or simply display it.

Humans can serve as props, too. I sometimes get some sideways glances when I reference people as things to be manipulated. But the fact is if it is something physical—be it animate or inanimate—it counts as a prop.

Consider, for example, whether you will need a volunteer from the audience. Or, do you plan to ask someone in attendance to hand out your materials. You need to manage these individuals' actions so that, first, they meet your needs and, second, you avoid placing them in an embarrassing position.

Finally, pause when it is time to introduce a prop. Give the audience a good look at it and let them catch up mentally and figure out what it means in the context of your talk.

Now you have a solid grasp of your Video Tools. *Action, facial expression, eye contact, wardrobe*, and *props* will go a long way in fortifying your presentations.

Your Audio Tools

Now it is on to the second ingredient in winning the Communications Trifecta, your Audio Tools. This discussion gives you some suggestions for improving how you sound when delivering presentations.

Where the Video Tools covered above help draw your audience's eyes to your talk, the Audio Tools attract their ears toward your message. You need to sound interesting in order for your audience to find your words interesting. Research shows by consensus that how you sound has an effect on how much information people recall, the degree to which their attitudes change, and how much credibility you earn.

You also need to sound confident. The more times you stumble and fumble while presenting, the more the audience is liable to think you are lying. Get rid of all that anxiety during your practice sessions. Your performance needs to be smooth if you want to sound credible.

Let us examine the five Audio Tools you have at your disposal. You will recall that this *PAVER* formula can help pave the way to your speaking success:

- **P**itch
- **A**rticulation
- **V**olume
- **E**motion
- **R**ate

I don't know anyone who wants to listen to someone speaking in the same tone, same volume, and same rate for twenty minutes or more.

Pitch Perfect

The first of the Audio Tools we will deal with in detail is pitch.

Who wants to listen to a dull monotone or a singsong approach? Speaking in a monotone is a surefire way to put an audience to sleep. These presenters are what I call "forehead bruisers." Why that name? Audience members are bored to sleep in no time, causing them to slump forward unconscious onto the table top in front of them. The result is a contusion on their foreheads.

The opposite of monotone is a singsong approach. This is a little more insidious than a monotone since some speakers go too far overboard when trying to compensate. Watch out that you don't fall into this category. The best I can say about singsonging your speech is that it makes you sound like a caring pre-school teacher. Of course, when addressing a group of adults, this nursery rhyme cadence makes you sound like Little Bo Peep instead of a renowned expert. You destroy your credibility and transform yourself into an airhead with zero knowledge and zero credibility.

Strive for the happy medium. Vary your inflection and modulation, but don't overdo it. And make sure your pitch remains consistent with your persona.

One of the most basic elements of pitch is to bring your vocal emphasis down at the end of each sentence. Unless you intend to pose a question, wrap up each statement emphatically by bringing your pitch down. Downward inflection exudes an air of authority; going up indicates uncertainty and timidity.

The register of your voice also comes into play. You may own a mellow bass voice or a high-pitched one. Yes, you can alter your register somewhat over time. But unless you sound like a cartoon character, my advice is to work with what you have by accentuating other strengths.

Pay attention to your intonation. How do you emphasize certain words with your voice? A rising or lowering pitch can frame words and phrases you want your audience to remember.

Finally with regard to pitch, vocal activity is important. In fact, variety makes a big difference in all of your Audio Tools.

I will stress once again that the goal with all of your Audio Tools, pitch included, is not to change your style, but to maximize the strengths you already possess.

The Art of Articulation

Articulation is the second of your Audio Tools. It seems so basic, yet there is no secret here. You must speak clearly using your mouth, tongue, and teeth to their full capacity in order to be understood.

Articulation involves a number of factors. Enunciation and pronunciation top the list. Also important are how forceful or relaxed you sound, the resonance or thinness of your voice, breathiness, hoarseness, raspiness, nasality, lip and tongue control, slurring, and disturbance frequency.

Let's dig a little deeper into enunciation since it counts for a lot when you offer a presentation. Regardless of how informal your talk appears on the surface, public speaking demands a more formal style. For example, don't drop the "g" in words ending in "ing." It makes you sound uneducated, not laid back.

If your enunciation is letter perfect, congratulations. People who speak in what researchers term an "upper class" dialect (think Boston Brahmin) elicit positive reactions from their listeners. But that perception turns negative if the speaker recognized as upper class, in a futile attempt to bond with his audience, starts talking about the workin' man instead of the working man or insists on using coarse language. Your image is what it is. Play to your natural strengths.

Articulation is also important given today's global village. Nearly every audience in this day and age is likely to include individuals whose first language is not the same as yours.

As an example, your first language may be English. If you were to deliver a speech in Asia—even if your audience spoke conversational English—they might need to strain somewhat to catch each word if they normally speak in another tongue. Help them out by enunciating clearly. I am not suggesting that you overdo it and speak as some people would to a two-year-old. Just make sure your enunciation is clear.

If you speak internationally, proper articulation is also vital even if you and your audience both speak English. At a presentation I once delivered in Ireland, all of us spoke the same language, but our accents and catch phrases were different. To make matters easier, I monitored my articulation to see to it that my American accent did not prove a barrier.

Eliminate words that cause you pronunciation difficulties. As comedian Mike Myers said in the utterly forgettable movie, *View from the Top*, don't put the em-pha'-sis on the wrong syl-lab'-ul.

We all have such words. President Gerald Ford insisted on pronouncing the word "judgement" as "judg-uh-ment." The problem became so acute, his speechwriters soon learned not to insert that word into his speeches.

And how many times have we cringed upon hearing certain politicians talk about "nu-cu-lar" weapons? Determine where your "judg-uh-ments" and "nu-cu-lars" lurk and keep them out of earshot.

Breathe Deeply

Proper articulation means that you have to breathe if you choose to speak. I know it sounds basic. But we have all witnessed presenters who forget to inhale and exhale effectively. On its most serious level, it can lead someone to pass out from oxygen deprivation. That is not an image most speakers want to cultivate.

When you practice your presentation, practice your breathing. If, for instance, one passage includes an overly long sentence, break it up by taking a breath at the end of a phrase (better yet, keep away from long, run-on sentences or thoughts).

The point is you want to pump enough air into your lungs to make it through your next phrase. A long thought means a deep breath. Otherwise, you may try to rush your words to get them out before running out of gas. That destroys the impact of your message since, in most languages, including English, our thoughts culminate at the end of the sentence. This is where your emphasis belongs. If you are not able to hammer home your conclusion due to a lack of oxygen, you can kiss your persuasive abilities goodbye.

Each individual demonstrates varying levels of breathiness, hoarseness, raspiness, and nasality. Some conditions are permanent. If you feel that your voice is overly nasal or breathy, vocal coaching can sometimes help. Just understand that changing any articulation patterns in your voice will not occur overnight. You need to commit to the long haul.

At times, nearly everyone faces temporary hoarseness or raspiness, such as when we suffer from a cold. The best advice I can give if you are ill is to slog through it if possible. No, it will not be your best performance of all time. But unless you are in the Typhoid Mary category, you may be able to do a serviceable job. If you are too sick to perform, find a capable replacement and concentrate on getting well for your next gig.

I find lip and tongue control and slurring to be related. In fact, this is one of the areas I need to monitor when I deliver long presentations. By afternoon time, my batteries can start to lose their juice. In my case, this tends to manifest itself in lazier action in the lips and tongue, causing articulation to suffer. With this understanding, I know that I must monitor this part of my performance closely.

The notion of disturbance frequency involves an excessive use of such place-holders as um, er, ah, and y'know. Nervous noises like sniffles, sighs, giggles, and throat clearing qualify, too. Speech disturbances also incorporate overly long silences (see "Rate Relevance" below for further details). A high disturbance frequency will lead your listeners to think you have a negative attitude or are trying to deceive them. It is also associated with speakers who deliver a negative message.

The Vitals of Volume

Volume is the second of your Audio Tools. Varying the loudness and softness of your voice periodically better engages your listeners' ears.

The main point here is, you need to throw in a change-up every now and then. The baseball pitcher who throws only 100 mile-per-hour fastballs may seem intimidating at first. But if that is all he's got, hitters will soon be able to time him and knock him out of the game. Conversely, if he works in a few change-ups or curve balls, he will most assuredly gain the batter's attention.

So it goes when you speak. You could talk louder to emphasize a certain passage. Later, you can soften your voice to draw attention to an important lesson.

That second approach is important. Most people turn their volume dial only one way and mistake volume for talking only louder. Shouting does not add to your charisma.

Lowering the volume of your voice when driving home key points is a powerful technique. The audience will be eating out of your hand when you drive home your point in a stage whisper. It is like letting them in on a secret.

Teddy Roosevelt's admonition to "speak softly and carry a big stick," was right on the mark. In this case, when you speak softly, your audience hears your "big stick" of a message much more clearly.

This is not to say that you want to change your volume all the time. That would be the equivalent of employing a singsong pitch. For most of your presentation, you will want to find a comfortable volume and settle in. But it is vital that you change things up when, for example, you hit on a key point or when you sense the audience needs a change of pace.

If you are trying to convince your audience about a certain point, that is the time to turn up the volume. Louder statements are considered more persuasive. Again, take care not to yell. But do pump up the volume somewhat when trying to persuade.

Of course you must project your voice in order to be heard. This means proper breathing is necessary. Breathe with your stomach, lungs, and throat, taking advantage of every ounce of air. You can supercharge your voice if you speak with authority using the diaphragm. Poor speaking habits leave you with a hoarse voice and sore throat. You will be of little use when the time comes for your next presentation if your pipes are in disrepair.

Emotion Essentials

The third section of the Audio Toolkit is emotion. This factor is ignored far too often. If you fail to transfer your passion to the audience, you cannot expect them to invest in what you are selling. Transmit a sense of urgency. Your audience members only buy your message if you demonstrate that you care.

Your emotion may be joy, outrage, excitement, gratitude, sadness, pride, disdain, or any other feeling. In some instances, coolly detached may be the best fit.

Your body language must serve to support your emotions. You can evidence a forward lean to show empathy, clench your fists with rage, or shake your head to connote disappointment.

As with everything else leading up to your presentation, you must plan in advance which emotions best suit your given situation. No matter your choice, you must put it on display for all to see.

A word of caution: Avoid coming across as a bad community theater actor, playing the ham who wears his emotion on his sleeve. Keep it at a reasonable level and refrain from going overboard. But do be sure to mix in the element of emotion as you practice your presentation.

Be sure to balance your emotion with the size of room in which you speak. Keep from overwhelming a small room with an overabundance of sentiment. At the same time, bear in mind that you will need to play it a bit hotter if you are to successfully portray your presence to a larger venue.

If you play to a large auditorium, you likely will appear on video screens spread throughout the room. Even though the space is huge, avoid getting too "hot" with your emotions. The camera brings it back to the level of an intimate presentation.

This also holds true if your remarks are being videotaped. Think no further than Howard Dean and his "I Have a Scream" speech during the 2004

Iowa caucuses. His boiling-over persona that night may have been appropriate for the roomful of avid supporters. But as a TV moment, it will continue to live in political infamy for decades to come.

Rate Relevance

The fifth portion of the Audio group is rate. Your rate of speech is also easily understood on an intuitive level. Some people talk fast, some talk slow. There is no single correct way. Just be sure your listeners can understand you.

Think of the times you have heard speakers who rave like the announcer at a horse race. You feel as though your brain is struggling to keep up with simply processing what they are saying, let alone soaking in the richness of their message.

Now reflect on presenters you have heard who speak as slow as molasses running uphill. You have plenty of time to ponder the choices for lunch or that evening's entertainment. Just like you, everyone else in the crowd is wondering when this guy is finally going to get to his point and wrap it up.

In general, you want to aim for a middle ground as regards your rate of speech. Not too fast, not too slow. Go for the Goldilocks approach—just right.

If you are delivering a persuasive speech, note that faster talking individuals are seen as more influential. I am not suggesting you mimic one of those hokey fast-talking hucksters on a used car commercial. But research does indicate that speeding up your rate of speech can make a positive difference.

Here is the real key in working with your rate of speech: Alter it throughout your presentation. As with all of your nonverbal qualities, mix up your pace to keep your audience engaged. Speak more rapidly for a sentence or two. At other points, slow things down for a few beats in order to keep listeners' ears refreshed.

In addition, most of us need to slow things down a bit when we speak formally. In everyday conversation, the average person speaks at a rate of about 150 words per minute. That slows to the low 100s for most public speakers. One reason for that slower pace is the need to enunciate with perfect clarity.

We not only need to ensure our listeners hear the words we say, we need to allow a bit of time for their brains to process our ideas and arguments. Your rate of speech, which we will discuss in a moment, also comes into play here. But too many speakers fail to heed the importance of enunciation.

There is another factor at play in the words per minute discussion. While we tend to speak at 100–150 words per minute, we can normally process more than 700 every 60 seconds. Does this help tell you why nonverbal cues are so important? Yes, our brains have all that spare time to process something beyond words. The audience can gaze about the room aimlessly or have your message reinforced by your nonverbal signs. I opt for the latter choice every time.

There is another aspect to your rate of speech. That is the pause. A pause is especially effective when you want to focus your audience's attention on a certain word or idea. Bracket key thoughts with a strategic pause and watch the reaction you get. Executed properly, a pause will lead people to sit forward in their seats, hanging on your next idea.

As with any technique, do not overdo the pause. Chronic lengthy silences give your listeners the idea that you are anxious, angry, disdainful, or condescending.

Consider that regional differences often play a part in people's customary rate of speech. Yes, it is true that, by and large, New Yorkers talk faster while individuals from the southern U.S. tend to talk more slowly. Take this localism factor into account if you speak in various geographical regions.

The Audio/Video Club

To summarize, your Video Tools can go a long way in strengthening your ability as a speaker. Let us review A FEW Pointers:

- **A**ction
- **F**acial expression
- **E**ye contact
- **W**ardrobe
- **P**rops

Similarly, your Audio Tools—using the PAVER formula to pave your way to the high road of speaking—also add to your legitimacy when you stand in front of the room. Use these techniques for maximum advantage:

- **P**itch
- **A**rticulation
- **V**olume
- **E**motion
- **R**ate

Of course, expert use of these nonverbal skills merely opens doors. The prize you want your listeners to win is the essence of what you have to say— your message.

Forging A Magnetic Message

It sounds so basic. The words you utter do make a difference. But it is important to recognize that the third section of the Communications Trifecta—a magnetic message—is more than merely a collection of facts. Properly constructed, your message is a systematic argument that serves to attract listeners to your point of view. It also makes it easy for you to stick to your story when delivering your speech.

Chapter Four introduced the concept of the magnetic message that attracts listeners to your argument. To review, a magnetic message requires four strong legs. These are the main tenets you want to impart.

Think of it as a sturdy, four-legged chair. If one of its legs is weak, the chair collapses, sending you to the floor.

There are no shortcuts to developing a magnetic message. Indeed, message development workshops can often be sweat-producing, headache-inducing affairs.

I will let you in on a little secret: Most organizations have never developed formal messages for their key issues. Or if they have, the messaging is extremely weak. Think of the opportunities this presents for you. You can top the competition by crafting a tight message and making the commitment to delivering it in every presentation.

The size of the organization often makes no difference in terms of message sophistication. I have worked with Fortune 500 companies that have abysmal messages for many of their endeavors. It is hard to imagine how they got to a position of strength in the marketplace with such shoddy craftsmanship. It is equally difficult to envision how they will maintain their leadership position.

The Acid Test

Now assemble your message team. Its membership will likely change for individual issues. Some teams, for example, may include the president, regional vice presidents, sales managers, technical advisors, lawyers, your public relations staff, and more. Other teams may involve some or none of these experts.

The important consideration is that everyone with a stake or special expertise needs to be there. Of equal importance, keep anyone superfluous to the issue out of the room. Avoid too unwieldy a process at all costs.

Your first concern is to get ideas on paper. Brainstorm without editing, either mentally or in writing. Begin to winnow down the thoughts only when you have exhausted everyone's "blue sky" contributions.

To smooth out the process, choose a facilitator who can remain impartial in directing your messaging deliberations. This person could be someone inside your organization who has no personal stake in the issue at hand. Or you could opt for an outsider to guide your discussions. Just be sure he understands and agrees that his role is not to jump in and take part in substantive matters.

Once you have achieved a first cut of your magnetic message, it is time to see if it can withstand rigorous questioning.

To test the magnetic attraction of your message, think of all the tough questions audience members could toss at you. If one of the legs of your message responds adequately, you have likely achieved success.

It is vital that you *practice* dealing with the hardballs. Going over them in your mind is not enough. Simulate a presentation by having co-workers pelt you with questions.

And invite the office skeptic. If one or more of your message points is responsive to the salvos of this cynic, you likely have attained the necessary magnetism.

Seek reaction from trusted colleagues and peers outside your organization. This outside criticism provides you with good insights into how "on target" your messaging is.

For higher stakes opportunities, you may wish to consider more formal measurements, such as polling key constituencies or holding focus groups.

Important note: Messages are constantly evolving creatures. There is no guarantee that today's magnetic message will suffice tomorrow. I strongly advise you to revisit your messages on a quarterly basis at a minimum, more frequently for rapidly shifting issues.

Messaging Strategies

How do you build a message with the strength of steel? Let me give you a jump start by providing some questions that can serve as your starting point:

- What is the problem?
- What is your solution?
- What is the next step?
- How can you put matters into context for your listeners?
- How does your issue affect them?
- Why should they care?

- What's in it for them?
- What do you want them to do about it?
- Who disagrees with you?

This list is by no means exhaustive, though it does give you a good foundation. I urge you to develop inquiries that fit your situation.

In addition, there are common traits of reliable messaging strategies and systems. Here are some of the factors you want to investigate:

- *Who is my audience for this particular presentation?* This is a basic question that demands an answer as you develop your message for your next speech.
- *What are my goals and objectives in delivering this specific presentation?* In one presentation, you may aim to persuade; in another, you may want to inform. Align your message accordingly.
- *How can I best make listeners aware of those goals and objectives?* Decide what words, phrases, and examples will best advance your goals.
- *What is the audience's current perspective and baseline of information?* If they know little about the matter at hand, your message will need to lay some groundwork.
- *What do they see as the big picture and how does my viewpoint mesh with it?* If your issue is one small part of an overarching concern, you may need to broaden the perspective before you can zero in on your role.
- *What matters to my audience and what benefits can they expect?* Forget about what is important to you. Craft your message from the perspective of your target market.
- *What do they care about on an emotional level, and how can I connect with that?* Data-driven individuals have a hard time with this one, but connecting emotionally is vital to the success of your message.
- *What do they need to hear from me?* Decide whether the tone of your message should be one of comfort, cheer, challenge, or confrontation.
- *How can I broadcast my message without sounding preachy?* Avoid a condescending tone.
- *What do I want them to support, condemn, or take action upon?* Clarity is vital. Spell out specifically how you want your audience to change its thought process and action patterns as a result of hearing your message.
- *What is likely to motivate them to take action?* Use your audience research to press their hot buttons.
- *Where are my vulnerabilities?* Your stance on any given issue can never be 100 percent airtight. Understand where the chinks in your armor

exist and see to it that your message preempts them.

- *Where is my data or proof weak, making me subject to attack?* Counter those weak points you anticipate during your messaging deliberations.
- *Is there a particular segment of the audience I need to address?* Not everyone is likely to agree with you. Decide whether you want to target your message to your supporters or the fence sitters.
- *What types of words and images will propel me to leadership status in their eyes?* Powerful language helps to drive a magnetic message.
- *What buzzwords specific to their industry can give me the appearance of an insider?* Do not overload your speech with jargon. A few catch phrases used judiciously will make you sound like an expert.
- *What facts, figures, and anecdotes are they most likely to identify with?* You have a storehouse of vivid images you can use to bolster your message. Pick the ones to which a given audience best relates.
- *Which are the most concrete proof points I can offer?* Some types of evidence are better than others. Prop up your message with your strongest contentions.
- *What facets of my personal background give me an edge in their eyes?* Your past may include a prime position or you may hold a special designation with which your audience identifies. Leverage your message accordingly.
- *What makes my contention better than my opposition's?* Consider the arguments of your adversaries and ensure your message preempts them.
- *What is the single best quotable quote I want them to recall and restate?* Plan your quotable quotes in advance, then salt your message with them.
- *How can I best transform them into disciples of my message?* You want your audience leaving your presentation singing from your songbook. Give them language that makes it easy for them.
- *What "call to action" must I sound?* Your message should make clear what deeds you want audience members to take.
- *Where do I want my audience's mindset to be at the end of the presentation?* Decide whether you want to fire them up or leave them pensive after taking in your message.

You will no doubt explore additional questions specific to your issue or industry. The important point is to unearth the concerns that put you on the fast lane of the message highway.

In the Real World

How do these factors play out in everyday life? Take the example of a company that wants to build a new plant but faces local opposition from neighborhood activists. The locals may decry faulty zoning laws. The company that develops its message skillfully knows enough to focus on the number of jobs created instead. Why? It's simple. People care more about jobs than arcane regulations.

Here is another illustration. An environmental group rallies against gas-hogging SUVs. While its goal is to conserve energy resources, the group's message meisters realize that most people are indifferent to wasting energy. As a result, the focus of their message turns on how much more expensive SUVs are in times of rising gasoline prices.

Note how in each case the organization is sensitive to what matters in its target audience's minds, and plays both to that logic and emotion.

The Message Box

One specialized messaging technique used frequently in the political arena is commonly referred to as the "message box." It is a simple concept that can prove valuable in adversarial situations.

The message box is based on an us vs. them format. You can develop your own message box by drawing it as a grid.

The upper left quadrant reflects what you would say about your issue. These points represent your strengths.

The upper right quadrant indicates your views on your opponent's position, or its weaknesses.

The quadrant in the lower left shows what your rivals say about you; in other words, these are your weaknesses.

In the lower right quadrant, characterize what your rivals would say about themselves. This shows their strengths.

Once you have defined these various assets and liabilities, use the tools described above to develop a leg of your message for each quadrant.

With this information in hand, the message box allows you to focus on your strong suits while anticipating your opponent's arguments. It also empowers you with a way of addressing your vulnerabilities while anticipating your opponent's arguments. Once defined, you have a much easier time deciding which part of your message best counters any attacks.

The 3-D Message Model

When multiple interests are arrayed against you, a three dimensional approach to message creation is often necessary.

This is not an uncommon situation for large organizations. Decisions about the siting of new facilities, launch of a new product, plant closures, and other similar issues draw interest from a variety of groups.

So, too, do crises like plant explosions, toxic waste spills, accounting irregularities, workplace violence, and death of a member of the executive team, to cite a handful.

A crisis does not have to be worthy of national headlines to activate the 3-D Message Model. Every organization encounters calamities large and small. A small business crisis, for instance, could include loss of a large customer, sudden collapse of its Internet service provider or web host, or a lawsuit.

Who are these affected parties that could line up against you? They could include workers, neighborhood associations, local government officials, competitors, labor unions, environmental activists, the governor, area chambers of commerce, and a host of other organizations.

The 3-D Message Model gains added importance when you plan to address an audience that consists of multiple interests, perhaps at a community forum, city council meeting, or through the media.

In cases like this, you need to anticipate the arguments of not just one critic, but of a host of adversaries with differing agendas. The 3-D Message Model provides the armor you need when facing challenges on multiple fronts.

How do you shape your 3-D Message Model? Begin with the Message Box outlined above. Then add columns and rows for each party that might step forward to oppose you.

The specific items you need to consider will vary from case to case. Some common categories include the name of the opposing organization, the individual leading the charge, how powerful or influential the institution or individual is, its position on the issue, tactics it customarily uses, and allies it can bring to bear.

Once you have anticipated the categories for your situation, form a grid or matrix that allows you to visually discern where your strengths and weaknesses, as well as those of your antagonists, lie.

Look for any common threads. This step allows you to adjust your message to best address the array of issues and interests lined up against you. For example, is money a central issue for all parties? What about safety, jobs, or legal rights?

Also, determine whether any of your opponents' messages run counter to those of another. In cold, hard terms, you may find you are able to play one adversary against another, in effect neutralizing them.

The fact is entire chapters and books could be written about crafting a magnetic message. In workshops, we can spend entire days devoted solely to message development. The strategies contained here are designed to give you some insights and a baseline of knowledge so you can begin shaping messages that will lead you and your organization to success.

Say It Again, Sam

Repetition is a good thing when broadcasting your message. It is not enough to state your message once and walk away. I repeat, saying your message once will not get the job done.

Nor is it enough to say it a second time and call it a day. In fact, repetition is one of the most important tools available if your speech is an attempt at persuasion.

During my days as a reporter, I was sometimes going from one event to the next, wondering where I was and what the issue at hand involved. If a news source told me his opinion several times, I would finally start to get it after hearing it for the third or fourth time.

So it is with many audiences. They may not be paying rapt attention to you (shocking, I know). They may be preoccupied with that deadline staring them in the face back at the office. They may be thinking about where they need to go next. They may wonder how their daughter is doing on that big test at school today. They may be daydreaming about going on vacation next week. In other words, they may be thinking about any number of things that have nothing to do with you.

That is why you need to reiterate your message often. Redundancy and repetition generate greater intensity of understanding among audience members. State it in different words, but be sure you broadcast the essence of your message frequently during your talk.

Message equals consistency over time. It might help to think of it as a mathematical formula in which M stands for message, C for consistency, and T for time:

$$M = C/T$$

Keep reinforcing your message and, as with that thick-headed reporter, your audience will start to absorb your ideas.

Add a Dash of Color

A powerful message is more than words on paper. Presentations are made to be spoken aloud. Words that flow on paper do not necessarily equate with silver-tongued oratory.

The spoken word must contain some color. It is your job to get your audience involved by adding some spice to your message.

Place your listeners at the scene of your conquest or defeat. Make them feel the joy of your success or the pain of your embarrassment. Plant an image in the audience's mind that remains with them long after you have parted company.

The most dynamic speakers appeal not only with their words, but with images. They aim for the senses, painting visual pictures, broadcasting auditory echoes, or cooking up an olfactory image. Such an approach makes your message more concrete than abstract.

Employ metaphors, similes, alliteration, onomatopoeia, personification (just as the plane aimed its nose for the runway), and other figures of speech. Just be cautious not to get carried away. There is no need to force overdone color into every sentence. That is the equivalent of a brochure that is too busy for the eye, using too much color and too many distracting graphics.

We have all heard speakers and read passages in books that apply the color too heavily. You only end up sounding like the hammy actor who couldn't portray a tree in the school play.

It makes your topic seem more real and more important to your audience. Let's review some of the instruments you have at your fingertips:

- Stories
- Numbers, fractions, percentages
- Extremes (the best, the first, the only)
- Case studies
- Jiu jitsu (citing the opposition)
- Quotations from famous individuals
- Anecdotes
- Analogies
- Topics du jour
- Clichés
- Personal experience
- Humor

Adding color to your message adds to your credibility as a presenter. Listeners want to learn from someone who was at the scene gaining real world experience, not a bystander with only secondhand hearsay to impart.

Now, Where Was I?

Have you ever experienced one of those moments where every valuable thought flew right out of your head? Sure, we all have times like this. Some of us even face them in front of a roomful of people!

What happens when your mind turns into a blank screen? This is where a strong message earns its keep. The message you worked so lovingly to craft during your preparation phase becomes your safe harbor.

Your message gains double importance. Not only do you want your audience leaving the room singing your words, your thesis gives you comfort that, when things go wrong, you have tossed yourself the life preserver that will get you back safely to shore.

When you have lost your place and your mental circuits have shut down, reach back for your message to get yourself back on track.

If you are working from notes or using presentation software, it should be relatively easy to find your place. If you are delivering a full text speech, it becomes that much easier.

Flashing Congruent Signals

Winning the Communications Trifecta requires an integrated package. Your credibility depends on it.

I recommend that you view your presentation as an organic whole. For example, your message and body language must not only be strong, but congruent. All signals need to match.

You wouldn't tell your children you love them with a frown on your face. Why tell an audience how excited you are to be with them while speaking in a monotone?

Your audience will think you are trying to deceive them if you fail to nod your head, offer few gestures, talk too slowly, or smile too much.

At the other extreme, they will dismiss you as too submissive if you overdo the smiling and nodding, speak with too high a pitch or too slow a rate, or blink profusely.

Strong Video Tools mean little if you ignore your message. Similarly, the most magnetic of messages will do you little good if your Audio Tools are weak.

What happens when you send inconsistent signals? It turns out that your nonverbal cues dominate. More proof of just how important your Video and Audio Tools are. Moreover, when your verbal and nonverbal cues are harmonious, the power of your message is strengthened.

Think of a finely tuned orchestra. If you omit the violin section, there is not much of a symphony. If you leave out the brass, your performance shows no pizzazz. Setting aside the percussion section takes away the rhythm.

Each segment of the Communications Trifecta—Video, Audio, and Message—are vital to your communications success.

The key to improving your abilities lies in utilizing your strengths to the maximum and keeping vulnerabilities to a minimum. For example, some of us take more readily to utilizing emotion when we speak but are wardrobe challenged. If that describes you, bring out that emotion while keeping your wardrobe simple.

To assess your strengths, complete the "Taking Inventory" exercise. It can heighten your performance in utilizing the two nonverbal parts of the Communications Trifecta. Taking Inventory allows you to gauge which of your Video items and which of your Audio items are strengths that you need to *maintain*, and which are challenges you may wish to *sharpen*. Flip to Appendix B to take advantage of this assignment.

Over time and with skilled coaching, "Taking Inventory" can sharpen your skill level, in some cases dramatically. I encourage you to take this quiz again in a few months and compare the results with your coach, comparing them to those you got today. You are likely to see that you have sharpened a few skills.

Home Stretch

When you make the commitment to Winning the Communications Trifecta, you earn an advantage not only when you speak in public, but when you talk to reporters or appear as a witness before lawmakers and regulators. Latch on to this system as a means to help communicate in public with greater impact.

Use each of the three components of the Communications Trifecta to demonstrate to your audience that you are both interesting and interested. Here is a quick review:

- Video Tools: The way you look
- Audio Tools: The way you sound
- Message Tools: The words you say

When you practice your presentations, focus on Winning the Communications Trifecta.

SPEAKING NONVERBALLY

THE THREE KEYS TO CHAPTER SIX

You can expect to learn the truth about the importance of non-verbal communications:

- The surprising percentage of your message you transmit via body language;
- How your audience takes its measure of you by assessing your nonverbal qualities;
- The necessity of ensuring your nonverbal signals are congruent with your words.

"IT'S NOT WHAT YOU SAY THAT COUNTS, it's what you don't say." That was the tag line from the 1960s TV game show, "You Don't Say." Host Tom Kennedy would wrap up every program with that reminder. Isn't his credo the truth?

Your audience is keeping an eagle eye on you as you speak. Yes, they are listening to your words. But they are also soaking up every gesture and vocal change you emit. Just how important are these nonverbal cues?

Earlier I referenced commonly cited statistics—55 percent of the communications signals we send result from how others see us; 38 percent flow from the way they hear us; and 7 percent come from our words.

When leading a workshop, I sometimes spring a pop quiz, asking which set of tools conveys the bulk of one's message. Is it the Video Tools? The Audio Tools? Or the Message Tools?

Some people guess right, some wrong. And while they may deduce the

The basis for this chapter comes from the white paper, "How Important Are Your Nonverbal Signals?" by Edward J. Barks. © 2003 Edward J. Barks.

correct order, the percentages are often way off the mark. Few people know the numbers. Yet it is surprising how many intuitively recognize the power of nonverbal communication.

The learning moment arrives when they grasp just how powerful a signal these "body language" cues send. Stressing that more than half of the average individual's ability to communicate is delivered via the Video Tools drives home the point.

A Closer Look at the Real Data

I am careful to point out that the 55-38-7 figures must be placed in context. Not for one moment do I suggest that a speaker or news media source will achieve success if they simply master their Video Tools.

The wizard behind the nonverbal curtain is Albert Mehrabian, PhD, a faculty member of UCLA's Psychology Department, who first advanced this arrangement. Mehrabian published his research in the 1970s and, while others have added to it around the edges, his work remains the guiding light even today.

Mehrabian's most important contribution, in my view, was his 1972 book *Nonverbal Communication*, for which he conducted rigorous research and enumerates his conclusions in a fairly straightforward manner. The previous year, he authored *Silent Messages*. That volume contains some interesting insights, but offers nowhere near the research heft provided by his later work.

Magnetize Your Message

Since we send only 7 percent of our message via our words, does this mean your message is not that important? Far from it. A magnetic message is critical.

Here is how I interpret Mehrabian's research and bring it into the real world—the one where real people deliver real presentations every day. You must make full use of your nonverbal tools, both Video and Audio, to make an audience receptive to your message and to persuade or educate it about the value of your position.

Some have tried to stretch Mehrabian's analysis beyond recognition. His research into what I call Video Tools, for instance, considered only facial expressions. Mehrabian is explicit about his approach, writing that total communications involves 7 percent verbal feeling, 38 percent vocal feeling, and 55 percent facial feeling.

Note that his equation includes only "facial feeling." While important, facial expressions are but one part of the Video Toolkit. Clearly, this limits the applicability of his research to a degree since such vital facets as action, wardrobe, and positioning vis-à-vis one's audience were not taken into account.

Does this invalidate his thesis? Hardly.

Using Mehrabian's findings as a communications training tool, however, means that matters must be kept in context. Simply stating that 55 percent of our communications can be chalked up to how we look ignores the original research.

Balancing the Academic with the Practical

It is my job as a communications coach to translate the research from the jargon of the ivory tower into the everyday language of the corporate boardroom.

Most people don't care about the research methods used to arrive at these findings, nor should they. They care about results. They are intently focused on delivering more persuasive presentations or garnering more positive news clips. These outcomes lead to a healthier bottom line, a shinier brand, an increase in membership, and additional volunteers.

I am forever conscious of remaining alert to the research without getting so bogged down in the minutiae that matters devolve into a college lecture instead of hands-on, practical information. As a university professor of mine was fond of saying, "those who can, do. Those who can't, teach."

The Error of Dismissing these Numbers

Some critics have launched diatribes suggesting Mehrabian's rule be rescinded. I disagree. His findings have merit if for no other reason than they paint at least a broad picture for many people of what they need to do in order to sharpen their communications skills.

Consider another factor: What if Mehrabian's research *had* included Video Tools such as action and use of props? It is hard to imagine those inclusions could have done anything other than *increase* the percentage of communication conveyed by use of Video Tools.

I am a great believer in the virtue of common sense. In this case, that quality clearly dictates that his landmark research may have, in reality, *underestimated* the value of one's Video Tools. While no research is apparent on that aspect, it is difficult to picture gestures, appearance, and other Video factors as doing anything but raising the proportion to something above 55 percent.

Keeping It Real

Let us remember to interpret the data so that it makes sense in the real world. This applies whether the correct percentage is 55, 75, or 95.

Here is how I frame the picture: Your message is vital. After all, you decide to speak before an organization because of the ideas you have to impart, not because you wanted to impress them with your ability to raise an eyebrow or talk with your hands.

Picture in your mind the times you have attended presentations and couldn't wait to escape the room. The speaker may have been a world renowned expert in her topic. Her content was top notch. But she stood still in the dark while using slides as a crutch. Or she spoke in a monotone or avoided all eye contact with her audience. Neglecting to utilize critical Video and Audio skills, she soon bored everyone to tears.

Consider the Christmas tree. You want the guests at your holiday party to notice the tree, comment on its loveliness and how it adds to the festivity of the season. Yet few of us trudge out into the woods, chop down any old tree, and plunk it down in our family room unadorned.

What do we do? We dress it up and make it attractive. The glittery ornaments and twinkling lights assume the 55 percent role of your Video Tools. Bing Crosby crooning carols in the background takes on the 37 percent role of your Audio Tools. The tree itself accounts for a mere 7 percent of that holiday glow.

So it is with your message. You want to make it attractive to your listeners. Adorning it with sharp Video and Audio performances gives your message a sense of magnetism. You need all of your communications skills operating at a high level if you are to achieve communications success.

Your Vocal Qualities Give You Away

People assess female and male speakers, rightly or wrongly, through different prisms. One Audio Tool quality used by a man could cause a wholly different perception when used by a woman.

In *Nonverbal Communication in Human Interaction*, Mark L. Knapp and Judith A. Hall examine the specifics of how certain vocal qualities can shape your effectiveness as a presenter. Here is a quick a look:

Breathy. Men are perceived as younger while women are viewed as more feminine, attractive, and shallow.

Flat. Both males and females gained a colder, listless, and withdrawn image.

Full-voiced/strong. Members of both sexes with strong voices are in luck. Women appear lively and gregarious. Men are viewed as healthy and energetic, in addition to being interesting and enthusiastic.

Nasal. In both genders, audiences believed nasal speakers held a wide variety of socially disagreeable traits.

Pitch. A wider range of vocal pitch allows women to be viewed as extroverted and dynamic. While men also seem dynamic, the lilting tone associated with increased pitch can make them seem more feminine.

Rate. Both men and women who increase their rate of speech appear more extroverted and dynamic.

Tense. This brings to mind the image of a cranky, old man. Conversely, women are seen as younger, feminine, and slow on the uptake.

Thin/reedy. Women were identified as having a better sense of humor and greater degree of sensitivity. At the same time, they were seen as more immature. Oddly, a thin-voiced male had no effect, positive or negative, on an audience.

Throaty. This brings to mind a host of negative qualities in women presenters: Uninteresting, lazy, stupid, careless, reckless, naïve, and even neurotic. With men, it is just the opposite: Mature, refined, and secure.

None of this is to say that if, for example, you are a woman who speaks in a reedy tone, you are immature. The important factor at play here is to realize your audience may well perceive you that way. If that is not one of the qualities you wish to emit, consider it as an area you might choose to sharpen over time.

Sending Congruent Signals

Nonverbal proficiency alone is not enough. Your communications signals must be congruent. No conflicts allowed.

These tools must work in harmony with one another. If the pitch of your voice, for instance, does not match your words (the academics call this "asynchronous"), the audience will sense that something is amiss. This impacts your credibility, driving down your odds of convincing your listeners.

Try this experiment in the privacy of your office or home. Furrow your brow as you enthusiastically tout a new innovation your company has developed. Or smile broadly as you announce a record financial loss for the most recent quarter. It is tough to do since it runs contrary to our desire for congruence.

Yes, these are make-believe examples. But think how often similar disconnects occur in the real world of presentations. How many times have we seen the speaker who says how excited he is to be here in a flat voice strangled by trepidation? Or the individual who says, "I'm having a great time," in a voice dripping with sarcasm? Then there are the politicians who tell us of their plans to cut our taxes while glossing over, with a Cheshire Cat grin, the fact that it will cause deficits to balloon.

It is important for presenters and media subjects to recognize the importance of congruence. If you claim to be excited, leverage your vocal inflection and widen your eyes, for example, to prove it to your audience. If, alternatively, you are reacting to a crisis, maintain a voice of dignity when discussing any victims and reduce the use of excitement-inducing gestures.

Unearthing Buried Treasure

Let us examine Mehrabian's findings beyond the mere numbers, for his research unearthed a treasure trove of specific cues that can help you become a better speaker while steering clear of some common pitfalls.

One of the most persuasive nonverbal indicators was the immediacy of communication. This comes into play when you take questions from the audience. People who answer more quickly are seen as more persuasive and truthful. I do not interpret this to mean that you should shoot from the hip during Q&A just so you can issue a rapid response. What it does suggest is the need to anticipate questions and map out which part of your message best responds to a particular issue. You will find more details on Q&A strategies in Chapter Eight.

A trait Mehrabian labels "speech disturbance frequency" also plays an important role in how the crowd perceives you. If you litter your speech with ums, ers, or overly long gaps, your listeners will build a negative attitude toward you. They will believe you are trying to pull the wool over their eyes and will quickly lose any positive feelings they had toward you.

Other types of speech disruptions—such as changing a sentence in midstream, delivering incomplete sentences, omitting words, repeating yourself unnecessarily, offering a slip of the tongue, and stuttering—signal heightened anxiety or discomfort. We all fall victim to such disruptions every now and then. But if they become part of your routine, your judges in the audience will subtract points from your score.

It is intuitive to sense that the more you use your Video and Audio Tools, the more believable and persuasive you will become. Mehrabian puts some weight behind this instinct by noting which tools add the most to your persuasive powers.

He discovered that a higher level of vocal activity makes a big difference. Think of the radio announcer vs. the person with a flat, colorless voice. Also of import is additional volume, a higher rate, increased facial expression, more gestures, smoother speech pattern with few disturbances, more eye contact, and a low incidence of distracting mannerisms, such as twirling your hair or rubbing your eyes.

Research by two contemporaries of Mehrabian, Paul Ekman and Wallace V. Friesen, found that stationary positions communicate attitudes while movements connote specific emotions. That is, the way you stand transmits your overall mindset whereas your hand gestures, facial expressions, and the like signal how you feel at a given moment.

From a presenter's perspective, this means your audience will, consciously or not, take its measure of you based on your decision to stand behind a lectern or roam throughout the crowd, as well as the steadiness of your posture. They will gauge your happiness, fear, or passion by the movements you make.

Taking Action

Highly accomplished communicators realize that self-monitoring to ensure congruence and a high level of nonverbal performance does not, in and of itself, get the job done.

Those who have not studied nonverbal interaction in depth—and I include top-notch communicators in this pool—simply do not know what to look for.

Review the videotape of your performance with your coach. If the two of you see and hear signals you did not intend to send, check for congruence.

Steel yourself for some honest and frank criticism. A skilled coach is able to help you accentuate your strengths and, in due course, minimize your weaknesses.

The stakes are high when you speak, too high to risk a nonverbal faux pas. Your next promotion, election victory, or new account may hang in the balance.

The precise percentages are not as important as the gist of Mehrabian's data. Your Video Tools may account for 55 percent of your ability to communicate, 95 percent, or anywhere in between.

Here is the irrefutable fact: Skillful use of your nonverbal tools raises your odds of forging a connection with your audience. That is a wager any speaker will gladly accept.

CHAPTER SEVEN

TALES FROM THE
FRONT LINES

THE THREE KEYS TO CHAPTER SEVEN

You can expect to learn the truth about sharpening your public speaking skills by observing other presenters:

- How to avoid common presenter pitfalls;
- Why you must be true to your own style and keep your cool when speaking;
- What steps to take when confronted with problems like balky projectors, substandard facilities, and undesirable time slots.

LEARNING BY DOING PROVIDES A POWERFUL EDUCATION. But it is also possible to learn from the mistakes of others.

My idea of a busman's holiday is to attend a lot of presentations. I normally just take a seat and observe. Rarely does the speaker know what I do for a living.

This pastime aids my education on the subject, gives me lots of ideas for books and columns, and, sad to say, can be a rich source of comedic entertainment. It also expands the treasure chest of examples I can offer while leading presentation skills workshops.

People often ask me if I always scrutinize with a critical eye. The answer is yes. It's like the next door neighbor who happens to be an auto mechanic. He cannot help but pop your hood when he hears your engine sputtering in the driveway. Truthfully, I wish I was able to move away from the reviewer's role at times. I may be attending a talk solely because I want to hear the speaker's point of view. Still, it is nearly impossible not to allow my critical eye to emerge.

What to Watch For

I monitor the speaker, checking to see how she forges her connection with the audience. Is she using her Video Tools effectively? Are her Audio Tools particularly strong? Is she demonstrating a healthy dose of emotion or does she appear stiff? Does she send congruent signals or does something not seem to match up?

I also keep an eye on the audience since it is the ultimate judge of a presenter's performance. Are members paying rapt attention or are they distracted, reading the newspaper and engaging in chit chat? Do they have lots of cogent questions at the end, or are they ready to run for their next meeting?

This is not to say you need to issue a detailed critique of every presentation you attend. But I do encourage you to take a look at these lessons and use them to your benefit.

Some of the miscues included below are howlers; others are fairly minor. But all offer a learning moment or two. The vital part is the *Key Takeaways* from each occurrence that can aid you as you work to sharpen your communications edge. Now let us shine the spotlight center stage for our parade of presenters.

Surprise, Surprise!

I once moderated a panel discussion where the organizer failed to give the panelists any biographical information about the other panelists in advance. This included yours truly, the moderator.

During my opening comments, I dropped in some references to my qualifications to give the audience some idea about why it made sense for me to take on the moderator's role. But the panelists had not been tipped off in advance that I was a presentation skills coach.

It wasn't until afterward that one of them—with a wealth of speaking experience, no less—confessed to me that she got a case of the jitters when she heard about my expertise during the introductions. She performed admirably. But those doubts, as she acknowledged, remained in the back of her mind throughout her talk.

Key Takeaways: When serving as part of a panel discussion, devote some time to learning about those sharing the stage with you. This applies both to fellow panelists and to the moderator. If your host organization fails to supply what you need despite your repeated requests, do some digging yourself by visiting relevant web sites, conducting an online search, or making a few phone calls.

Can You Direct Me to the Women's Room?

This is a hall of fame blooper involving a certain faux pas with a wireless microphone. Trust me, you never want to fall victim to this classic blunder.

I was in attendance at a seminar led by an individual who made a really big deal about how much experience she had as a speaker. I had never heard of her before and her braggadocio sounded a bit puffed up, but I gave her the benefit of the doubt—until she got caught with her pants down—literally!

For those of you who are fans of the crime spoof movie *Naked Gun* with Leslie Nielsen portraying Detective Frank Drebin, you may recall the scene where he appeared at a news conference. The same fate befell our "expert" presenter.

The presenter I witnessed had the advantage of wearing a wireless microphone that clipped to her blouse and allowed her to roam the room when interacting with the audience. But in her case, it turned out not to be a plus.

She asked us to break into small groups to participate in an exercise, after which she proceeded to leave the room.

As you may be aware, the battery packs on those wireless microphones have an on/off switch that controls whether the mike is live or not. She committed the cardinal speaker sin of leaving the switch in the on position. Those of us in the room listening through the speaker system were treated to the sound of the door opening followed by a number of conversations she held in the hallway. Amused glances filled the room. Our "experienced" speaker had already lost most of her credibility.

Once she had wrapped up her personal chats, we heard the sound of her footsteps muffled on the carpeting in the hallway. Next, the sound of another door swinging open, and then her footfall echoing on a tiled floor. There were some smiles, some guffaws, and some horrified looks. By now, we all knew she had hit the restroom.

What really brought down the house was the squeak of a stall door being pushed open, followed by the distinctive click of the lock and a rustle of clothing.

Then silence. Our presenter had finally caught a break. One of the female audience members had taken pity on her and made a beeline for the women's room to warn her to turn her microphone off.

Sure, some of us were disappointed that we didn't get the full monty. But at that point, it really made no difference. There was no way she could have regained her credibility. The status she had tried to claim was shattered. Oddly, when she returned to the room, she compounded the damage by refusing to acknowledge her mistake. That elephant remained in the room for the duration of her presentation.

By the way, you may have picked up on a number of additional errors this speaker made. When she left the room, she sent several signals to her audience. First, if you have questions as you conduct the exercise, tough luck; I'm out of here. Second, who wants to listen to (and perhaps learn from) your deliberations? Third, I could gain a lot of insights into audience members that I could weave into my presentation later, but I don't really care about customizing things for you.

Key Takeaways: Familiarize yourself with any electronic equipment you plan to use. And unless it is an emergency, limit your restroom visits to the official breaks you give your listeners. Better still, take off the wireless mike during break periods.

No Cursing in Public

Rule number one: Never curse at people who honor you by coming to hear you speak. Communicating successfully in public means never having to say you're sorry. And if there is one situation that is guaranteed to warrant an apology, it is cursing and making obscene gestures at a member of your audience.

That was the situation in San Diego one September when Rep. Randy "Duke" Cunningham (R-Calif.) tore into one of his constituents at a forum for, of all things, prostate cancer survivors. As reported in the *San Diego Union-Tribune*, a seventy-four-year-old man, a retired Navy veteran like Cunningham, interrupted the Congressman to call for further defense spending cuts. "That's when he gave me the finger and said (expletive) you," the retiree said.

Impartial observers at the event seemed to concur that Cunningham was the first to flip the bird, though he claims his questioner gave him the one-finger salute first. No matter. If you have been invited to share your special expertise with a group of people, respect is an absolute must. They have graciously invited you to speak about an issue of import to you. Never abuse that privilege.

That is not the only public speaking offense Cunningham committed. He also uttered a tasteless anti-homosexual reference targeted toward openly gay Rep. Barney Frank (D-Mass.) in the same set of remarks.

More's the pity that Cunningham lost his cool since he was scheduled to shed light on such a worthy cause—research and treatment of prostate cancer. By disrespecting his audience, the politician's message turned into a negative despite his noble intentions.

Cunningham's outburst thoroughly drowned out his intended message. News accounts that followed his appearance at the prostate cancer forum centered on his misbehavior, not on education efforts intended to reach men at risk from the disease.

He had the potential to deliver his message in a powerful and personal fashion since he had previously undergone surgery for prostate cancer. He can present firsthand testimony about the wisdom of screening for the disease. Although the affliction is nearly 100 percent curable with early detection, it kills almost 40,000 men each year. Unfortunately, the Congressman's outburst drowned out a most valuable message.

Key Takeaways: Maintain your professionalism at all times. If you should blow your stack and act inappropriately, apologize quickly. To his credit, Cunningham did express his regrets. "I am sorry. I was out of line," the Associated Press quoted him as saying. Of course, you should never put yourself in the awkward position of having to apologize in the first place.

Be True to Yourself

Former Vice President and 2000 presidential candidate Al Gore came in for a lot of criticism when he kept trying to change his style. He tried to segue from a policy wonk in the Senate to a comedian appearing with David Letterman to an alpha male wearing earth tones and no tie. It was also interesting to note Gore's attempts to change his speaking style. He struggled to go from his natural earnestness to a cadence more suited to the fire of fellow Democrat Jesse Jackson. All of it appeared fake in the public's eyes.

Gore violated one of the cardinal rules of great presentations: If you really want to become better on the stump, you should imitate the style of only one person—yourself.

Allow me to reiterate one key fact: This book is not intended to change your style. Rather, I want you to maximize the strengths you already bring to the party. Try to turn yourself into a carbon copy of someone else and you will succeed only in appearing phony and insincere.

Let me be clear on this point. You do want to analyze others to continue to sharpen your communications edge. Perhaps you notice one presenter use the volume of her voice to great effect. Another has a nice way of weaving stories into his talk. Do learn from their talents. But do not try to ape them 100 percent.

Key Takeaways: Analyze proficient speakers. Borrow what they do well if it fits your approach. But don't try to clone yourself into that person. Let your personal style shine.

I'm Late for a Very Important Date

I was once seated at the head table of an association's meeting, awaiting a presentation about sports marketing. Dinner began and the speaker had not arrived. Fifteen minutes later, there was still no speaker in sight. But there was a table full of very nervous organizers.

Mr. Big finally arrived a precious few minutes before he was scheduled to talk, much to the relief of the meeting planners. He thought he got there just in time. I argue he was an hour late.

Don't ever make your hosts sweat. Let them know you care. Demonstrate some respect. Show up early. And be sure to track down your meeting planner, conference chair, or program liaison to let them know you are on the scene. This simple action sends their comfort level sky high. That is important to your future relationship.

It all comes back to preparation and planning. If it normally takes you thirty minutes to drive to your venue, give yourself a full hour. All it takes is one fender bender to turn your quick trip into an agonizing crawl. Better to arrive with plenty of time to spare. If you get there super early, you can use the extra moments to make a few phone calls, finish up some paperwork you stuffed into your briefcase, or drop by to see a client or acquaintance who has an office nearby.

If you are arriving from out of town, fly in the night before. Why risk getting delayed by weather and either missing your speech or showing up late and panicky? In fact, I sometimes arrive the morning or afternoon before. I gain a few hours to catch up with friends or business contacts I haven't seen in a while, make contact with people I want to meet in that city, or attend a networking event. That still leaves my evening free to rehearse one last time or to kick back and rest in my hotel room for the big day ahead.

Key Takeaways: An on-time arrival is an absolute must. This means getting there a minimum of sixty minutes before you are scheduled to speak and flying in the night before if your engagement is out of town. It helps remove stress from both you and your contacts at the organization that invited you.

The Gang That Couldn't Project Straight

I once witnessed a presentation that left me shaking my head, wondering how supposedly smart people could be so ill-prepared. It involved five panelists, all with separate laptops for their segments. Predictably enough, every time the moment came to switch speakers, the new computer took forever to attain warp speed. As it happens, they had been stuck with an older projector incapable of handling rapid transitions.

To add to their woes, only one of the speakers was savvy enough to eventually solve the problem (as is often the case, the hotel audio/visual crew was nowhere in sight). It was unfair of the organizers to put her in that situation. Her focus should have been on delivering her remarks.

Ironically, this was a panel whose members all claimed a high level of expertise in the information technology field. In reality, their difficulties made them look like the Keystone Kops of computers. Their integrity was shot and the audience quickly grew restless, with some heading for the doors well before the program ended.

On a positive note, there are fixes for this if you prepare properly. Systems exist that allow users to switch effortlessly among laptops. Ask the organization sponsoring your talk if they have access to such a capability.

Alternatively, you can load each presentation onto one central laptop. That makes it a simple matter of calling up one slide show after another. Just be sure you know *before you take to the stage* how to open your presentation. And remember to delete your slides from that computer when the show is over. Your valuable intellectual property has no business residing on someone else's PC.

Key Takeaways: For presenters, be ready to roll if your slides are inaccessible. If you are unable to solve the problem within thirty seconds, move on. Use that hard copy of your slides you printed in advance. Do not continue to fiddle with the laptop and keep your audience cooling its heels!

For sponsoring organizations, give your moderator clear and specific instructions to keep the flow going. Unrest in the audience reflects poorly on your group.

A Room with a View

During my days in the association realm, I always made it a point to "advance" the room where my president would appear to be sure all was as it should be.

One time, he was scheduled to appear on a panel discussion held at a beautiful beachfront hotel. I walked into the meeting room about 30 minutes before the panel was due to begin. The room was drop-dead gorgeous. It featured a tantalizing, panoramic view of the beach just beyond a wall of floor-to-ceiling windows.

The person who escorted me to the room stepped inside and commented on the beauty of the space. Indeed it was perfect for a party, wedding reception, or bar mitzvah. But it was terrible for a business meeting.

If we didn't do something quick, that audience would be admiring the view and paying attention to not one word my president spoke.

The hour was too late for a wholesale rearranging of the room. As a solution, we drew the thick curtains, shutting out the lovely scenery. We would likely have had a revolt on our hands had any of the spectators ever got wind of the picturesque sun, sand, and surf hiding just behind those curtains. While they were not able to soak up the rays, they did absorb my president's message with no distraction.

Key Takeaways: Pay attention to the backdrop at your locale. You do not want to be overshadowed by very beautiful or very ugly surroundings, or by a setting that conflicts with your message. If the location is not set up to your specifications, do what you can to change it. Remember to tell yourself that you are the owner of that room for as long as you will be speaking.

No Big Deal

If you speak often enough, something will go wrong at some time. One of my most vivid recollections along these lines occurred when I spoke in San Francisco. There were a number of presenters on the program. As we edged toward late morning, there were still two speakers to go before I hit the stage. All of a sudden, the slides disappeared from the screen. Yup, the projector bulb had burned out, resulting in a thoroughly flummoxed presenter. He was incapable of continuing without his precious slides on the screen. Same story for the next scheduled presenter.

This occurred in a hotel and, as typically happens in that type of facility, the audio/visual staff refused to leave a replacement bulb with the projector for fear of theft (those bulbs are not cheap). Of course, it took the better part of an hour to get a replacement.

The somewhat panicked organizers had not thought out their Plan B. I had. I suggested we switch the order of the presenters because no one else was ready to go on without their slides. I was prepared. So after what turned out to be only a brief delay, I hit the stage, minus my presentation software slides, but ready to perform. The organizers were profusely thankful, most pleased that I was able to solve their problem for them.

Key Takeaways: Be prepared with your Plan B. Decide ahead of time what you will do if, for instance, your projector bulb dies or your laptop freezes.

Set an Early Wake-Up Call

Speaking at a breakfast event can be tough. People are not fully awake. They may be grumpy before that first cup of coffee. And they may be distracted, thinking about what they need to cram in to the rest of their day.

Yet there can be a positive side to the early morning presentation. You can become the cavalry riding to the rescue of your host organization—if you prepare and perform properly.

This story involves a presentation I delivered beginning at 8:30 a.m. Despite the early start, another speaker had preceded me, hitting the stage at 8:00. I had my usual post-speech curiosity about whether I had made a sufficient connection with the audience, given it was still the breakfast hour. I prepared a presentation that called for a bit more interactivity than usual to combat the normally sleepy time slot.

When I concluded, an audience member stepped forward to offer congratulations on getting everyone involved. Boy, didn't that make my day! He noted that the earlier speaker had lulled listeners to sleep by reciting a litany of dry facts. He much preferred the livelier atmosphere, noting that it allowed him to benefit from content that proved useful in his business on a day-to-day basis.

Key Takeaways: In time slots when audiences may be naturally drowsy or inattentive, make an extra effort to engage them with interactive exercises or by using an extra dose of your Video Tools or Audio Tools.

The Post-Lunch Lull

After lunch engagements also carry risks. I once spoke before a medical meeting in which the morning speakers ran overtime. In order to accommodate the flight schedules of others on the program, the organizers decided to change the order of some presentations. I suddenly found myself slotted immediately following lunch instead of late morning.

The upside? I witnessed the presentation of the scientist who was originally slated after lunch. We avoided a lot of napping that day by moving his droning persona. I may not have had the most alert audience in the history of speechmaking, but at least I was able to turn up my nonverbal performance and include some audience participation to keep things interesting.

Key Takeaways: Similar to the early morning speech, raise the level of interactivity and pay extra attention to your nonverbal performance.

How Not to Win a Campaign

The political convention season always brings a plethora of speeches. A keynote speaker at a political party convention a few years back offered many a lesson in how *not* to deliver a rousing, inspiring address to the faithful. His sins occurred at a state convention. The state shall remain nameless in order to protect the guilty.

The worst part was this should have been an easy crowd for him—a gang of political animals who were salivating for red meat. Yet our speaker managed to alienate the party loyalists and put a dent in his own political future. Here is how he managed that feat:

- Offered an emotionless recitation of what should have been burning issues;
- Insulted his First District audience by telling them he thought he was talking to the Second District;
- Asked who the actors were in a semi-obscure 1950s era movie, then actually waited for a response from the audience (as you may have guessed, he was met with stone silence);
- Expressed the belief that one county has no business being in a particular part of the state, thereby making that section of his crowd feel like interlopers;
- Told stories to which his audience could not relate.

When you want to score with an audience, especially if you are trying to rack up political points, offensive techniques like these will guarantee you a Harold Stassen-like political future.

Key Takeaways: Your advance research into your audience should tell you what they want to hear and what could alienate them. Use stories and examples that will resonate with those in attendance and leave the little-known references at home.

The Plague of the Purple Pantsuit

Garish wardrobes and loud colors prove highly distracting, as these examples illustrate. I once advised a certain association president who fancied an absolutely horrid-looking purple pantsuit. When she came around a corner wearing that thing, it positively screamed at you. There was nothing else you could think of at that moment except "purple pantsuit!"

She liked it so much, she sometimes delivered speeches wearing it. Big mistake. I made it a point to observe audience members as she spoke, and many of them just could not get past that purple pantsuit. It clearly interfered with her message.

In a similar vein, accessories can also detract from your message. I worked with an elected official who insisted on wearing a very noticeable lapel pin. My team and I advised him constantly to stash it in his pocket, at least when he spoke or dealt with reporters. Yet that pin signified something important to him and he refused to remove it from his lapel. It gleamed when he spoke under bright lights, leading some watchers to wonder what it represented. In smaller chats, it proved to be a conversation starter. The problem was, it had nothing to do with the message he wanted to impart.

Here is another quick example of accessories getting in the way. During my early days as a college radio broadcaster, I knew one reporter who wore clunky bracelets on air. I am skeptical that her broadcasting career advanced very far since radio microphones, sensitive as they are, picked up every tinkle. No news director will stand for that.

Key Takeaways: Avoid those lapel pins, brooches, dangling earrings, bracelets that rattle, and other distracting wardrobe items. And above all, steer clear of that loud purple pantsuit when delivering a presentation.

Open Your Eyes

The organization's president displayed great emotion, replete with energy and excitement. That was his job, to whip up enthusiasm among the crowd celebrating at his organization's fiftieth anniversary dinner.

He followed a number of other speakers, all of whom were sharing a wireless lavaliere microphone.

Our president's passion for his organization and its mission came through loud and clear. You could hear it in his voice and see it in his eyes. Well, at least some of the audience could see it in his eyes.

A good number of us missed it because he kept his back to fully one-quarter of the crowd. Rather than position himself in the front of the room where everyone would have an unobstructed view, he clung to the security of his own table. To further detract from the power of his words, he held the clip-on microphone in his hand instead of clipping it on his shirt or sport coat. Similarly, he insisted on holding the battery pack for his wireless microphone in his hand rather than attaching it to his belt or sliding it into his pocket. In doing so, he removed any possibility of using hand gestures were he so inclined.

How could an experienced speaker allow this to happen? He no doubt failed to plan in advance how he would manage his props. It painted him as inexperienced and, more important, erected barriers between him and his listeners.

Key Takeaways: If you follow another speaker and need to share a microphone, give some thought as to how you will accept it from him and how you can effortlessly attach it to your clothing. In addition, pay attention to your position. Block out your movements just as an actor would. Decide where you will stand to give your audience a clear view.

Hang Together or Hang Alone

Let me tell you a story about a training I once led. As I always do during the preparation phase, I asked the client to send me the key messages. Over the years, I have worked with organizations that have never committed to paper any formal messages. I have also worked with a select few that have successfully constructed tight messages. Then there are the rest. That is the category into which this organization fell.

What I received was a twenty-five-page slide kit with a bunch of facts, but no central theme that allowed it to hang together. It was like a rock collection gathered by a four-year-old. Lots of volume, but no value.

Ben Franklin talked about hanging together or hanging separately. If your message doesn't hang together, that loose collection of facts will see to it that your spokespeople hang separately.

In the case of the organization described above, we had to essentially turn the training for one of their key executives—who sorely needed all the practice he could get—into a message development session. Don't get me wrong. Message development workshops are valuable and many groups need exactly that. Unfortunately in this case, the executive was forced to sacrifice valuable practice time.

Does it really matter that your messages are as limp as that bouquet of flowers you got last week? That depends on your goals. If you are indifferent to lost income, fewer members, losing in the political arena, and being embarrassed in public, you have no problem.

But consider the opportunities. When your rivals use weak messages, or no messages, it presents you with the opportunity to top the competition.

Key Takeaways: Constructing a tight message and delivering it in an attractive package has major implications—increased revenues, more members for your community group, achievement of public policy goals, and greater personal prestige among them.

Pop Go the Props

Let me add one caveat about the use of props. I once coached an individual who was adamant about using a prop in every speech she delivered. Whether it made sense or not, we had to find a prop of some sort. We were forced to come up with more lame ideas and waste more time that could have been dedicated to better endeavors.

The worst part was we knew the audience either would miss the connection she was aiming for or wouldn't be able to see the prop because it was so tiny. But our executive was adamant. Her props not only failed to enliven her presentation, they actually detracted from it. The audience had to spend so much time trying to figure out the relevance of the prop, they lost track of her message.

If you have to think really hard to wedge a prop into your speech, your audience won't get it. You will succeed only in losing their attention and stumbling over your message.

Key Takeaways: Props are great when they make sense, but don't force the issue. If the shoe fits (and, yes, a shoe does qualify as a prop), wear it. If not, leave it in the closet.

The Agenda Hog

I witnessed the classic Agenda Hog (see Chapter Eight for a definition of the Agenda Hog) when attending a National Press Club forum about the search for weapons of mass destruction in Iraq following the U.S. invasion of 2003.

During the Q&A portion, a man rose and, in a booming voice, identified himself as a former CIA analyst. His question was not really a question, but a harangue about, as he called them, "weapons of mass distortion." He wanted only to air his gripe that intelligence analysts have been ignored. It was clear that this guy had personal issues he needed to resolve. Unfortunately for everyone else in attendance, he tried to resolve them by sapping valuable time from a forum designed to educate the press and public about a critical issue.

The moderator unfortunately failed to rein in the questioner until he had blathered on for quite some time.

Key Takeaways: In a case like this, the moderator should deal with the Agenda Hog. If he fails to do his job, it may be up to you to deflect such rants or to erect roadblocks (see Chapter Eight for details on those strategies).

The Audience Rides to the Rescue

I experienced another Agenda Hog moment when speaking to a group of health care professionals in Orlando, Florida. In this case, the Agenda Hog didn't even wait for the Q&A to begin. After listening for less than ten minutes, she interrupted me, launching into a lengthy treatise on her belief that I was not delivering what audience members needed. It is ironic that this individual was in charge of public relations for the organization that hired me. But she had studiously avoided any involvement in the planning process and was now trying to play the big shot in an attempt to save face.

She jumped right in, suggesting that the audience needed to hear more in-depth information about how to deal with the media. All the preparation I had logged told me just the opposite. I had spent a lot of time reading the background info supplied by the organization and holding numerous conversations with those who did get involved with the planning. As always, I also conducted some independent background research to sniff out any issues they were ignoring or trying to hide.

I also held discussions with several audience members before the presentation. That intelligence reaffirmed that there were more than a few novices in the crowd who needed a baseline of understanding before we could proceed to more complex issues.

What happened? First of all, I kept my cool. Then an interesting dynamic occurred. Before I said anything, several audience members chimed in to say they believed the presentation was on target. They made it clear to the communications manager that her comments were off-base and less than tactful.

I would like to think this dynamic unfolded because I charmed them with my brilliance and wittiness during the first few moments of my remarks.

The fact is, although I knew not one person in that room before that day, I made it a point to talk with a good number of folks beforehand to break the ice and to ask them what they wanted and needed from the day's session.

They already knew I was going to cover areas of interest to them since we had discussed it. Needless to say, the Agenda Hog failed to avail herself of the same research strategy.

In addition, I attended the session scheduled just before mine. This allowed me to observe the dynamics and to be seen. Familiarity, after all, breeds comfort.

Key Takeaways: Allow your audience time to get comfortable with you. If you are confronted by a hostile questioner, familiarity can be your best line of defense—provided you have completed your homework and done a solid job of audience research.

Drop Back to Punt Formation

One of the all-star classics in terms of disrespecting an audience comes to us courtesy of football great Reggie White, then a star defensive end of the Green Bay Packers.

White provided a case study for the ages on how to offend every member of a diverse audience. When he was honored by being invited to address the Wisconsin state Assembly in March 1998, he was expected to offer remarks lasting five to ten minutes. His agreed-upon topic centered on his efforts to help his community and on a recent trip to Israel. However, he ended up sacked by his own words.

In fifty agonizing minutes, White managed to offend homosexuals, several ethnic groups, and the legislators—both Democrats and Republicans—who invited him to speak.

The gridiron great demonstrated the clumsy moves of a journeyman free agent in the message department. His rambling comments touched upon such matters as television talk shows, the definition of the word "synergy," the Roman Empire, and the TV program *Touched by an Angel*.

To top off matters, White later expressed amazement at the negative public outcry. The all-pro says he wanted to deliver a message about unity. Ironically, he raised nearly every wedge issue imaginable, contradicting his intended message time after time.

Key Takeaways: Stick to your knitting. If you are invited to give a light talk, keep it free of controversial issues. On the flip side of the coin, if you are expected to talk substance, give your audience plenty of data, examples, and opinion.

That's Me

You may one day find yourself in the audience critiquing a stunningly bad performance when you hear someone sidle up to the speaker and whisper, "We should talk. You can use a bit of polish." Please make it a point to say hello. I would love to meet you.

TURNING QUESTIONS INTO ANSWERS

THE THREE KEYS TO CHAPTER EIGHT

You can expect to learn the truth about emerging victorious when you field questions from the audience:

- Ideas to keep you on track with your message and maintain control;
- Strategies for handling hostile, off-point, and outright dumb questions;
- Secrets for dealing with Agenda Hogs and hecklers.

AUDIENCES REMEMBER STUPID THINGS IF a speaker gives them good reason. They will long carry a vivid memory of the presenter who stammered, shook, sweated, and recoiled when asked even the simplest question.

The question and answer session is the make or break part of any presentation. That is one of the basic truths about public speaking.

You may have wowed the crowd with your arguments and speaking abilities during your prepared remarks. But if you fall flat at the end with your Q&A, you will leave them with a bad taste in their mouths. It is akin to topping off a perfect meal with bitter coffee and a spoiled dessert.

I want you to think of Q&A as an integral portion of your presentation, not a separate entity. Like the point after touchdown at a football game, if you fail to execute flawlessly, you could well find yourself on the short end of the score when the final gun sounds.

One of the benefits of fielding questions is your ability to emphasize your message a few extra times. That is, after all, the reason you accepted this engagement in the first place. Responding to any and all questions with your message is vital, and is, I contend, a sure-fire way to show your audience your respect for them.

In this chapter, I will talk about the need to prepare for Q&A every bit as much as you prepare for your planned presentation. You do this by anticipating the toughest questions audience members could ask and planning which parts of your message best address those issues. Also, I will dig into how to perform your due diligence and unearth those potential hardball questions.

This chapter demonstrates how you can become more effective at managing questions from any audience. It also explains the advantages of encouraging Q&A and shows you how to avoid common hazards to which many speakers fall victim.

The Advantages of Q&A

There are numerous advantages to opening up the floor to questions. It tends to keep the audience engaged, making them an active part of the show and giving them a chance to contribute. Be generous in sharing your spotlight, provided your questioner doesn't morph into an Agenda Hog, of course.

Q&A also allows you to extend your presentation. Audience members tend to get restless and bored just listening to one individual prattle on. All it takes is one listener glancing at her watch or shifting uncomfortably in her seat. Soon, you will be looking at an entire roomful of clock watchers and seat squirmers.

The solution? Rather than speak for forty-five minutes, aim for thirty minutes, then go interactive for the final fifteen. This stimulates the brain by giving people license to gaze in a different direction, hear another voice, and look at another face.

Q&A also comes into play in your ongoing efforts to assess feedback. It gives you an instant reading of the audience's pulse.

It is important to consider another dimension of Q&A from the audience's perspective. When you are part of the crowd, posing a question represents your best opportunity to distinguish yourself. Fellow audience members tend to view questioners as leaders when they step forward to become part of the discussion.

Your question often spurs fellow audience members to approach you afterward to continue the discussion about the issue at hand. Thus, even if you are sitting in the audience, you can transform Q&A into an outstanding means to position yourself as an expert.

When to Field Questions

Speakers sometimes wonder when they should solicit questions: During the speech or after the presentation is complete?

No matter which method you opt for, make sure you tell the audience in advance if it is okay for them to ask questions as you speak, or if you prefer they hold them until the end. Your audience will appreciate the fact that you clued them in to the ground rules.

What is my personal preference? I normally choose to take questions. An interactive format fits my style. In addition, so much of my efforts are educational in nature, I want to be sure I address what the audience wants and needs to learn.

Deciding when you will field questions is also a matter of individual choice. If you prefer that your listeners hold their issues until the end, let them know in your introductory remarks. If you don't mind being interrupted as you speak, tell them.

If you are delivering a formal speech to a large auditorium, it is usually advisable to hold questions until the end. If, on the other hand, yours is an educational talk about a technical subject, you may want to encourage questions as you go to ensure that everyone is learning at an appropriate pace.

What happens if you find yourself inundated with questions during the course of your talk, so much so that you fear running over your allotted time? It is okay to ask listeners to hold their questions for a few moments. Simply explain that there is a lot of material you know they want you to cover (your advance research told you so), and you will be glad to entertain more questions as time allows at the end.

If, despite hours, weeks, and months of diligent practice you still fall apart when a question comes your way, it may be best to avoid Q&A until you find that extra reserve of steel. Every speaker must decide what is best for her individual style.

Getting Yourself into Trouble

It is one of the best ways I know for a presenter to get herself into a jam. And I see it happen time and again.

Far too many speakers exhale a sigh of relief when they complete their prepared remarks and turn to the audience for questions. You have no doubt experienced it sitting in the audience. An almost audible whoosh courses through the room as the puff of wind from the stage passes. But beware. This is the precise moment when, as a speaker, you need to be on your toes.

Recall your newfound mantra, Practice! Practice! Practice! This dictates the need to rehearse your presentation if you want to succeed and improve. It is also imperative that you rehearse responding to questions, for Q&A could be the highest hurdle you will face all day.

Why? Because you have lost a great deal of control. You no longer have an unencumbered opportunity to broadcast your message. Audience members can now raise all sorts of static and interference.

Your message may center on a new product your company is bringing to market. But that crank in the second row only wants to harp on why your last product still faces lagging sales.

You may be touting a new environmental initiative championed by your non-profit organization. But the plant in the audience insists on turning the discussion toward why you oppose the president's policies at every turn.

You may be educating the world about a new pharmaceutical breakthrough. But the house skeptic dwells on side effects and wants to know how much the drug maker is paying you to make these claims.

Anticipate the Tough Ones

Your goal as a presenter is to advance the ball down the field and score. You do that by playing offense, not defense.

Take charge of the Q&A session. Your first step in doing this is to anticipate the tough questions that could arise. Write them down. This is important, so I will repeat it: Write down a list of tough, hostile, off-point questions that audience members might pose.

You may well be too close to your subject matter to see the chinks in your armor. So enlist your co-workers, advisors, peers, friends, and family to draw up lists of questions.

During your Preparation phase, ask your colleagues to pepper you with the most challenging questions on those lists. Decide how you will respond if someone in the audience raises them. In every single case, your reply should include a strong dose of your message.

A point of clarification here: I am not suggesting that you develop trite, word-for-word replies. That approach makes you sound like a pre-programmed machine. Rather, get a sense of which leg of your message chair best addresses the question, and bring forth those mental file cards when the time comes. This keeps your message in the forefront of your listeners' minds. At the same time, it prevents you from sounding like a robot.

Change the Equation

Some speakers become overwhelmed by Q&A, worried that they need to memorize answers for dozens of possible questions. Not so. The trick is to think in a different way.

Here is the mental model I want you to use from now on:

> *A question is nothing more than an issue that*
> *ends with a different punctuation mark.*

Yes, the question mark replaces the period, and the questioner's vocal inflection goes up at the end of his sentence. But boiled down to its essence, a question remains nothing more than an issue about which an individual wants more information.

As you work to define potentially difficult questions, sort them into what I call "baskets" of issues. This helps organize your approach and makes your task much more straightforward. Instead of having to remember how to answer 100 specific questions, you have now neatly sorted the material into a mere handful of key issues. You will probably find that you end up with only four or five baskets.

Let us take this issue—how to deal effectively with audience questions—as a case study. If I were presenting on this topic before an audience, I might get dozens of questions. But in my mind, I know there are basically four things I want to talk about. I should be able to sort any of those inquiries into one of those four areas.

For instance, I want to stress that Q&A time is an important part of a presentation. Or I might choose to highlight the fact that, if you choose to engage in Q&A, you must prepare for it just as you prepare for your planned presentation. Also, I could shed light on the idea that this book and my presentation skills training workshops can teach you how to become more effective at managing questions from any audience.

All I need to do is listen closely to the question, sort it into one of those baskets, and respond accordingly. This not only ensures I will be responsive to the question, but helps me live up to my end of the bargain by giving the audience the information they expected to gain when they decided to attend.

Want some more examples of how this works? Here you go:

- The speaker above who discussed a new product launch might end up with baskets including past product failures, high cost, low manufacturing capacity, and the threat of a potential strike by workers.
- The environmentalist might be faced with such baskets as opposing political views, cost of the initiative, the odds for success while being vastly outspent by industrial interests, and recent financial shenanigans on the part of one of its leaders.
- Our spokesperson for the wonder drug could sort challenging issues into baskets like side effects, a lawsuit by a company that was formerly a development partner, issues raised by federal regulators, and whether health insurance plans will pay for the new therapy.

Your specific baskets will vary depending on your issue.

As you practice for Q&A, decide which part of your message best responds to each basket. The result? No need to beat yourself up trying to memorize replies to dozens and dozens of pointed questions if you face an adversarial grilling from your audience. With this system, you need to remember only four or five key directions. Most people can handle that with a minimum of sweat.

Let me stop here to make an important point about Q&A. In the vast majority of cases, you do not need to worry about audience members attacking you verbally, although I will give you some strategies later in this chapter for dealing with disruptive individuals.

Most people genuinely want to hear your point of view or learn what you have to teach. The intelligence-gathering effort you plotted during your advance preparation will tell you if this is a crowd that plans to bring over-ripe tomatoes to hurl at you.

Whether your audience turns up the heat or not, preparation for Q&A pays dividends.

Listen Closely

Make it clear to your audience from the start that you will entertain questions. And make it clear that you welcome questions, not statements. This won't stop everyone from trying to steal your spotlight, but it might dissuade some who came prepared to launch a diatribe rather than ask a question.

Queries may come your way that have little or nothing to do with your topic. Assign these off-point questions to the "Bullpen." This is a running list of miscellaneous issues you track on your flip chart or white board. Or you can appoint a scribe to keep a list. You may decide to deal with these matters later, time permitting. Or you may choose to discuss them one-on-one after your talk.

Explain the Bullpen up front. Make it clear that issues sometimes arise that may not fit into your presentation, but you do not want to lose track of potentially valuable ideas. The Bullpen demonstrates your respect for the questioner while preventing you from becoming bogged down in extraneous issues.

As you field questions from your audience, stop your old habit of focusing on the specific question. Instead, begin your new regimen of listening closely to determine what issue your questioner is raising. Then it is a fairly simple matter to sort it into the appropriate basket and respond with the portion of your message that best addresses the issue. This makes your life much easier since you have already weighed the issue in advance.

What is the most important tack you can take to raise your level of persuasiveness? Mehrabian's research shows that an immediate response is the single biggest determining factor when you are aiming to persuade your listeners—no ums, ers, or pregnant pauses.

Get right to the heart of your message. Then back up your argument with proof points, examples, facts, and figures. Tie your answer into a nice, neat package by ending with a brief summary of your message.

Some advisors suggest you pause for a second or two before answering a question, on the theory you will look pensive and deliberative. Some even tell you to twirl your eyeglasses or stare up at the ceiling for a moment. Wrong!

This may work if you are in a collegial, academic environment. But if your goal is to convince others of the truth and accuracy of your position, don't delay. Be prepared to launch right into your reply. This is the best persuasive tool you possess.

Every Question Has a Nonverbal Answer

Consider how things look when you are part of the audience. In fact, the next time you are in the peanut gallery, watch the speaker closely as a listener asks a question.

Chapter Five detailed the benefits of Winning the Communications

Trifecta during your presentation. the Trifecta also comes into play when answering audience questions.

When I am seated in the audience, my eyes are more frequently on the presenter than on the inquisitor. Who cares how the questioner acts? That is not who I came to see. My interest is focused on the person at the front of the room.

I stay attuned to his reactions while the question is on its way. What do his nonverbal signals tell me?

- Does he smile, indicating openness and understanding?
- Does he recoil as if shot by a verbal arrow?
- Does he break off eye contact in a futile effort to manufacture an answer?
- If he is close enough, can I see if his pupils dilate, indicating receptivity to the question or questioner?

Monitoring the speaker's nonverbal reactions during Q&A can tell me just as much as his stated response. Most speakers have no idea they are giving up such transparent answers unintentionally.

There is one other critical nonverbal signal that merits discussion: The nod. A lot of speakers nod their heads as a question is coming. I suggest you avoid this trap. Your nod leads your audience to assume you agree with the questioner's thesis.

If that individual calls you an ax murdering, treasonous, lying wretch (or simply disagrees with your position), you had best avoid nodding in assent.

Add Value to Each Inquiry

Some speakers would rather answer questions literally, just as they might if they were involved in a casual conversation. Well, have I got news for you. A presentation is far from a chat over the backyard fence.

This desire to shoot unprepared from the lip is particularly strong among those in fields that rely on reams of data—doctors, scientists, engineers, and information technology executives, for example. This seems to hold sway for one of three reasons:

- *The Data Driver.* They personally get a kick out of digging into all the minutiae they can. Instead of getting to the heart of the matter, they usually go straight for the capillaries. In most cases, this serves only to give their listeners' yawn muscles a good workout.
- *The Crusader.* These fact-driven individuals are positively convinced they can overwhelm their audience with the "truth" (as they see it, at least).

- *The Ego Tripper.* They emit an aroma that says, "I am more important than the audience." This type tries to convince everyone that the person in the front of the room has more factoids crammed into his brain than anyone else alive.

Dealing with Q&A involves a different mental process for some people. Responding to audience queries is not a conversation in the everyday sense.

Here is the case I make: Your audience came to see you for a reason. You entered into a verbal contract with the people who walked through the door to see you. You pledged to discuss a certain topic they found of interest, agreeing to educate, inspire, or persuade. Give them what they came for.

Do not confuse your overall audience with a single audience member. Refuse to let one individual with a conflicting agenda bait you into getting off topic. One loner should not be allowed to dictate to everyone else.

I contend that you are treating your audience with ultimate respect when you stick to your topic. Message discipline assures that you will uphold your contract with the audience and give them the benefit of the valuable information they came to gain.

Build the Bridge

I want to open the door to a crucial concept known as *bridging*. Bridging empowers you to respond to a question by building a verbal bridge to one of the four legs of your message. This technique works particularly well with the off-point or hostile question.

Bridging takes some practice, for it is a new style of communication for many people. Think about it. In our everyday conversations, we ask questions and respond with literal answers.

During a presentation, however, you need to add one more element: Your message. The conversational flow proceeds from question to acknowledgement to your message. Your goal with each and every question is to reply with at least one of the main points of your message.

Let me add one very important caveat: It is important to disabuse you of any attempt at "spin." By this I mean neglecting the question altogether. Here is an example of spin: Someone asks whether it is day or night; the presenter launches into a dissertation on how much he likes the color red.

In my book, spin is a sin. Show respect for those who came to hear you speak by acknowledging their questions, no matter how off the wall they may be. You score no points by being a smart aleck and attacking someone in the audience.

How do you build your bridge? The first step is to acknowledge the question. Step number two involves use of a transitional phrase like the following:

- "Let's look at the big picture…"
- "I can best answer that by telling you…"
- "Let me give you an example…"
- "It is also important to remember…"
- "Before we wrap up today, I want to be sure to mention…"
- "And that's not all."
- "There is even more exciting news."
- "I have some examples to prove it…"

That transitional phrase is your bridge. After building your bridge, it is imperative that you delve right away into the portion of your message that best addresses the inquiry.

Let me give you an example based on the topic of the preceding section. If, during a speech, an audience member told me he prefers to answer questions literally, I might respond as follows: "I understand that a first instinct might be to answer questions literally. Let's look at the big picture. My goal is to respect my audience at every turn. If this fine organization wanted me to have a casual chat with a few folks, they would have invited me to the cocktail hour, not to stand in the spotlight in front of a roomful of people. We all came here today to learn more about delivering winning presentations. Responding with the highlight of my message keeps me on track to fulfilling my end of that bargain, giving you the knowledge you came to gain."

I contend that bridging to your message at every turn demonstrates respect for your audience. You entered into an agreement with the people who walked in the door to learn from your point of view. You pledged to discuss a certain topic they found of interest. They showed up expecting to gain your expertise and hear your opinion. Give them what they came for. Sticking to your message assures you will uphold your part of the bargain and give your audience members what they came for.

Wave the Flag

Now let's talk about another compelling technique useful in handling Q&A called *flagging*. Your intent here is to plant a verbal flag that tells your audience, "This is what I'm here to talk about." Preface your message with a signal that you are about to say something of high importance, a quote of which they will want to make special note.

To review, flagging is essentially what the name implies. You plant a flag—in this case a verbal flag—to highlight the main ideas for your audience.

When you really want to draw their attention to an idea, principle, or fact, put it in neon lights for them by waving a flag. Sample flagging phrases include:

- "The important issue here is…"
- "Here is the key to this issue…"
- "If there is one thing you need to remember…"
- "The main point is…"
- "Here's the bottom line…"

Phrases like these give listeners a cue that something important is about to cross your lips. It serves to perk up their attention to the points you want to emphasize.

You can also employ the flagging technique in your writing. The bottom line is you will notice verbal flags throughout this book helping to reinforce key points.

Just be sure not to overuse this technique. Using an occasional flag is effective. Forcing one at the beginning of each thought makes you sound trite.

Control the Flow

It is important that you control the flow during Q&A. Keep reminding yourself that you are in charge. You decide who asks questions, and when. It is your right to recognize one questioner—diplomatically, of course—over another so that no one person or section of the room begins to dominate.

Identify your preferred questioner as specifically as possible. For instance:

- "The man in the red and blue striped tie."
- "The woman in the back row."
- "Right up front, in the blue dress."

When a question comes, look at the questioner as she speaks. Then move your eye contact around the room while answering. This is important for two reasons. Number one, it serves to draw the entire audience into the conversation, allowing you to maintain everyone's interest. Number two, it helps avoid those annoying dialogues that sometimes occur when a disgruntled audience member tries to hog the microphone during Q&A. Those exchanges are insulting to the bulk of your audience.

I am sure you have been present when a totally off-point harangue thinly disguised as a question is lobbed at the presenter. You may even be, like me, one of the people who rolls his eyes in exasperation. Think back to that time. Wouldn't you have paid anything if the speaker had been skilled enough to bring the discussion back on track?

Let me tell you the story of one workshop participant of mine who drove this point home in no uncertain terms. I had counseled his group to respond to the entire audience—not strictly the questioner—by using eye contact. A panel of his colleagues was responding to questions with this star pupil and others assuming roles of audience members. He was recognized for a question. After getting his response, however, he kept firing question after question at the panelist.

Why did he feel he had license to take over the floor? The panelist maintained eye contact with him and him alone, reducing his presentation to a dialogue. Sure enough, at the conclusion of the exercise, our interrogator said he continued launching his salvos in order to prove the point I had made about not locking in eye contact with one listener. I love seeing that light bulb flick on over a learner's head!

The Deep Echo of Silence

Here is another Q&A situation you need to anticipate: What if you open the floor to questions and no hands go up initially? It is your job to avoid that awkward silence and keep your presentation moving in a positive direction. Occasions like these really make audience members squirm in their seats, feeling embarrassed for the speaker. One of your roles is to make your audience feel comfortable. So don't force them to sit there writhing with anxiety. Have a strategy.

For starters, be ready with a question of your own. There are many transitional phrases you can use to start the Q&A process. Among them:
- "A question I am often asked is…"
- "You may be surprised how often I get this question…"
- "Here's an issue that comes up frequently…"
- "I delivered a presentation last week and here is a question I got from the audience…"

Then respond with a brief story. In addition to maintaining your forward momentum, lobbing a softball to yourself is also an easy way to keep you and your audience focused on your message.

I vividly recall speaking to a roomful of Washington, D.C., public relations professionals. I knew from talking to them in advance and from their nods and note-taking during the speech that I was giving them what they needed and wanted. Still, when I opened the floor to questions, not one hand rose. I began matters by tossing myself an easy one. Sure enough, by the time I had completed the answer, four hands shot up into the air, eager to ask questions.

In fact, I wound up with more questions than I could squeeze in to the remaining time. No problem there; I stayed afterward for some one-on-one and small group conversations. I consider it an honor to be flooded with listeners seeking some personalized advice.

Priming the Pump

Another approach when no questions arise is to acknowledge the common problem of nobody wanting to break the ice. Bringing it out in the open and even making light of it with an offer to start with the last question instead of the first can comfort audience members.

What explains this phenomenon? In most cases, I believe it amounts to nothing more than fear of embarrassment. People worry about getting tongue-tied or asking what others might consider a stupid question.

Think how many times you have been in this situation yourself. You may have felt ill at ease being the first to raise your hand, despite the fact you had a burning issue on which you desperately wanted to gain some advice.

The lesson? When Q&A seems to falter, don't stare your audience down waiting for a question that may never come. Sometimes it takes a bit of cleverness to generate questions.

Break your audience into small groups (even pairs will do the trick) and assign each group the task of fashioning a minimum of two questions. There is safety in numbers and people are often more inclined to participate under cover of a group.

How you ask for questions makes a difference. A general statement calling for questions can be interpreted as a signal that you are finished. I might prime the pump with phrases like:

- "What element of the Three Keys to Great Presentations do you want to discuss in more detail?"
- "What other means for assessing feedback can you think of?"
- "How can I help you establish your personal lifelong learning plan?"

Another tried and true technique is to ask for written questions. This has a couple of advantages. Most obvious, it normally increases your supply of material since shy audience members will feel more free to become engaged. Additionally, it gives you greater control over the issues raised during Q&A. Would you prefer not to talk about that thorny issue? No problem; simply pass on that question in favor of another.

It is perfectly fine to solicit questions in advance. Let me suggest two methods here. Number one, ask those who plan to attend to bring up a certain issue. Is this called planting a question? Yes. Is there anything wrong with it? Not in my book. Number two, as you talk with your audience immediately before your presentation, listen for issues that are of import to them. Assuming their issues track your message, enlist them to be sure you cover it during your talk.

I encourage them with a phrase like, "If time runs short and I don't deal with that during my remarks, it would be a big help if you ask about it during Q&A." You have succeeded not only in buying a question that targets your message, you have created a valuable ally amidst your audience.

Watch those Traps

Responding to questions is not all sweetness and light. It's hard work. Although your preparation allows you to minimize your creativity while speaking (the front of the room is not the place to get inventive), it still involves a fair degree of thinking on your feet.

So let us get specific and talk about some common pitfalls and, importantly, key takeaways for handling these situations:

- *Let down your guard.* Your presentation is not over when you wrap up your prepared remarks. Q&A is very much a part of your talk, not a distinct address.
  - □ *Key takeaway*: Don't exhale a sigh of relief, thinking you have crossed the finish line. Stay sharp and stay on message.
- *Ignore the question.* No matter the nature of the question, you must acknowledge it before you bridge to your message. Reporters call this "spin," and an audience can smell it a mile away. You will lose their respect if you try to play them for suckers by ignoring issues they raise.
  - □ *Key takeaway*: Acknowledge the question, then build a bridge to your message.
- *Fake it.* Yes, you are the expert. But you cannot be expected to have every factoid on the tip of your tongue.
  - □ *Key takeaway*: It is okay to say, "I don't know." Just be sure to

include one important addendum that many speakers neglect: "I will be glad to get you an answer if you leave me your phone number or e-mail address when our session ends."

- *Give long, windy answers.* Avoid coming across like a blowhard. Q&A is no time to devolve into a filibuster. One exception: If you are facing an overwhelmingly and overtly hostile audience, a filibuster works to your advantage since it minimizes the number of questions you will receive.
  - □ *Key takeaway*: Practice Q&A until your replies are crisp, concise, and message-oriented.
- *Lose your vocal sharpness.* There is a tendency to relax after concluding your prepared text. Not only can this lead to a mental letdown, it can drain the energy from your Video and Audio Tools.
  - □ *Key takeaway*: Stay on guard. Monitor yourself or have an aide signal you if your nonverbal performance starts to slip.
- *Allow Q&A to drag on too long.* If there are still lots of questions when it is time to wrap up, that's a good thing, for it indicates you have struck a responsive chord with your audience. Nonetheless, some people need to leave at the appointed hour.
  - □ *Key takeaway*: Have a timetable and stick with it. You can stay a while and talk one-on-one or in small groups, but end your presentation on time.
- *Make eye contact only with the questioner or moderator.* Time and again, I see even the most experienced speakers commit this error. This is not a monologue, it is a presentation to a group. Audience members will soon feel left out if you zero in exclusively on one individual.
  - □ *Key takeaway*: Move your eye contact around the room as you reply to a question.

Never Surrender Control

Most of us have witnessed this occurrence: A presenter is stumped for an answer, and, in desperation, decides to turn the question over to his audience. What do I think of that technique?

I don't like it. You relinquish two important advantages. First, you lose control, which is always more of a challenge during Q&A, regardless. Why would you want to turn the spotlight over to an audience member who may well have views diametrically opposed to yours? Second, you concede your position as the resident authority—the expert your audience honored with its attendance. Relinquishing the question diminishes your standing in their eyes.

What do you do? Hey, everyone understands that you are not going to have all the answers on the tip of your tongue. There is no shame in admitting it. If it is a legitimate question for which you don't have a ready answer, tell your audience. But take two additional steps.

One, tell them you will find the answer and offer to get back in touch with the individual asking the question. This tells your audience that you really care since you are willing to go the extra mile for one of its members. Be sure to ask that person to give you her business card after your talk is finished. (Make sure this exchange occurs after; you do not want anything interrupting the flow of your presentation. Plus, it gives you a ready-made excuse to wade into the crowd following your remarks.)

Two, build that bridge back to your message. You are always looking to add value to your responses no matter the question, so be sure to give the audience something of substance.

Avoiding Hostilities

Most audiences you encounter are going to be friendly. This is not to say there won't be challenging questions, but they will most often be posed in a respectful, collegial tone.

But on occasion you can expect to run across audiences that are not 100 percent welcoming. Your advance preparation and research should give you the intelligence you need to discern whether the room is full of supporters or detractors.

Your best defense is to be prepared for questions that are off-point or outright hostile. We have already talked about the wisdom of anticipating tough questions that might be percolating in your listeners' minds.

Once you have defined those issues, and the day of your presentation arrives, you need to stay alert for the audience member with an agenda: The Agenda Hog or the Heckler.

If you are speaking before a defined crowd—the workers at one business or the board members of a single non-profit organization—these individuals are relatively easy to recognize ahead of time.

Some of the following advice builds upon Chapter Four's treatment of how to handle disruptions. When it comes to Q&A, we take this knowledge into the deep end of the pool.

The Agenda Hog

If, on the other hand, you appear at a public forum that anyone can attend, these Agenda Hogs are present nearly every time. How can you spot an Agenda Hog? They crave the spotlight.

They typically feel they have been wronged or slighted and will try to hijack any public setting in a vain and sad attempt to right that perceived injustice. Perhaps they have an opinion that runs counter to yours. They may even think they deserved that speaker's slot instead of you.

The Agenda Hog takes things personally. Everything revolves around him. The reason he got fired from his last job or couldn't get his research published drives him to seek recognition. His questions are rarely questions, but tirades, and they go on endlessly. He normally talks in a loud, urgent-sounding voice.

I use the term "him" advisedly in this instance. In the vast majority of cases, the Agenda Hog is a male.

The Agenda Hog is not easy to spot by appearance alone. He can be dressed in denim or a Brooks Brothers suit. His hair can be perfectly coiffed or tied back in a scraggly ponytail. He can be a degree-laden medical researcher whose arrogance leads him to believe he has answers to questions no one else has ever considered, or the guy who never graduated high school.

I do not mean to suggest that every Agenda Hog is mentally unhinged. But it does take a certain amount of imbalance or arrogance bordering on megalomania to think people will hang on your every word if you could just get them to listen.

Corralling the Agenda Hog

If your presentation is part of a panel, you should have less direct dealings with the Agenda Hog. It is the moderator's job to handle this type of distraction. I suggest you chat with your moderator beforehand to gauge just how savvy she is. Casually ask how many times she has served as a moderator in the past.

If she is an experienced moderator, ask her about the toughest situation she ever encountered in that role. If she does not possess the needed know-how, you must mentally prepare yourself for the fact that you might have to handle this yourself. No, that's not fair. You should not have to assume that task. But this is one of the little curveballs life loves to throw at us. In this instance, reality dictates that you may have to do her job for her.

If you are flying solo and not part of a panel, it will also be your charge to politely but firmly deal with the Agenda Hog. You are within your rights to shut him down. You struck a bargain with your audience. They entered that room to hear you and benefit from your experiences. They don't want to hear the Agenda Hog any more than you do.

In fact, many times they themselves will be embarrassed by his conduct. It is not unusual for audience members to approach you after your remarks to apologize for the conduct of one of their compatriots (see "The Audience Rides to the Rescue" in Chapter Seven for a good example).

Deflect Rude Questions

It sometimes takes more than the bridging strategy I explained earlier to rein in the Agenda Hog because his question is so off-base, argumentative, or long-winded.

It is time to introduce another technique: *Deflection*. I recommend that you deflect the Agenda Hog's wild questions. Here are some methods for dealing with various situations in which you need to deflect:

- Indicate a willingness to talk with your questioner one-on-one about the specific issue after your presentation, then immediately bridge to your message. Do not wait for the Agenda Hog to agree to your proposition. Assume agreement and move on. Your bridge in this case may not be paved as smoothly as you would like, but in the end, you will put yourself and your listeners back on course.

- Tell your audience that you have not seen the information referenced by the questioner if he raises some arcane data or brings up a new study with which you are not familiar. Here, too, you want to build a bridge immediately, using a phrase like, "What I can tell you is..." and getting into the details of your message.

- If the question has little or nothing to do with your topic, feel free to say, "Unfortunately, that is not the issue I was asked to address. What we need to remember is..." or, "You know, I'm not the expert on that, however concerning the subject at hand, I do know...."

- Even more simply, you can politely and briefly tell your grandstander, "Thanks for your perspective," or, "That's an interesting viewpoint," and immediately recognize the next questioner.

- If you get the onion question—you know the type; you can peel layer after layer and still have no end in sight (plus, it stinks as bad as an onion!)—reply, "That is a complex issue we could spend hours discussing. The important point is, as I mentioned in my presentation...."

- Deflect the "what if" question. Unless you are a charter member of the Psychic Friends Hotline, it is difficult to peer into the future and guess what might happen in a hypothetical situation. Issue a response like, "I would not want to mislead you by speculating. What I can tell you is, in the real world...."
- Address rumor-mongers by saying, "Our industry always seems to be ripe for rumors. Let me stick to the facts and tell you...."

Think through these tactics in advance and know how you will handle such distracting inquiries. Again, creativity comes before you speak, not while you are on the platform.

Put Up a Roadblock

Deflection helps you redirect such questions. Consider this technique particularly with overtly hostile attacks. You need to shut these down. They are an affront not only to you, but to your audience as well. Take charge and dispose of them quickly.

You need to maintain your professional attitude and an air of respect and diplomacy.

Yet you also need to remain firm and in control. Under no circumstances should you let the lone prickly individual in your audience dictate your temperament. Remain calm, cool, and professional. But also remain firm and in control.

Do not repeat any negative or pejorative language used by your inquisitor. If such words pass your lips, you take ownership. You want your audience to take away your positive message, not a vivid memory of someone dragging you into a street fight.

You can diplomatically close the verbal door and shift the tenor of the conversation with such introductory phrases as "In reality..." or "The fact of the matter is...." Then build a bridge to your message.

For example, you may deliver a presentation designed to recruit new members for a charitable organization. Out of nowhere, this question comes flying at you: "Isn't it true that you mismanage your money, and that very few of the dollars we donate actually go to direct services? And don't you just create make-work for volunteers. I have heard you don't really give them anything worthwhile to do."

What can you say in response without repeating the negative assertions? Try this: "In reality, over the years our track record shows that more than 90 percent of our funds go right back into our community. Plus, we maintain the average volunteer for more than five years. That is how we measure their happiness with the opportunities we provide to help them help their neighbors. I see another hand up in the back of the room. Your question, please."

Another technique: Restate the question to smooth out the rough edges. You may hear, "Why do you want to raise our taxes? You're nothing but a tax and spend politician." Turn the inquiry around by saying, "What are the programs we need to fund with these additional revenues? They are programs that serve you and your neighbors—school lunches, library books, ambulance service, flu shots for the elderly, and more. The woman in the third row with the blue sweater, you have a question."

Note the importance of moving right away to your next questioner, who is in all likelihood less antagonistic. Do not leave even the slightest opening for your aggressor to take another bite at her wormy apple.

Finally, when you are ready to end questioning, send a signal to your audience by telling them you have time for one or two more questions. Recognize a friendly face or someone who has not been pressuring you, and use her question as the springboard for your message-driven conclusion.

Maintain Your Dignity

Every so often when the going gets rough, you will see a speaker abruptly cut off questions. I strongly advise against using that tactic.

These unskilled presenters are one of two things. The first type is the thin-skinned, boorish lout who cannot stand the least bit of criticism. He evidences no respect for his audience in the first place. When the waters get choppy, he abandons ship and crew without a second thought.

The second category consists of people who are simply not skilled at managing the flow of questions. They have failed to study and practice what it takes to succeed during Q&A. As a result, they are unprepared and scared out of their wits.

If you fall into the first category, what can I say? Anger management is not the topic of this book. You need to work on getting your ego in check and viewing your audience as a treasured group.

Those in the second category, take heart. Practice the Q&A techniques outlined in this chapter. And I mean really practice. Enlist those skeptical colleagues or cranky old Uncle Phil to hurl some high, hard fastballs your way. Practice fouling a few balls off. Before long, you will be knocking them over the fence.

The lesson here is, once you have opened the floor to Q&A, you are committed to it. Your audience will gain respect for you if you show them you can deftly and diplomatically deal with the hardball questions.

The Extreme Agenda Hog

Be forewarned, an Agenda Hog has no reluctance whatsoever about standing up and firing away, whether you formally recognize him or not. These people are extremists who either don't recognize the bounds of polite society or choose not to live within them.

They are masters at assuming that any gesture, no matter how vaguely in their direction, is a signal to launch into their broadside. Some are looking for the tiniest crack of limelight. Others honestly believe that no one else could possibly be as fascinating as them. The Agenda Hog will try to slip through the narrowest opening.

Once he begins, you can settle your brains for a long winter's nap. You are in for a rant, not a question. How do you stop him in midstream? First of all, remember to retain your dignity.

I know I sound like a broken record stressing this point. But you cannot let the Agenda Hog drag you down to his level. Oh, it might feel good to get off a barbed one-liner at his expense. But you could well lose face in the eyes of your audience.

At the same time, do not be afraid to push him if he starts prattling on for twenty or thirty seconds with no question in sight. You are well within your rights to interject, "We have a lot of people here with questions on their minds, and I want to be sure to recognize as many as possible. Can you state your question, please?"

In the vast majority of instances, the audience will be on your side and sympathetic to your effort to shut down the Agenda Hog, assuming that you do so respectfully.

What do you do if he continues, in the process evidencing a high disrespect for his fellow audience members? If that happens, you are clearly dealing with an individual who has more issues than the one he is trying to raise. Unless you choose to let him exhaust himself (this could take a long time), you have no option other than to interrupt. Once again, try to do this as tactfully as you can, indicating that, now that he has had his chance to speak, you would like to show a sense of fair play and give someone else the same opportunity.

Alternatively, you can try to recognize another questioner, but most people are understandably reluctant to jump into the middle of a spat.

By this point, it is clear that he is severely disrupting the proceedings. A senior person from your host organization should step in and take the heat to spare you from having to do so. She can even signal the audio crew to shut off the Agenda Hog's microphone if you are speaking in a larger room with microphones for the audience. Again, arrange in advance who will fulfill this mission on the rare chance a severe disruption occurs.

If nothing works in the end, your only choices—and they are admittedly drastic—are to let him go for a few minutes or to walk off the stage. Use these only as very last resorts. Try to utilize every avenue available to you before turning to this radical move.

The Heckler

The heckler is an extreme version of the Agenda Hog. This oaf doesn't even have the good manners to disguise his disruption as a question. He will just shout out his viewpoint to the world in the middle of your delivery.

I must stress that your odds of ever encountering a heckler are extremely slim. While Agenda Hogs are rare birds, hecklers are an endangered species.

Understand that there is no magic formula for dealing with hecklers. It depends on the specific situation and on your own talents and preferences. This section contains some strategies for you to consider.

As we discussed, you can often dispose of an Agenda Hog with indirect methods—bridge away from his irrelevant issues or give him one last chance to pose his question. Not so with the heckler. Here, you must deal decisively.

This is not to say you want to get into a verbal sparring match with the heckler. You don't. Keep your cool and your sense of professionalism. Your audience is normally on your side in this debate, and you want to keep them there.

Tell your heckler that you have a lot of ground to cover and want to be sure to discuss everything your listeners told you they wanted to hear. Offer to meet with him after you conclude your remarks when you can zero in on the concerns that affect him.

One way to avoid encouraging him is to break off eye contact, just as you did with the Agenda Hog. Engage other members of your audience; steer clear of the heckler.

Ask the heckler to stand and identify himself by name and organizational affiliation. Hey, you have identified yourself. It is only fair that others who want the limelight also tell the crowd who they are. Requesting that he stand brings him out into plain sight, allowing the rest of the audience to see who is disrupting the proceedings.

Stripping the heckler of his anonymity may serve to soften his diatribe. Once the rest of the audience knows his identity, he has to tread a bit more lightly for fear of damaging his personal reputation or losing customers who will never want to do business with a firm that employs a dope like him.

Silence can sometimes do the trick. If you receive a rude comment from the peanut gallery, stop, stare, and shush. Stop speaking. Stare at the heckler. Shush your mouth for a pregnant pause.

Alternatively, you could try a bit of humor to ease the tension created by the heckler. But beware. If your style does not lend itself to humor, you will only dig a deeper hole for yourself. And be sure that any levity does not come at the expense of your heckler. Stay above the fray by respecting your audience—yes, even hecklers.

If your heckler strikes during a longer presentation with built in breaks, take a scheduled time out a bit early, if need be. Buttonhole the offender at the beginning of the break and, in no uncertain terms, explain why his behavior is unacceptable. If he does not explicitly agree to behave—and make sure you get his assent that he will refrain from acting up—offer to show him the door.

If the heckler becomes persistent and openly disruptive, it is time to stamp out this overt distraction by playing to the audience's sense of fairness: Even people who may vehemently disagree with your stance respect the principle of freedom of speech. Tell him, "Some of us look at issues through different lenses. I think that's healthy. I hope you do, too. Now is my opportunity to share my opinion."

A slightly stronger version goes, "This is my turn to express my freedom of speech. I am going to give you your turn in a few moments and will allow plenty of time for everyone to ask questions that are important to them." Then resume your presentation immediately.

Refuse to give the heckler an opening. And never cede your control by asking him a question. Do you reward bad behavior from your children? Of course not. Why reward the heckler for displaying ill manners?

The truth is most hecklers don't wait for an opening. If they come back for another bite of your apple, it is time to let the organizers remove him. If you anticipate trouble, arrange in advance for your host organization to appoint a "sergeant-at-arms" charged with alleviating such disruptions. Plan what this person will do and when. Just be sure he or she does not acknowledge that you had a role in setting this up. As the speaker, you should not be a part of this equation.

A note of background: If you run into hecklers more than once, take a good look at your own performance. You may lack energy. Your pace may be too slow. You may be unintentionally insulting the audience. Consider what proactive steps you can take to eliminate the cause of the derision.

The Accidental Heckler

You may at times encounter unintended hecklers. These are the people who chat during your presentation, snap the newspaper as they read it, or take a call on their cell phone.

You can attempt to bring the unintended heckler back into line by indirectly calling attention to him. Start by making eye contact if possible. Sometimes this will do the trick, but many times they are so oblivious you need to dole out stronger medicine.

Silence may prove effective. A hush will call any private chat out into the open. They may realize they are interrupting and cease their rude behavior. Or their peers in the audience may pressure them to put a lid on it.

If you are not speaking from behind a lectern and have the freedom to move about the room, get as close to them as you can while you continue speaking. If they still don't get the hint, pour them a glass of water and set it down conspicuously in front of them, or hand it to them (nearly every room should have pitchers of water and drinking glasses on the tables).

What if none of that works? Then what you have is not a minor interruption, but a full-blown distraction. You must deal with this directly and dispatch it quickly. Give these rude individuals a choice by asking them (diplomatically, of course) to join the rest of the audience and cease their distracting behavior or to move their conversation into the hall. If that fails, this is a case for your sergeant-at-arms.

In an absolute worst case scenario, call a break, investigate the situation, resolve it as quickly as possible, and move on with your remarks. Level with the offenders and tell them you expect one of two things: Either their attention and cooperation, or their departure. Then enforce it.

End with Strength

How many times have you seen a presentation fade away weakly after the last question? The speaker, unsure of how to conclude, flashes a meek smile and mumbles, "Well, okay, I guess that's it then. Have a nice day."

Wrong! Your presentation is not complete when you finish Q&A. You need to end with a bang. Wrap up by offering a clear summation of your message.

What benefits do you gain when you cross the finish line strong? Your audience will aid you when they:

- Walk out the door as disciples of your message
- Tell colleagues they see in the hallway about the main points you want to stress
- Rave to the meeting planner about the outstanding value you just delivered
- Hire you to speak before their organization

Seize the opportunity. Take advantage of your final response and drive your message home powerfully one more time. Transition from that last question to the conclusion you have prepared. This tactic will help you earn the disciples you deserve.

The Show Must Go On

I want to return for a moment to that feeling of relief some presenters experience when their presentation is over. This is to be expected to some degree. It is natural to feel a sense of achievement. But the show is not over when Q&A time arrives.

Think about it: It is no longer just you stating your point of view. You may be challenged to defend those principles. Or you might be prodded to think about them in a new light.

It is important to remember that Q&A is an extension of your remarks. It is your job to restate your message at every opportunity. How can you gain the discipline needed to return to your story consistently?

Let us recap some important preparation and practice techniques:

- *Anticipate.* Forecast the toughest questions that could arise and sort them into baskets of issues you can deal with more readily.
- *Research.* Conduct your due diligence and decide what your audience members would ask if you were in their place.
- *Survey.* Take the pulse of part of your audience in advance to find out what is on their minds.

- *Role play*. Enlist the most skeptical people you know and have them pelt you with questions.
- *Practice*. Give yourself plenty of rehearsal time.

Think of the Q&A at the end of your presentation as your encore. Do you think Bruce Springsteen wings it during his encore? Not likely. He anticipates and no doubt rehearses his encore numbers every bit as much as the tunes in the body of his show.

Final Keepers

How you answer questions from your audience can make or break your presentation. Responding with your message really drives your point home and exhibits respect for your audience. The Q&A process also gives you an added bonus: It allows you to reinforce your message a few additional times.

Return to your message as you respond to each question, even the hard ones. You now have a lot of valuable tools at your disposal—bridging, flagging, deflection, and the roadblock. Use them strategically and you will earn success and learn to enjoy the give and take with your audience.

Keep reminding yourself: A question is nothing more than an issue that ends with a different punctuation mark.

THE THIRD KEY: ASSESSING FEEDBACK

THE THREE KEYS TO CHAPTER NINE

You can expect to learn the truth about the third of the Three Keys to Great Presentations—Assessing Feedback:

- How to go beyond an evaluation form and gain in-depth feedback that improves your presentation skills;

- Specific methods for soliciting feedback both during and after your presentation;

- The warning signs that flash when you are in danger of losing your audience—and how you can recover.

TWO OUT OF THREE AIN'T BAD. So sang Meat Loaf in his 1980s ballad. But two out of three ain't necessarily good when it comes to sharpening your public speaking skills.

The vast majority of presenters focus on Performance, the second of the Three Keys to Great Presentations. Preparation, the first key, comes in a distant second. The truth is most neglect the vital third key: *Assessing Feedback*.

Measuring how you performed is vital to your continued improvement as a speaker. Why? Because better speakers get better results. They convince more people more readily. They are more effective educators. They rise to the top of the corporate ladder. They win the respect of their colleagues and competitors. You may have a different goal in mind. Regardless, leaders tend to be effective presenters.

Just as the first chair in the orchestra is won by the violinist who absorbs the master's teachings year after year, the standout leader gains knowledge from a trusted coach who can sharpen her speaking skills over time.

Begin with the End in Mind

It is a well-worn maxim: You need to know where you want to go before you can plan how to get there. That same principle applies to assessing feedback.

Decide what your speaking goals are. Aim for goals that are measurable and achievable. Then write them down and review them before every presentation you deliver. This makes them more concrete and achievable.

Next, envision what will change. How will you look and sound that differs from your present image? Is your intent to persuade, educate, or entertain a key audience? Keeping these types of specific goals in mind helps you both to assess feedback and to clarify your ambitions.

Strike a balance with your speaking goals. If you set the bar too low, you won't be challenged sufficiently. If you attempt to reach for the stars, you will end up frustrated and your improvement curve will flatten out, and perhaps even dip downward.

The goals of a novice speaker vs. a polished presenter will diverge. As a beginner, you may be satisfied simply to stride to the front of the room, complete your speech, and walk offstage in one piece. If you are a speaking pro, you may decide to sharpen your vocal pitch to a fine point or concentrate on using props more effectively.

Work hard to ensure that your goals are the right ones for you. If you find yourself struggling with this aspect of assessing feedback, an expert coach can help you clarify your specific objectives and work to attain them.

Your measurable goals will change over time. That is as it should be. As you improve one set of tools, you will want to zero in on assessing others in months ahead.

Form Counts

Many people believe that assessing feedback begins and ends with an evaluation form. I suggest you use one, by all means. Make your questions open-ended and leave plenty of room for comments.

Be sure to spend some time designing a form that unearths the data you need while keeping your form to one page. After hearing a presentation, audience members are ready to roll. They are in no mood to complete a *War and Peace* length questionnaire.

Ask about the program and about you as a speaker. Here are some sample questions to consider. Of course, you will come up with queries appropriate to your situation:

- What benefits did you gain?
- Which passages were most effective, persuasive, or educational?
- Was your speaker effective? Why or why not? Please be as specific as possible.
- Did the speaker have command of the subject material?
- If time had allowed, what else would you like the speaker to have covered?

Numbers Don't Tell All

You learn and improve by reading suggestions from real human beings, not by scanning a bunch of meaningless numerical averages. Forget numbered scoring systems.

Such forms may make sense for personnel people because they create nice, neat pigeonholes. But they cannot provide you with the critical information you need as a speaker. Even with large crowds, I much prefer narrative feedback. Trust me, I will read those comments no matter the size of the audience. That is how I get better.

You can see the basic form I use in Appendix E. I may change, add, or subtract a question or two depending on the audience, but this is the model I generally employ.

There are drawbacks to the evaluation form. For instance, not everyone will fill one out despite your pleading. In addition, it is typically those in the extremes—listeners who either strongly liked or strongly disliked your message and performance—that are motivated to complete them.

Respect your audience's time when you hand out your evaluation form. They may feel rushed if you distribute it at the very end of your session. They are more concerned with returning to the office, getting home in time for dinner, or moving on to the next meeting.

If you are leading an all-day workshop, you can remedy this by handing out your questionnaire at the end of your last break. When participants return, ask them to take five minutes to complete it. This sends a clear signal that you understand evaluations are an integral part of your talk since you are dedicating time from your program, not their personal time afterward.

Compliance is a real issue. It is difficult to prod 100 percent of attendees to fill out the form. But that should be your goal. To get there, you need a strategy that goes beyond a meek request for them to fill out that colored sheet of paper they found on their chairs.

You might designate an assistant (someone from your office or a willing volunteer from the sponsoring organization) to distribute the forms and collect them. The compliance rate also goes up when you assign one or two people to stand at the exits to collect the forms as people leave. Be sure to tell everyone that aides are standing at the door to take their forms as they depart. Instruct your aides not to be shy about asking for completed forms as the audience streams out.

Some organizations are moving their evaluations online. A day or two after the event, they will e-mail attendees with a link to a web-based survey form. This makes it easier to collect the information in an electronic database that can be referenced at any time.

Evaluation Is More Than a Piece of Paper

One last thought about your evaluation form. Once you elicit this good information, use it. Judging from their performance, I suspect that too many speakers collect their forms after a presentation and stuff them in their briefcase, never to be seen again.

While an evaluation form is important, you should not rely exclusively on that lone sheet of paper. No matter how well structured, it cannot give you a complete picture.

The truth is evaluation forms embody several key weaknesses. As noted above, time is a factor. Your audience wants nothing more than to get on to their next chore when you are finished speaking. Unless you sell its value, they will see the evaluation form as a waste of time.

In addition, some people are too polite to give you a poor evaluation. They figure it is better to fudge their answers or not respond at all rather than insult you. They will not understand honesty leads to learning and improvement unless you tell them.

Then there is the fact that they are not likely to be critical if they think you will personally review their form, particularly if they think you can identify them. This is a particular problem for small crowds in which it is easier to narrow down who believed what.

Sure, some individuals will be highly forthright, giving you all the criticism you can tolerate. But most want to remain anonymous. That is why I am careful to stress that including one's name is optional.

Beyond the Evaluation Form

You are missing out on a wealth of information if you stop assessing feedback with a mere evaluation form. Fortunately, there are plenty of additional means of gauging your performance. Number one, record your presentation.

This is important: Record yourself either on video or audio tape every time you speak. You can learn and develop new improvement strategies based on each talk you deliver if you take advantage of this opportunity to grow.

If you or the meeting planner has arranged for a professional videographer to shoot your speech, great. You may even be willing to negotiate a lower fee if your sponsor throws in a copy of a professionally edited video that you can use for marketing purposes.

You can even create products using the video or audio that you can sell at future presentations and on your web site. A professional camera crew is, needless to say, mandatory if you plan to distribute or sell the video. Just be sure your contract grants you the rights to do so. Consult your lawyer on such matters.

If, on the other hand, your only interest is in assessing feedback, all you need is cousin Joey who loves to videotape weddings. He may not be the best. He may frame his shots awkwardly and cut your head from the frame now and again. But yours does not need to be a flawless product. You just need a record of how you performed. So ask Joey to put on his suit and tie, set up his camcorder in the back of the room, and shoot your presentation. Treat him to a nice dinner afterward and you will both come out ahead.

If videotape is not an option, make an audio recording. If the host organization is recording all of the proceedings for posterity, ask for a copy. This will at least give you a sense of how your Audio Tools are functioning.

Taping yourself is yet another possibility. There is a range of reasonably priced digital voice recorders on the market that are small enough to clip to your belt. Add a basic microphone you can clip to your dress, shirt, or tie, and you are ready to record yourself.

Another benefit they offer: The digital format allows you to quickly upload the audio to your web site. If people can hear you speak at the click of a mouse, they are more likely to hire you for future engagements.

As an alternative, you can place a small cassette recorder on the lectern or on a table near the front of the room. While the sound will not be crystal clear, it likely will be good enough to allow you to monitor your audio performance.

Once you have your video or audio tape, don't let it gather dust. Watch it or listen to it as soon as possible and critique yourself honestly. With tape in hand, you are ready to conduct the "Taking Inventory" exercise found in Appendix B to measure your nonverbal qualities.

Are you looking to gauge your Video Tools more closely? Try this tip: Turn down the sound as you view your videotape. This permits you to zero in exclusively on your Video performance.

Do you want to monitor your Audio Tools? In that case, darken the screen and listen to the playback. This leads you to focus intently on how you sound to your audience.

Also, play the tape on fast forward or rewind. If your Video Tools are weak, this quick scan will show you that you are not sufficiently animated. But if you look too "hot," you will observe yourself flapping your arms as if trying to send a message with semaphore flags.

Skilled Analysis

You may opt for any number of feedback tools—the evaluation form and videotape are just two possibilities.

But let me lay the cards on the table. Your expertise is probably not in presentation skills. You may be a top-flight cardiologist, financial planner, information technology expert, or politician. But you haven't dedicated your days and nights to learning about the craft of public speaking.

Successful communicators realize that self-monitoring to ensure a high level of performance does not get the job done. They need a set of expert eyes and ears.

Remember the old maxim, "He that is his own lawyer has a fool for a client." Most people who have not studied public speaking and oral communications in depth simply do not know what to look for without an expert's guidance.

The stakes are high when you speak, far too high to risk a faux pas in front of an important audience. Your next promotion, election victory, or new customer may hang in the balance.

Draw up a plan destined to lead to real improvement. Decide in concert with your coach what you want to work on. It could be anything from how you stand when speaking to sharpening your articulation to perfecting your use of props. The choice is up to you based on how you assess feedback you receive from your audiences.

Defining those items that are critical to you allows your coach to monitor those areas more closely. He should offer concrete suggestions that will polish your strengths and, with a lot of time and effort, help minimize your weaknesses.

Appendix C holds the keys to selecting the individual who is right for you: Twenty questions that help you define what you are looking for and point you in the right direction.

A Good Match

A professional trainer is sensitized to your individual needs. Spend some time with this person beforehand to ensure a good match. You do not, for instance, want someone who is accustomed to dealing only with volunteers from a local non-profit board if you are a president in a Fortune 500 operation.

Of equal importance, you should seek out a good match from a personality standpoint. For better or worse, there are people who grate on our nerves for no apparent reason. Then there are those who we get along with swimmingly no matter how rough the sledding becomes. Hire someone with whom you are comfortable. If your coach is working diligently to improve your performance, expect him to offer advice that will, in some cases, lead to a bit of personal discomfort. It is not easy for some of us to hear the unvarnished truth. A strong bond will see you through those times.

Once you have selected your coach, bring him along on a speaking engagement or two and ask him to offer immediate feedback. Like shopping for vegetables, advice is best when it is fresh. Arrange for a debriefing session right after your presentation.

But don't stop there. He will likely have some additional suggestions after reflecting on your performance for another day or two. If you videotape your speech, he will want to review the tape to further analyze your approach. Set up a second debriefing a few days later to further fine tune your presentation skills. Be clear if you want a written analysis. Most trainers are pleased to offer this if you request it.

Monitor the Crowd

Even with an experienced guiding hand, you need to be conscious of watching for audience reaction as you speak.

Do not ignore the need to analyze your performance in real time. Scan your audience continually as you speak.

These days, we are all accustomed to instant replay when watching a sporting event. As a longtime baseball fan (and somewhat of a purist), I must admit that even I look around for a replay screen at the ballpark. As you speak, monitor the instant replay camera in your mind's eye so that you can rewind your performance and aim toward improvement.

If you receive positive feedback throughout your talk, you have likely hit a home run. Standing ovations may be few and far between. But there are other signs your listeners will send that tell you things are on target:

- Solid eye contact
- Smiling
- Nodding
- Leaning forward toward you
- A general sense of quiet in the room as you speak
- Applause at key moments
- Everyone staying seated, with no one exiting or milling about
- Plenty of relevant questions during Q&A

Then there are the negative signals for which you must remain vigilant. Albert Mehrabian, whose research into nonverbal signals was discussed in depth in Chapter Six, found the following factors were the strongest indicators of relaxation. Note that this is not relaxation in the restful sense. When you note these traits, it means your audience is bored:

- Sideways lean, particularly if they are leaning with head in hand.
- Backward lean, a clear sign they are tilting away from you.
- Asymmetrical arm and leg positions. If, for instance, the arms are open but the legs are crossed, you have some work to do.
- Extreme open arms. This is a sign of someone who is too relaxed and probably not paying attention.
- High rocking rate. People who rock vigorously in their chairs are ready for the next act.

There are also other signs that will tell you when you are on the verge of losing your audience. Also among the signals that you need to sharpen your skills:

- Crossed arms
- Side conversations
- Reading of newspapers or magazines
- Doing paperwork
- Applying makeup
- Congregating in the back of the room
- Heading for the exits
- Taking a catnap

If you receive positive feedback from your audience, keep doing what you have been doing. It is obviously working for you with this group of people. If, however, you detect negative signs, come prepared with a strategy for shaking things up in order to re-engage the audience. If you let the negatives fester, rest assured they will snowball into an out-of-control avalanche that will bury you and your audience.

Your antennae need to be sensitive to the signals your audience sends. Think of your brain like the weather radar we all see on TV. Its beam scans the skies every few seconds for signs of storms. You need to do the same type of scan with your audience.

Placing Matters in Context

Even with the nonverbal information outlined above, it is dangerous to try to put too fine a point on your attempts to interpret nonverbal signals transmitted by other people.

Unless you know the individual and his habits, reading specific meanings is difficult. You will realize he is displaying some type of emotion and may even be able to narrow it down to a range of feelings. But it will be next to impossible to pin down his exact mood without a broader context.

For instance, we tend to consider solid eye contact a trait of an honest individual. Yet researcher Paul Ekman found that pathological liars are highly adept at faking sincere eye contact.

As another example, we typically think that someone shifting in his seat is bored or restless. Yet it is possible he has a bad back and needs to move frequently for comfort's sake.

You will be on much firmer ground if you gain intelligence from a variety of signals, not just one.

The central idea is to put every nonverbal action you observe into context and consider the range of reasons for their coming into play. Don't make the mistake of overreading your audience's reactions.

Walk and Chew Gum at the Same Time

A lot of speakers become perplexed when I tell them to scan the audience. They see their main job as delivering their presentation. The reason they neglect this real-time check is that they are so busy thinking of what they are going to say next, they fear they will lose their train of thought and blank out on stage.

There is no question that performance is important. Here is the crucial point: I contend that a speaker's main job is to communicate, not to simply present. And communication is a two-way street. You must train yourself to communicate in both directions—sending and receiving.

We were born with two eyes to see with and two ears to hear with, but only one mouth to speak with. Use them in proportion. On stage, you are the one doing the talking. However, you must find ways to let communication flow *to* you, not just *from* you.

A well-rehearsed talk allows you to take heed of the signals you receive instead of focusing strictly on those you send. Yes, our old friend practice comes into play in assessing feedback.

I will stress here again the need to **internalize to verbalize**. If you are comfortable with your remarks and have practiced sufficiently, you will have more opportunity to receive feedback from your listeners.

Practice your remarks so that you know when you will make certain gestures, when you will pause, when you will temporarily turn off your slides, when you will toss a question out to the assembled multitudes, and the like.

Internalize to verbalize.

Knowing when you need to cue yourself to perform a specific action frees your mind to soak up any warning signs the audience is transmitting. Are they gazing off into space? Reading the newspaper? Tapping their toes? If you train yourself to zero in on these silent alarms, you will be better able to dispatch them quickly. The last thing you want is for other audience members to get attuned to this impatience. If you miss these signals and prove unable to deal with them right away, the boredom can spread like a virus, infecting everyone in attendance.

Shake It Up

If your feedback sensors witness any of these mannerisms while you speak, it is time to shake things up—right away. The longer you permit your listeners to stay disengaged, the more difficult it will be to pull them back to your train of thought.

What can you do? Use your nonverbal abilities to lively up the room. For example, take a few steps so the audience gets to redirect its gaze and shift ever so slightly in its seats. Raise your voice—not to a shout, but to a higher level that perks up your listeners' ears. Toss in a pregnant pause to get them wondering what is coming next. Pull out a prop and demonstrate your point.

In addition, use your words more carefully. Punch up your language with a sparkling anecdote, an analogy, contrary assertion, or shocking claim. Or ask the audience a question. It can come in the form of a rhetorical question, or you can take a snap poll. Asking your audience to raise their hands and shout a loud "yes" or "no" will help to get their juices flowing again.

All of these techniques make you a more interesting speaker and help guide the focus off their daydreams and back to you.

Heed those Questions

Your audience Q&A session will also give you lots of feedback. When the audience poses in-depth questions centering on the main parts of your message, take that as a good sign they were paying attention as you spoke. They are asking for deeper details about the essence of your speech. That is a highly positive sign.

If, however, their questions largely focus on basics you thought you covered adequately during your introduction, it is time to assess whether your comments lacked clarity. Perhaps you failed to define key terms they needed for a baseline of understanding. Or your pre-program research might have proved faulty, leading you to aim over their heads.

Listen, too, for the tone in your questioners' voices. Is it a respectful tone, one that indicates they are on your side? Or is there an edginess in their voices that could indicate they are impatient with your shortcomings or that you have more to do to convince them?

Factor feedback from the Q&A segment into your future presentations. As you practice for upcoming engagements, pay particular attention to any issues that lurked behind the questions.

Post-Presentation Feedback: Stage One

It is essential that you monitor audience indicators as you speak. You also need to take some steps immediately upon the conclusion of your presentation in order to gain critical, time-sensitive information.

Sure, your natural reaction following a presentation may be similar to most of us who speak: You let out a deep breath and pat yourself on the back for a job well done. Perhaps you even treat yourself to something special like a decadent dessert or a mini-shopping spree.

I am not suggesting you stop doing those things. But I heartily encourage you to hold off just a bit on the self-congratulations. Your job is still not done.

The time will never be as ripe for measuring audience feedback as it is immediately upon the conclusion of your speech. Unless you have a flight to catch, stick around. It is important if you want to better assess your performance. There are lessons to be learned that could all but disappear as even the briefest bit of time passes and the audience's short-term memories begin to fade.

As noted earlier, it is important to mingle with your audience in advance of your talk. Take some time to chat them up after your presentation, too. This can be a real eye-opener. Stay away from such vague questions as, "How did I do?" or, "Did my speech work for you?" Try to ascertain some deeper opinions with probing questions:

- Were there one or two points that really hit home for you?
- I sense the audience reacted a bit more positively when I talked about the yellow widgets. Did you notice that, too?
- How will you do your job differently as a result of what you heard today?
- If time had allowed, was there something else of value to you that I might have covered?

Then do some plain, old-fashioned listening. Remember our two eyes, two ears, and one mouth equation. You have done your talking. It is your audience's turn now.

Monitoring conversations that go on around you is a great way to pick up added intelligence. Some people will not enumerate your weaknesses face-to-face. They will be much more candid if they don't realize you are standing right behind them, soaking up every word and using it as a learning opportunity.

A note of caution here: If you are involved in a conversation, stay involved. Don't let your eyes glaze over while you try to eavesdrop on the couple next to you. This is an insult to your conversation partner.

Analyze the feedback critically and honestly. Solicit opinions from a variety of audience members. Talking to a lone individual or a single cluster from one department, for example, could give you a skewed impression. They could be nabobs of negativism who cast everything in a bad light. Or they could be Little Miss Sunshines who wouldn't say "ouch" if you were standing on their feet.

If you receive positive feedback from your audience cross-section, congratulations! But realize that most people will shy away from insulting you to your face; most of us are not hard-wired to dole out bad news. As a result, they tell you only the good things, in some cases whether they are true or not.

Dig Deeper

Do the comments you receive relate to some amorphous ability you possess that allows you to connect with your audience? Such general remarks don't tell you much. Dig deeper and ask what helped solidify that connection. Without leading their opinions, ask some open-ended questions that will help you discern what contributed to your strong showing. Was it something about your emotion? Your eye contact? Your smile?

Is there a distinct shortage of feedback about a trait you thought was a particular strength of yours? That could be an indicator that you are not as skilled as you imagined in that area. Or it could mean this audience was not tuned in to that factor. That represents one more reason why you need to put feedback into context and analyze what you hear.

Before you wade into the crowd, it is important to steel yourself for negative feedback. There are few things more embarrassing than the frozen smile or wounded countenance of a speaker upon hearing criticism. Be prepared to accept such evaluations gracefully and constructively.

If someone offers assurances that your audience wasn't really snoring, just practicing deep breathing exercises, you know you have some work to do.

Most people have no interest in insulting you. When they offer negative feedback, they are likely to couch it in sugar-coated language. Listen to these individuals. You can gain valuable improvement strategies from them.

Of course, there are people who are totally insensitive to your feelings. They may inform you in their undiplomatic way that you royally stunk out the joint. Again, put this feedback into context. While there may be useful learning experiences underlying their comments, these are the same people who criticize the Easter Bunny for not hiding the eggs in the right places.

Also, prepare yourself for some heartwarming feedback. People will open up to you, revealing intimate challenges they now feel able to conquer thanks to your advice. I encountered one such individual after I presented remarks to one of the world's preeminent medical schools. This audience member had just completed authoring a book about the institution. She sought me out afterward to tell me how my insights would help her as she launched a speaking tour to promote her work. Gratifying moments like this make all the hard work of public speaking worthwhile.

Check in with representatives from your host organization before leaving the scene if time allows. Ask them the same open-ended questions you asked of your listeners.

Important note: As soon as you depart, jot down some notes about the feedback you received. These comments are too valuable to lose, and your memory will never be as sharp a few minutes, let alone days, from now. Writing down key bits of feedback allows you to factor them in to practice sessions for future presentations.

Leave Your Calling Card

To gain future feedback, give your audience a lovely parting gift. No cars or diamonds are necessary. But you should give them a high-quality remembrance.

What can you give them? Tip sheets are great. Offer a concise ten-point plan for improvement or the six secrets to success. If you have a booklet, so much the better. Books, audio and video CDs, and cassette tapes also serve the purpose. If you have a book or audio product, you may be able to convince the event organizer to spring for a copy for each attendee. I always give a price break for group purchases.

Your leave-behind serves a number of functions. First, it keeps your name "top of mind." You never know who needs to hire a speaker for her company's next meeting. Second, it extends their learning beyond the day of your presentation. As a firm believer in lifelong learning, I swear by the importance of creating a strong learning resource.

In addition, you get one more chance to solicit feedback. Your leave-behind materials can include a self-addressed post card containing a few questions about your performance that respondents can mail back to you. Your response rate is likely to go up if you print your business reply permit or place a stamp on the back of it.

As an alternative, you can include a separate sheet in your handout as a feedback form. Or you can use the last page of your booklet for the same purpose. Just be sure to include instructions on how they can mail or fax it to you.

Another possibility: Your leave-behind materials can include the address of a page on your web site containing an online evaluation form.

Not only is this one more opportunity for feedback, it represents one more opportunity to promote your services in a low-key manner. Display your contact information—name, address, phone, e-mail, web address, fax—

on everything you distribute. Again, you never know who may want to get in touch with you to book you as a speaker.

This last point bears repeating: Make it easy for people to get in touch with you via their preferred means of communication. I am constantly amazed by the number of people and organizations that fail to put their web site or e-mail contact information on their promotional materials. You had better give the impression that you are part of the twenty-first century.

Post-Presentation Feedback: Stage Two

The second stage of assessing feedback takes place when you complete your fact-finding conversations with your listeners and review the comments from your evaluation forms. Now is the time to have a conversation with yourself. This is your moment for self-analysis. Ask yourself some tough questions, and be frank with your responses.

You should enter each presentation with a checklist of items you want to work on. Your personal list might include these areas:

- Ability to make a connection with your audience
- Powerful delivery of your message
- Effective use of specific nonverbal tools
- Success at seamlessly integrating your slides or presentation software into your talk
- Capability to persuade, inform, or entertain your audience
- Degree to which you succeeded with those elements you chose to sharpen when answering the Taking Inventory exercise (Appendix B)
- Talent to stick to your message when dealing with Q&A

I suggest you prepare more than a mental inventory. Make this a formal exercise. Take ten minutes or so shortly after your presentation to write down your reactions. You can return to your hotel room to write, jot some notes in the car on the way to the airport, or find a reasonably quiet corner of the hotel or conference center. But find somewhere to jot down your ideas and impressions. Don't worry about proper grammar or spelling right now. Concentrate on putting basic thoughts down on paper so you don't lose those irretrievable gems.

Writing it down in the form of a personal improvement checklist encourages you to treat your need to improve more seriously. Determine in advance what specific areas you want to sharpen, then review your list shortly after your speech to measure your performance.

It is important that you write down your answers. Even if you have a terrific short-term memory, I can guarantee that in a week or so you will conveniently forget how you did. Do not waste this opportunity for improvement. Once your memory has lost its sharpness, you can never recapture those images that can guide you toward growth as a speaker.

Committing your thoughts to paper, your PDA, or your laptop's hard drive allows you to review your progress prior to your next speech. That is the way to blaze the path to improvement.

Important note: Don't beat yourself up by being hyper-critical. Self-flagellation does no one any good. But do be realistic in your personal evaluation. If you fell short in one area, keep it on your list and pay it some extra attention during your next presentation.

Post-Presentation Feedback: Stage Three

The third phase of assessing feedback comes a few days after your presentation. The organization to which you spoke can provide a rich source of information. Call your contacts there a few days after your engagement. Tell them you are always striving to improve so you can be even better the next time you speak to their group. Ask them some focused questions designed to steer you toward improvement.

Are you wondering what to ask them? Use the questions on your evaluation form as a starting point. Then mix in the items from your personal improvement checklist.

There are two clear signs that you have delivered a five-star presentation. The first one flashes when your hosts invite you back to speak at their next meeting. The second lights up when they offer referrals to colleagues in other organizations in need of speakers. When you achieve either one of these goals, consider it a feather in your cap.

The Best Is Yet to Come

Great speakers realize they have not yet delivered their best presentation. Neither have you.

I encourage you to conduct a self-check to see if you still have that fire in the belly for your next presentation. After your speech, you should still feel secure in your belief that standing in front of a room and speaking to a crowd presents wonderful opportunities. But if you find yourself beset by nightmares and breaking out into a cold sweat at the mere thought of your next talk, it is time to examine seriously your commitment to this endeavor.

However, I cannot think of a better way to position yourself for securing that promotion at work, winning that new customer, achieving your organization's fundraising targets, attaining your public policy goals, gaining election to public office, and so much more.

The path to improvement is long and often winding. You can straighten that road by actively soliciting feedback in the three phases described above:

- Phase one by talking to your audience immediately after your talk
- Phase two by conducting an honest self-assessment
- Phase three by debriefing with the host organization

Assessing feedback will help ensure your next presentation is your finest ever. The best is yet to come.

CHAPTER TEN

TO SLIDE OR NOT TO SLIDE?

THE THREE KEYS TO CHAPTER TEN

You can expect to learn the truth about the use of presentation software and overhead slides:

- When to use—and when not to use—your laptop as part of your presentation;
- How to create a winning look for your slides while avoiding distracting bells and whistles;
- What to do when your audio/visual equipment dies.

HOW SIMPLE IT WOULD HAVE BEEN TO LIVE in medieval times. The only technology you needed to concern yourself with was the hit-or-miss guesstimate of whether your catapult was set for the right trajectory to land inside the castle walls.

No phone, no fax, no e-mail. And none of the ubiquitous presentation software that makes life so daunting for today's presenters.

Once they got past the gee-whiz factor of the technology, I am quite certain that, were a knight from the Middle Ages to be plopped in the midst of a darkened room showing a series of slides, he would soon fall into the same deep slumber many of us are tempted to try when forced to bear witness to such proceedings.

A Place for Everything

Don't get me wrong, one of today's truths about public speaking is that presentation software programs can be good tools. If you need to demonstrate something visual, there is nothing like showing a concrete example or giving your audience a step-by-step tour of a process they need to learn.

Most of us vividly remember the things we see. But this software is no more than a means to an end. You must recognize that your audience is there to see you: To hear your opinion, gain your wisdom, or be entertained by you.

Ask yourself, when is the last time you attended a presentation to see the speaker's cool slides? I pray the answer is never.

The most boring talks you will witness are those in which the speaker reads his slides word for word. You should proceed on the assumption that your audience can read (unless your advance research has told you otherwise). Your job is to add value to the key concepts spelled out on your slides, not to drone on with a dry recitation of the written word.

As a presenter, it is up to you to make a conscious decision whether or not slides will enhance your remarks or detract from them. When your presentation leans heavily on storytelling, slides are not likely to add much value to your capacity as a raconteur.

People ask me if I use presentation software when I deliver presentations to businesses and associations. The answer is, sometimes.

I do use a slide show when it is appropriate. As a presenting tool, it can be a good fit for some audiences, and not for others. I gauge during my preparation phase whether there is a compelling reason for using presentation software. If not, it stays out of the mix.

Simple and Elegant

Here is a critical point overlooked by too many speakers: Start your preparation phase by deciding what you want to say, then build your slide show around that message.

It sounds so basic, yet is forgotten by many people. You need to decide what you are going to say before you can begin to choose what visual tools are appropriate. Let your message—not your slides—drive your presentation.

You may draft a formal outline, jot down some talking points, or work from a few notes as you start the process of drafting your remarks. Whatever method works for you as you organize your thoughts is fine. But don't begin by assembling your slide kit right off the bat.

The slides are not the main portion of your speech. That role belongs to you. Slides exist strictly as a support mechanism.

If you decide they will add value to a particular speech, keep your slide show simple and elegant. The goal is to make slides strengthen your presentation, not become the centerpiece. Make them easy for the audience to see by avoiding busy, dense slides; keeping your text short; using only three to four brief bullet points per slide; and staying away from overuse of animation and sound effects.

This chapter explains some of the ins and outs that can make you a more effective presentation software user. This section offers pointers on:

- How to rearrange the order of slides
- How to edit using mouse or keystrokes
- How to print handouts (or "handups," as I like to call them)
- How to use speaker notes
- How to recover when something goes wrong

Nothing Is Mandatory

It seems nearly everyone is using their laptop computers to deliver slide shows these days. Some speakers seem to think an edict has been delivered from on high proclaiming that presentation software is to be used throughout the land.

Congress has not gotten around to that one yet, fortunately. A slide show can be a good tool, but that's all it is. The slides are not what your audience comes to see, although the sad fact is some audience members do view a slide show as a birthright. In truth, people are there because of you and your expertise.

Using slides is strictly a matter of personal preference. If you find them useful in a particular presentation and you feel comfortable with the technology, great. If you are frightened by your laptop or simply don't care for the technology, keep it out of your repertoire.

If you tend toward clumsy when trying to shuffle overhead transparencies, find another means of communication. If you are tired of loading your 35 mm slides upside down, leave the slide carousel at home.

It boils down to two choices: Avoid using technology in your presentation or embrace it and make the commitment to learning how to get the most from it.

The first camp was well represented by a speaker I witnessed at an event sponsored by the University of Virginia Darden School of Business. Some audience members were astonished that the speaker did not use his laptop. In fact, he used no visual aids at all.

He acknowledged that he did not feel comfortable with the technology.

Moreover, he made it clear that he wanted no part of putting his audience to sleep by forcing dozens of slides down its collective throat. Despite his no-slide rule, the talk was riveting. He had clearly practiced sharpening his Audio and Video Tools to such an extent that he had little need for slides.

The ironic piece to the presentation was a conversation I had with another attendee while networking beforehand. My newfound colleague got to talking about the use of presentation software and asked my opinion of it. I raised that program's omnipresence as a real complicating factor for many speakers, suggesting that too many presenters view it as a crutch—an easy way out of preparing thoroughly.

As a result, too few speakers know how to utilize it properly. They stand in front of the screen or on the wrong side, or they insist on leaving a slide up throughout their talk.

The Oops Factor

The time has come to remodel your home. You need a carpenter to do the job. Would you hire someone who didn't appear to know which end of the hammer to use?

You need a caterer for that big wedding reception or your boss' retirement party. You are not likely to sign up the cook who cannot separate a whisk from a spatula.

Similarly, it mystifies me why some presenters who use presentation software know so little about their equipment.

I got a first-hand look at this ignorance factor while attending a workshop in San Francisco. The speaker had trouble getting her laptop to talk to the projector. She owned the laptop and had set everything up properly there. But the projector came from the facility where she spoke, and she had not taken the time to familiarize herself with it ahead of time. To make matters worse, it was an evening talk and all the A/V help had gone home for the day.

Here is my point of view, and I realize it may sound blunt: Speakers who are unfamiliar with their tools have no business in the front of a room. If you cannot take the time to become a master craftsman with the tools of your trade, it is time to find another trade.

The sad thing is our speaker arrived in plenty of time to set up, but she failed to use her time wisely. Rather than give her slides a quick run-through, she decided to eat dinner. Now, I am all for eating dinner. An empty stomach can be quite a distraction. Then again, a full tummy can make you sleepy.

Eat light before you present. But before you sit down to your salad, make sure your technical preparations are complete.

Predictably, our speaker encountered some bumps in the road. Imagine the surprised look on her face when she clicked her first slide only to see that the bottom quarter of it was lopped off, invisible to the audience. It wasn't a matter of the projector being aimed too low. For some quirky reason (I always chalk up such events to computer gremlins), her laptop was telling the projector to display only the top portion of every slide.

Of course, she halted her presentation to wrestle with the technical difficulties. One audience member stepped forward in what proved to be a futile attempt to help. He began to tinker with the laptop settings. A valiant effort, but he tried to perform his fix without blacking out the screen. You get the picture. While the speaker was trying in vain to proceed, the audience was distracted, paying rapt attention to the fiddling plainly visible on the screen. Any flow she might have had quickly dried up.

What to do when technical snafus strike? The most obvious solution is to recognize them in advance so you will have at least a few moments to implement Plan B. Nothing says fear quite as succinctly as the deer in the headlights look on a speaker frozen by a mechanical failure. Arrive early and run through every slide transition so you know exactly how things will look to your audience.

If it turns out you cannot fix the problem, it is decision time. If the predicament is relatively minor (perhaps a slightly off-color font or a tiny portion of the slide cut off) you may decide to move forward with your slide show. Be up front with the crowd if the problem is obvious by acknowledging the difficulty at the beginning of your remarks. Come prepared with some light humor about the situation you can toss in if need be.

Then, forge ahead with your speech. Do not belabor the point again. Speakers who apologize throughout their talk do nothing but undercut their legitimacy. Get it out of the way up front, then work around the problem.

If the situation is so obvious that it proves distracting, you probably need to ditch your slides and go with your pre-planned backup. Even if you choose to use slides in 100 percent of your presentations, you need to practice without them for that one time conditions make it impossible for you to project your slide deck.

Make a List and Check It Twice

Let's talk about a checklist that can help you decide when it is appropriate to use slides. One of the biggest factors is the size of the room and the audience. If you are speaking before an intimate gathering, why would you want to overwhelm attendees with a formal approach?

The room layout also comes into play. Is the room big enough to accommodate a screen, projector, and laptop? Trying to jam all that gear into a tiny conference room is a losing proposition. Not only does it look crowded and uncomfortable, but those projector bulbs emit a lot of heat. Before you know it, you will have a roomful of people daydreaming of being in their swimsuits sipping drinks adorned with tiny umbrellas.

Consider the technical capabilities of the site. Does the venue have knowledgeable troubleshooters who can assist with problems? These individuals are vital to me. I am not a techno-whiz. Sure, I know how to hook up my laptop to a projector in most cases. But if something goes wrong from a technical perspective, I am the last person you want poking around under the hood. Just ask my wife; there is a good reason she is the one in charge of repairs in our household.

Assess your own comfort level with using a laptop, projector, or slide carousel. Do you find the technology easy to use or are you befuddled by it? If the facility does not have a projector, are you okay with lugging your own?

Another factor to take into account: Can you afford to darken part of the room in order to make your slides visible? You only need to turn down the lights in the very front of the room (don't be shy about asking someone from the facility to climb a ladder and unscrew some light bulbs if that is what it takes). It is very important to leave the audience bathed in light. In particular, early morning and post-lunch audiences are notorious for being sleepy. A well-lit room helps them stay sentient.

Finally, in terms of guidelines to help you decide on the appropriateness of slides, consider if you can deal with any information you need to distribute by using another method. For instance, it may be best to provide hard copies of dense, data-packed charts or graphs since they do not translate well to the screen.

Nasty Backlash

It is important to realize that an anti-presentation software backlash is fomenting. While there remains a fair share of organizations that believes slide shows are mandatory, there is a growing number that frowns on this tool. Some companies have, in fact, instituted an outright ban.

The point is you need to have a handle on the culture of the group you address. When it comes to slides, do they expect them, accept them, or prohibit them? Avoid a political faux pas by doing your research and learning the answer.

Your slides are not a crutch. The use of presentation software does not automatically make you a better speaker. It can, in fact, erect an invisible force field between you and your listeners. Some speakers frequently avoid using this tool for precisely that reason: They want to tear down barriers between them and their audience.

If you are able to effectively get across your story without using slides, think twice before tossing them into the mix just for the sake of having a neat plaything.

And above all else, remember not to bore your audience by reading every slide verbatim. If that is your intent, you might as well just hand them copies and let them read for themselves. They will find it quicker and less tedious.

The Look of a Winner

Is there one single look that tells me someone has crafted a winning speech when they decide to use presentation software? Not really. I realize that may not be the response you wanted. But the fact is there are as many good models as there are good speakers.

Understand that the software is a powerful tool, loaded with features. You may have the hottest car on the block. But if you don't know how to operate it responsibly, it does you more harm than good. Think of all those points you could pile up on your driver's license when you are ticketed for speeding and reckless driving. Drive responsibly when using your presentation software. It is up to you to harness that power and not let it run wild with you.

Although there is no single best practice, good design does have some consistent elements. Chief among them is the need to aim for simple and elegant. Here are some rules of thumb accomplished presenters use:

- Headline each slide with a message-oriented title.
- Use no more than three to four bullet points per slide, and make sure any charts and graphs are easy to read.
- Create your slides so that each one is easy to understand. Root out any jargon.
- Use a font large enough to be seen from the back of the room without

straining anyone's eyes. A 20-point font is a good rule-of-thumb minimum. Be sure to test this yourself as you prepare. Put up your slide, go to the very back of the room, and be sure you can read it.

- Ensure the image on the screen is level. Do not distract your audience and force them to crane their necks to one side because your slides are crooked.
- Do not let the image on the screen appear as a "keystone." This occurs when the image is broader at the top than the bottom. Some projectors have a keystone control that allows you to remedy this. Failing that, weighing down your screen and pulling it back toward the wall can help alleviate this keystone effect.
- Test your font of choice to be sure it is legible on the screen. Those that look good in print may not show up as clearly in a larger format.
- Stay away from cute fonts for professional presentations. Curlicue lettering explaining your company's weak financial performance creates a jarring disconnect.
- Employ font size to draw the audience's attention to central concepts. The bigger the font, the more important the idea.
- Resist the urge to cram every bit of information onto a slide, forcing your audience to fumble for a magnifying glass in order to read it. Remember, it is your job—not that of the slides—to impart crucial information.
- Use colors and color contrasts that are easily visible to the eye. For instance, steer clear of a yellow font on a white background.
- Be conscious of any symbolism your audience will attach to the colors you use. Corporations, sports teams, and universities often are closely identified with certain colors. Avoid unintentional use of a rival's color scheme.
- Leave plenty of white space to assure your slides are easy on the eyes.
- Stay away from the "artist's palette" approach. Use of an added color on occasion can help draw attention to key points. But overuse of color makes it hard to focus on content.
- Leave the crazy animation and sound at home. These features are, for the most part, useless for a professional presentation. If you use presentation software for your youngster's third birthday party, go to town with it. Otherwise, minimize your use of distracting bells and whistles.

Building a Better Slide

You also have the ability to "build" your slides one line at a time. This can work particularly well if you have three bullet points you want to stress, for example. You can create your slide deck so that the bullets appear one at a time, allowing you to spend a few moments singling out each one.

Get familiar with your software of choice and learn what it can do, such as fly in a bullet point. Many programs have slightly different commands. Even different versions of the same program from the same manufacturer operate differently. I suggest you create a dummy slide deck and play around with it. Gain a hands-on understanding of the software's strengths. Decide which features may be useful to you on some occasions and which are superfluous bells and whistles.

For instance, you may find it practical to record some audio and insert it in your deck. Or you may decide to slip in a different slide transition if you want the audience to make particular note of a key slide. As with other techniques covered here, be sure not to overuse these approaches.

Many programs allow you to time your slide presentation so that the slides change at a time you specify rather than advancing them manually. I advise you to stay away from this as you speak. It can lead to riotous confusion if your planned timing gets thrown off by an audience question or a distraction of some sort.

There is one case where timing can be effective: When you choose to show a slide loop as your audience enters the room and gets settled. You can give them a preview of your talk, pose some stimulating questions to get them thinking, or project quotes you gleaned from audience members during your preparation phase. Here again, familiarize yourself with the power of your software so that you know how to use this function if desired.

Trimming Your Slide Kit

One of the great benefits of presentation software is the flexibility it offers you. Perhaps you are speaking on a topic nearly identical to one you covered elsewhere a few weeks ago. The problem is, your upcoming talk is only fifteen minutes, as opposed to the thirty minutes you had last time. No problem.

It is incredibly easy to slim down your slide presentation by hiding or deleting slides. When you delete a slide, it disappears from your slide deck permanently; hiding keeps it as part of the file, concealing it only temporarily.

You can execute these commands with the mouse, from the drop down menus on the upper toolbar, or in many cases with keystrokes. Of course, the exact steps depend on which program and computer operating system you use. I strongly suggest you get comfortable with these methods by reading your manual or checking the help screen on your software.

The easiest slide to knock out of your file is the difficult to read one. If you find yourself saying, "The squiggly lines may be hard to see, but it's worth showing," it is not worth showing! Get rid of anything the audience will not be able to see clearly.

Should You Give Your Audience a Handup?

How many presentations have you attended where the speaker places printouts of his slides on each attendee's chair? What does this do? It gives his audience a ready-made excuse to check out early. Not only that, they manage to interrupt his talk with incessant paper shuffling; as he changes slides, they flip pages.

Save the paperwork for the end. Let them collect it on the way out, or distribute it once you are finished. The one exception: If you are speaking on a technical topic that your audience is expected to learn, such as a training for a bunch of information technology workers on how to get the most from their new server. They need to be following along. Otherwise, take every step to ensure that your listeners rivet their attention on you.

I am sometimes asked whether a presenter should use slides as handups. (remember, it is a handup, not a handout; you are presenting your audience with a rich resource they can use as part of their lifelong learning, not with a table scrap.)

When it comes to distributing your slides, use your personal judgment on the wisdom of handups. If you want the audience to take away a copy of your slides, fine. Review the printout to be sure it is easily readable. This may not be the case if your kit includes dense charts and graphs, or detailed photos and images. Printouts of web site pages are normally difficult to read clearly, too.

Also, perform a thorough quality control check on your handups if you use background colors or different shades for your fonts. Your audience is likely to receive duplicates in black and white, and these quick copies may appear as big, fuzzy gray blobs.

As a bonus, you can put the slide deck on your web site and provide them with a dedicated URL (web site address) to access it. This gives you lots of options. You can leave the file there for only a specified time. In addition, you can password protect it so that only that specific audience can view it.

If you opt for the hard copy route, familiarize yourself with the different printout possibilities for your handups:

- Slides that print one per page, just as they view them during your talk;
- Handups on which you can put anywhere from two to nine slides per page;
- Notes pages, which let them see any speaker notes you have entered;
- Outline view that shows only your outline, not the slides themselves.

Your specific options may vary depending on what software and system you use. In general, you are likely to find these different printout possibilities by going to the Print command.

Don't Get Caught Short

Whether or not you opt to distribute your slides, be absolutely sure to bring a hard copy for yourself. If your computer goes down or the projector blows up, your notes will prove invaluable as a reference.

Remember to bring two hard copies: The first bound with a paper clip, the backup stapled in the event of an emergency.

It is also imperative that you bring an electronic backup of your presentation on CD and floppy in case your laptop crashes. You can also use an electronic storage key that plugs into an ISB port. Keys store lots of data and represent a fast means of transferring files.

When you have your file available via those portable media, you may be able to load it on a borrowed laptop and proceed as if nothing happened. Note carefully that I suggest bringing more than one format. Some older laptops lack a CD drive or ISB port, while newer models sometimes are missing a floppy drive. Best to be prepared for any eventuality.

While on the subject of fail-safe precautions, always run your laptop with AC power; that is, plug it into an electrical outlet. Running a presentation saps battery life quickly. Plus, you may have forgotten to recharge it fully after you used it last. You do not want to risk running your batteries down and having your system die just as you prepare for your big climax.

Take a Note

Earlier, I talked about the speaker notes feature included in many presentation software programs. Let me go into a bit more detail now, since many people find this a useful feature.

As you are creating your presentation, you will see that you can enter notes for yourself at the bottom of each slide. Your comments appear only on the hard copy you print out and not on the slides your audience sees. These notes serve to jog your memory about key points, facts, or figures. They can also jog your memory on how you want to transition from one slide to the next. You can edit and change these notes any time you wish. For instance, as you unearth new research, you can easily add a reminder to yourself in your speaker's notes section.

Speaker's notes can reduce the tendency to try to cram every single point onto your slides. You will still be able to reference the information while keeping your slides clutter free. Remember, simple and elegant carries the day.

Use the Gizmos Wisely

Have you ever been to a luncheon buffet that spread out dozens of options before you? Perhaps you opted for a salad, entrée, vegetables, and dessert, leaving a multitude of other choices on the table.

This is how I want you to think of using your presentation software package. You can use varying templates, fonts, colors, and video clips while leaving the rest of the doodads alone. This includes, in most cases, leaving animation and sounds on the shelf.

Let me give you some quick examples of each. With regard to animation you can:

- Create slide transitions that, for example, fly in from the top left or dissolve in;
- Add some video from a previous presentation of yours;
- Make objects spin, rotate, flip, or do handstands (okay, I haven't yet found a program that allows you to perform handstands, but you get the point).

As for adding sounds, you have the ability to:

- Mix in effects like applause or a drum roll that will play during slide transitions;
- Add an audio sound bite from an old radio show;
- Insert a video clip from your organization's new promotional video;
- Make sounds go off when you move your cursor over a certain area of the screen.

These are attention-grabbing tools. But I urge you to think long and hard before you include any animation or sound effects in your talk. If you decide they add to your performance, think about it a second time. Then a third time.

Such effects are very cute—and very distracting. Your audience will zero in on the sound of breaking glass or the cute spinning globe you have onscreen while totally tuning out your words.

I once witnessed a presentation in which the speaker dropped some video from a movie into his slide presentation. There are a number of problems here. One, it totally interrupted the flow of his remarks. Two, audience members grew so curious about what movie it was from, they tuned out the speaker. Three, it raises some serious copyright issues. This speaker was a lawyer and should have known he was treading on thin ice. It is difficult if not impossible to obtain rights to film clips.

If, after much deliberation, you decide to use images, video clips, or audio, be sure you have the rights to that material. In general, you can legally use such items in only three cases:

- You are the original creator of the material;
- You have express written permission to use it for commercial purposes;
- It is material in the public domain.

Important note: This probably also applies to the clip art that comes with your presentation software program. Do not assume that because you purchased the program you can do anything you want with it. You may, for example, have the right to use such clips to educate but not for commercial purposes. Manufacturers make you agree to those one-way licenses for a reason—to maintain their rights, not yours. In all cases, check the fine print and consult your lawyer.

When it comes to animation and sound, remember this key point: Your audience is there to see you, not some cute tricks.

Living on Borrowed Time

Airport security lines are no fun these days. Perhaps you have decided to travel laptop-free and use a unit supplied by the hotel where you are speaking or by another presenter. Can you still run your own presentation? Sure.

But there are some extra items you will need to attend to. First, create a copy of your slide deck on a CD or key and diskette (remember, you need to carry multiple formats to cover yourself in case the computer you are using has only one type of portable drive). You could even e-mail the file to yourself as an attachment for backup purposes if you have a way to retrieve it once you arrive at your destination.

In advance of your talk, load it onto the computer you will use for the presentation. And I do mean well in advance of your time in the spotlight. Under no circumstances do you want to be fiddling with this in full view of your audience.

Why load it onto the computer's hard drive instead of running it directly from your CD, key, or floppy? Simple. It will run faster. This is important. You do not want the floppy drive grinding out painfully slow slide transitions. It will interrupt your flow and draw your listeners' attention away from your message.

When you have finished your presentation, there is one more very important step you must remember: Delete the file from the laptop you used. Your work is valuable intellectual property. You do not want it to fall into someone else's hands and allow them to claim the rights to it.

On some presentation software programs you cannot lock a file, as you can with many word processing documents. Delete that file from the hard drive to prevent someone from tampering with or modifying your creation.

On a related note, it is a good idea to copyright all your presentations. A simple © with your name or your company's name and the year will go a long way toward protecting your rights. It is also a good idea to file your written works with the copyright office at least once per quarter. Why leave things ambiguous and open the door for some unscrupulous soul to steal your hard work?

Hold the Presses

Human nature being what it is, there are occasions when your host organization will get last minute information to you and expect you to incorporate it into your slide show. One of the advantages of using presentation software is the ease with which you can add, subtract, or edit slides the morning of your talk.

I caution you not to rely on making these last minute edits. You should have everything ready to go well before the date of your speech. Just because you can insert "breaking news" right up to the last minute doesn't mean you should make a habit of it. I recommend having the final product finished well before zero hour so that you can rehearse effectively.

Yet there are times when such eleventh-hour adjustments are beneficial. To add new data to your slides, just edit them on your PC or pop open your laptop in your hotel room and get to work. Keep in mind, however, that you will also need to make the same changes to the hard copy you bring with you to the podium. You do not want to be surprised by your own slides. Also, remember to make fresh backup copies on both CD or key and floppy.

It is also a simple matter to change the order in which your slides appear. In most programs, you can use the slide sorter view to drag slides where you want them. You can even create new slides and insert them where desired. I will spare you the full and rather tedious details here. Suffice to say this is another facet you need to rehearse on your specific software package.

Build a Brand

Some presenters try to get by with a plain vanilla set of slides. Or, worse yet, they use one of the templates that comes with the software. Everyone in the audience has seen those humdrum bars and globes far too many times in other presentations.

It adds a lot in terms of consistency when the speaker takes the time to build a template that includes his company name and colors. It is also an easy matter to import your logo into your template. All you need to do is copy the graphic file into your master slide (hint: Usually this will be a .jpg, .gif, or .tif file extension).

It is easy to create a master slide, and it can be a real time saver. Once you design the master, you can use it in all your slide presentations. Simply create a title box that contains your logo, importing any graphic files, such as your logo. Then add in your company's name and web address if you wish. Avoid overloading this title or headline slide by keeping it to a maximum of two lines. Here, too, simple and elegant carries the day.

I use master slides regularly with presentation software. I have a template ready to go. This avoids wasting time creating a new look. Not only is it a real time saver, it keeps my brand consistent from speech to speech.

Building a master slide allows you to dictate which font style and size will appear on all your slides, and what background color you will use. You can even do things like insert footers, page numbers, date, and time.

What if you want to change the look of a single slide in a given presentation? No problem. Even if you create a master slide, you can still change individual slides manually whenever you want.

These techniques are not rocket science. However, it does take some time and elbow grease to make them second nature.

One client, a New York-based public relations agency, once sent me a presentation software deck that had a dark blue background on each slide.

They wanted to print the slides then copy them in black and white for distribution to an audience. But the only thing evident when they tried that was a huge ink blot with no words visible.

I suggested they simply use the slide master command to change the background color on every slide. There was no need to laboriously go through and alter each individual slide. That simple command solved their dilemma. The best part? When they called to thank me, they also booked me to lead a presentation skills workshop.

Stay Professional

Most people find it distracting when presenters use lots of bells and whistles in their slide presentations. I cannot stress enough the point that your audience comes to see you, not some overdone slide show with distracting sound effects, bizarre color schemes, amateurish-looking clip art, and slides that go flying every which way across the screen.

The majority of clip art that is available for free is worth exactly what you paid for it—nothing. If you absolutely need a graphic to demonstrate an idea, you are better off paying for it or having a graphic artist create it expressly for you. Those images of stick people scream out "unprofessional" when you use them.

If you are a clown interested only in entertaining a group of three-year-olds, loading up your slide deck with such effects might make sense. If you are a business executive attempting to persuade your audience or a non-profit leader trying to win over new donors, professionalism is important. Stay away from the whiz-bang special effects unless you are convinced they enhance your pitch.

The Creativity of Youth

You may at times feel as though your slides are too "plain vanilla." Look around you for help. Assistance may be as close as your son, daughter, niece, nephew, or the neighbor's kid.

Try this solution to add some sizzle to your slides: Ask a young person to enliven them. Many teenagers and pre-teens have a high degree of computer literacy. That adolescent who frowns every time you ask him to clean up his room may well light up when you pose this request. Enlist their creativity and talents.

One note of caution, however: You are the ultimate judge of what is appropriate for your presentation. Don't be carried away by certain elements of youthful exuberance like cool looking purple text on a black background, a clip from the latest hot music video, or certain sound effects related to bodily functions.

While youngsters can enhance the feel of your slides, it is your responsibility to ascertain that the package is suitable for a professional audience.

Know When to Hold 'em; Know When to Fold 'em

Here is a question that stumps many an individual: Why do you need to use slides during your entire presentation?

In many cases, you only need to reference them for part of your talk. When you must display something visually or graphically, or drive home a really important point in big, bold letters, slides make sense. But why keep them up there 100 percent of the time? It siphons attention away from you.

I make no bones about it. I want the audience's attention locked in on one place and one place only during my speech—me, me, me!

You can achieve this, for example, by beginning your talk with a darkened screen. Thirty seconds into your program, pop up a slide. After making some critical points, darken the screen once again. Using your slides with this strategic approach keeps your audience engaged and serves to capture their attention. And that is what you want: A crowd that is soaking up your viewpoint. So few speakers think of this, but it really is a way to show respect for your audience. Leaving slides up unnecessarily serves only to sidetrack their attention. Minimizing distractions makes it easy for them to internalize your message.

Change the pace of your presentation every now and then to keep your listeners more fully engaged. Discuss one slide for two minutes, briefly reference the next, then keep another up while you pursue a longer interactive discussion with audience members. Shaking things up in this way is vital to keeping interest levels high.

I encourage you to make a special note of this next fact and commit it to memory. Too few speakers realize that an easy way exists to disable the projector and get a black screen. Here's how.

When your slide show is running in many popular software packages, you can black out the screen by simply hitting the "B" key. Would you rather have a white screen? Hit the "W" key. To make your slides visible again, just hit the same key one more time—"B" for black, "W" for white. It is a simple toggle switch.

It amazes me that, given all the people who use presentation software, very few know this technique. I once led a workshop for several dozen account executives and supervisors at a public relations agency. The group included the rainmakers who pitched new accounts regularly. My goal was to teach them how to present themselves more effectively in such pitch situations.

They nearly always used presentation software when pursuing new clients. Yet, amazingly, not one person among them knew how to blacken the screen by using the "B" key trick. You should have seen the jaws drop when I demonstrated it. They looked at me as if I was Moses coming down from the mount with the Ten Commandments.

Out Go the Lights

If you speak often enough, something is going to go wrong. You may not have been a victim of the Summer 2003 blackout in the Northeast. But I can guarantee that if you present on a regular basis, the power will go out at some point. Or your laptop will freeze or the projector bulb will burn out. It is a matter of when, not if. That necessitates having a Plan B in your pocket.

When a noticeable failure occurs during your electronic presentation, you do need to acknowledge it since it will be clear to your audience that something has gone wrong. Assure them that you have the situation under control and that you are set to continue.

However, do not belabor the point. There is no need to apologize after every breath. Hey, a bulb burned out. It's not your fault. But it is your responsibility to hold up your end of the bargain and give your audience the performance they came to see.

How do you forge ahead? As I said earlier, it is important to have a hard copy of slides with your speaker notes at the ready. Move on. Don't waste your audience's valuable time trying to make repairs. Investigate quickly—once—and if the problem appears beyond your ability to solve within thirty seconds, continue with Plan B. Part of that fallback plan should include getting someone else to manage the repairs. And be sure to instruct them to do so out of sight of the audience. The last thing you want is the audience tittering as the technician curses out the projector while blocking their view of you.

It frightens some presenters when I tell them that something will go wrong at some point. Yes, it can be scary when such technical hiccups occur—if you fail to travel with a solid Plan B at the ready. Solid preparation keeps the demons at bay. So be prepared. Expect the unexpected. Keep your contingency plan in mind.

Be of good humor and realize that ninety-nine times out of 100 the audience wants to see you succeed and will cut you a lot of slack. Never let them see you sweat. If you stay cool, so will they.

Untangling Spaghetti

It can be intimidating. One glance at the spaghetti of wires you need to deal with when connecting your laptop to a projector is enough to strike fear into the most technical of hearts. Here are some suggestions to help you overcome this challenge.

Most of this goes back to Preparation 101. Talk to someone at the facility where you will speak well in advance of your speech. Do they have a projector? Do they (or you) need to rent one? Are there adequate power outlets in the room in which you will appear? Is there one near where your laptop will be resting?

I recommend you talk with someone who knows the technical set up of the room. Your initial contact there may not be intimately familiar with these matters; if you detect any hesitation in her voice, ask her who you should check with. You absolutely need answers to these questions in order to do the best job possible for her organization.

Then take some time to familiarize yourself with the specifics of the laptop you plan to use. Play around with it a bit. Here are some essentials you need to know:

- The location of the on/off switch. Don't laugh. If you are using someone else's laptop, this could stump you for a few moments;
- Where the power cord plugs in;
- The location of the CD, key, or floppy drive. Again, if you are using an unfamiliar laptop, you will need to load your presentation onto it;
- Where the cable to the projector connects;
- How to adjust screen brightness and contrast. If you are using the laptop's screen as your return monitor, you may need to fiddle with those settings;
- How to turn off your screen saver. Nothing says "I'm embarrassed" like some cute animations popping up on screen unexpectedly;
- How to arrange the power settings so your laptop doesn't go into sleep mode.

The day of your presentation, remember the cardinal rule of arriving at least one hour early. If you expect the set up to be complex (perhaps there will be multiple laptops if you are part of a panel), get there even earlier. You need to give yourself plenty of time to connect all the cables, scope out the power outlets, see if you will need an extension cord, give your laptop a test run, and acclimate yourself to your surroundings.

Travel with the basics. Beyond your laptop and its power cord, stuff an extension cord in your kit; the facility may not have one available or it may not be long enough for your needs. While you're at it, toss in a three-pronged adapter in case you find yourself in an antiquated facility that lacks proper electrical outlets. Include a cable that connects your laptop to the projector. Even if your contacts there have agreed to supply all this, things happen. They commit the gear to other rooms without thinking, or the equipment grows legs and walks away. Come with your own self-contained system.

Eyes on the Prize

You will notice we have been talking so far about what it takes to prepare your slide show. Now let us move on to some of the factors to consider when the spotlight shines on you.

The biggest downfall of speakers who use presentation software is poor eye contact.

Here is a question I hear a lot: When should I look at the screen and when should I look at the audience? The answer becomes obvious with a simple rephrasing of the question: Who do I need to connect with, the people who come to hear me or my slides?

I don't care what type of audio-visual tools you prefer—presentation software, 35-millimeter slides, overhead transparencies, or cardboard panels on an easel. You do not assume your position in the front of the room to teach or convince a screen, but to share with a group of people.

Your focus needs to be on the audience. Sure, you can look at the screen periodically and briefly when you want to emphasize a point on a slide. But return your eye contact to the audience quickly.

Novice and unprepared speakers do feel uncomfortable not checking the big screen all the time. Two things will help here. The first is our old friend, practice. The more you internalize, the better you will be able to verbalize without sneaking a peek at the screen.

The second method is to ensure you can see your slides on your laptop or, in a larger venue, on a return monitor (this is a separate screen set up to allow you to view the same thing your audience is seeing). I guarantee that you will see exactly the same thing as those in the crowd. This relieves you of having to turn around and look at the screen. Part of your preparation of the room involves placing your laptop or return monitor in a direct line of sight with your audience. That way, when you glance at that monitor, you can bring your eye contact back to the audience quickly and effortlessly.

Make it easy for the crowd to keep its focus on you and not on the slides. Do this by standing to the left of the screen as viewed by the audience. Positioning yourself on that side keeps the center of attention on you, and here's why. As we read, our natural tendency is to scan from left to right. When people read slides, their gaze will naturally return to you first if you stand on their left (the contrary rule applies if you are delivering a presentation in a language that reads from right to left; in that culture, stand to the right of the screen).

Also, ensure that everyone has a clear view of the screen. When you arrive at your venue, block your stage just as an actor would. Draw an imaginary line from the seat at your extreme right to the closest edge of the screen. When you cross that line, be conscious of the fact that you will be obstructing the view of the individual in that chair. If you need a helpful reminder, place a strip of masking tape on the floor as a mark.

There may be times when the room set up forces you to block that person's view. If possible, rearrange the seating or at least remove that chair so no one has to crane his neck to see your slides.

Lights and Lasers

You may need to darken the front of the room to show your slides. If so, make sure the light remains sufficient to illuminate you. In a larger hall, have a spotlight follow you or point to front center stage. In a smaller room, keep at least one bank of lights on toward the front but not shining on the screen. When audience members lose track of you, their interest wanes. Plus, a darkened room provides a cozy atmosphere for a nap.

Let us talk for a moment about laser pointers. Personally, I don't have much use for them. They can distract both the audience and the speaker. But, as with so many presentation niceties, a laser pointer is a matter of personal preference.

If you decide to use one, employ it sparingly. There are few things more disconcerting than a presenter who paints the screen with that annoying red dot. Or someone who highlights the wrong part of his slide. Or the individual who belies his nervousness by trying to keep the laser motionless on one spot, only to have it bob up and down like a plane going through a thunderstorm because his hands are so shaky.

This tool can get downright dangerous. I once witnessed a doctor who was unsure of how to use his laser. He proceeded to point it the wrong way, nearly blinding an audience member or two. The worst part was, had he zapped someone's eye, he wasn't even an ophthalmologist.

Conduct a Tech Run-Through

Despite your best preparations, never leave anything to chance the day of your speech. Yes, you have practiced with your laptop as part of your preparation phase, timing your presentation and rehearsing your slide transitions (by the way, this need for practice also applies if you use a slide carousel or overhead transparencies).

Familiarize yourself with your equipment beforehand in order to avoid technical snafus. Nothing says "incompetent bozo" to an audience more emphatically than a speaker who begins a talk by fumbling with the remote and displaying no idea how to work the controls.

There is simply no way to tell how the room is going to "behave" when showtime arrives unless you give it a test drive. Once you have completed connecting all the wires, it is time for your tech run-through. I suggest you enlist a trusted colleague to monitor this from the audience's perspective. Make sure there is one other person in the room, too—the individual responsible for managing the audio and video during your presentation. He needs to be ready to fix anything that goes haywire. In addition, it is a good idea to clue him in to your preferences.

Here is what you need to check carefully:

- Your slides appear on the screen
- The focus is clear
- The image is not crooked, too high, or too low
- The remote control device works properly
- The lighting is bright over the audience and dim near the screen
- Your microphone works
- The audio in the room is neither too loud nor too soft
- There are no audio dead spots that will reduce the attention span of the audience in that section

A word about remote control devices: You need to know where to aim your remote control device if one is available. There are many different models, so if you don't travel with your own, be sure you take a few moments to learn how to use the one supplied. Take a few moments to figure out if you can go back one slide or jump to another slide elsewhere in your deck.

Also, if someone is using a remote control in an adjacent room, your slide show may act as if possessed. Why? Your laptop can receive signals from their remote control device if it operates on the same frequency. The solution in this case is to unplug the key that receives the signal from the back of your laptop, then advance your slides using the keyboard.

Don't Overload Your Circuits

There is a lot to learn when it comes to using presentation software like a pro. As with any endeavor, start with the basics and build from there.

Acquaint yourself, for example, with developing the template you want. Once you get comfortable with that aspect, work on utilizing some of the shortcuts outlined in this chapter. Then continue to build your skills over time.

Here is the bottom line:

- Use your slides to strengthen your presentation;
- Make them easy for the audience to see;
- Avoid busy, dense slides;
- Keep your text crisp, with only three to four bullet points per slide;
- Avoid overuse of animation and sound effects.

These presentation software programs are good tools, but it is important to remember that your audience is there to see you. Bear in mind these key facts:

- They come to hear your opinion, gain your wisdom, or be entertained by you;
- None of us attends presentations because we have heard rumors the speaker has cool slides;
- As a presenter, you have a responsibility to make a conscious decision whether or not presentation software slides will enhance your remarks or detract from them.

When all is said and done in the world of presentation software, simple and elegant wins the day.

CHAPTER ELEVEN

CREATE YOUR OWN LIFELONG LEARNING PLAN

THE THREE KEYS TO CHAPTER ELEVEN

You can expect to learn the truth about the crucial role lifelong learning plays in sharpening your communications edge:

- Why a follow-up plan spelling out your lifelong learning objectives will put you miles ahead of run-of-the-mill speakers;

- How to start creating a lifelong learning plan that makes sense for you;

- What resources are most effective as you strive to improve your public speaking skills.

THE THREE KEYS TO GREAT PRESENTATIONS—Preparation, Performance, and Assessing Feedback—can go a long way toward sharpening your public speaking edge, if you let them.

In the final analysis, how much you improve—indeed, if you improve—is up to you. This is one of the essential and all-too-often ignored truths about public speaking.

Failing to Learn

Let me once again be blunt. Too many professionals fail to commit to developing their speaking skills on an ongoing basis. In fact, if the percentages I have observed over the years hold true, you yourself are likely to put this book down and do little else to enrich your presentation skills in coming months.

People are under the impression that reading a book or participating in a public speaking workshop is an end in and of itself. Can those steps help? Certainly. Will they contribute toward making you a better presenter? Sure.

But let me be up front: I cannot lay my hands on you and bless you with all the knowledge and skills you will need, even in an intensive and personalized full day workshop. It is a good start, but it is merely a single step on a journey.

Attending a workshop can make you better incrementally. The practice helps, as does the opportunity to learn some of the whys and wherefores behind public speaking. But real improvement comes only with practice, experience, commitment, and expert guidance.

You're in It for the Long Haul

That is why it is essential that you invest in your own personal plan for improvement. It is an integral part of any true learning experience.

If you commit to diligently following your lifelong learning plan, you will be miles ahead of most other presenters. How do I know this? Let me tell you a little secret from the front lines of the communications training skirmishes.

Very few speakers express an interest in moving beyond their workshop without some prodding. They walk in the door thinking their heads will be crammed full of every bit of knowledge they need, then walk out boasting they have been "trained" as if sanctified by a magic wand.

If someone ever brags to you that they have been "trained to speak in public," you are likely face-to-face with an individual who lacks commitment to lifelong learning. In the final analysis, this person is not likely to be a good speaker because the flame of improvement fails to burn within him.

If, on the other hand, he tells you that he participated in a public speaking workshop, consults with his coach regularly, and refers you to a helpful article he just read, you are in the presence of someone who is on the right track toward becoming a great presenter.

The Benefits of Lifelong Learning

Lifelong learning involves a constant commitment to your personal education. If I can instill you with one value as a result of reading this book, let it be this: You will commit right here and now to search for a system that will serve you well in months, years, and decades to come.

Develop a system of learning through your personal experiences as well as through reading, observing, and listening. Keep your mind open to those learning moments that spring up at the most unexpected times and places. Perhaps you happen upon an article that strikes you as particularly insightful. You may attend a presentation from which you can take a tip or two. Or you might gain an idea on the spur of the moment from a colleague. Such instances will crop up as you walk through life. Be attuned to them.

Watch other presenters, not with the intent to mimic their good qualities, but with the curiosity that will aid your lifelong learning by noting their positives as well as their gaffes.

You are quite likely to need a coach to help set you on the right path, one who can offer you regular check ups to ensure you are achieving the progress you want to attain. You should, in concert with your coach, decide what your benchmarks are. Improvement means different things to different people. You may want to scale the heights and capture the ability to address thousands in a convention hall. Or you may need to simply get better when delivering a chalk talk to half a dozen co-workers.

You are in school for the rest of your life: Public speaking school. This educational institution is one without walls, without report cards, and without grades. You have the benefit of being able to spend your time learning whatever you want to learn whenever you want to learn it and at whatever pace you choose. Think how overjoyed we would have been to have such possibilities as high schoolers!

Dedicate time to learning what you need to walk tall down your chosen path, whether that be a better job, a shinier public image for your company, higher status as a community leader, success in winning elective office, or any other goal that is important to you.

Create Your Own Solution

Commit to curiosity. Read the great speeches from history. Ask questions of leading coaches and read what they have to say.

One note of caution: Be sure that you carefully vet your sources. There is a lot of bad advice out there, especially online, but also in books and articles. Lifelong learning involves understanding how to separate gold from fool's gold.

A high level of expertise is a must in choosing the right advisor. But don't neglect the intangible "right fit." You are seeking to build a long-term relationship based on trust. Make sure it feels right to you.

If you are looking for direction, I encourage you to start at www.barkscomm.com, where we make it a point to post lots of fresh information for free. Plus, you can get in touch with me easily via e-mail through the site.

When it comes time for you to seek out your communications coach, remember to reference Appendix C, "Securing Expert Advice." It contains a list of twenty questions designed to help you narrow your search for the coach who best suits your individual needs.

Your Next Steps

I want you to commit to taking two "next steps" if you truly want to sharpen your public speaking edge.

The first is a psychological step: Promise yourself that you will take one action each day, week, or month (the choice of frequency is yours depending on the path you have mapped out with your coach) that will move you farther along the path toward improvement as a speaker.

Some learners maximize their wisdom by reading books. Others learn better and faster by listening to audio CDs. A number of us prefer to dial direct and have no problem calling an expert coach to bounce ideas around, while some prefer e-mail. Figure out what works best for you. Mix it up if you like. Read an article on Monday, listen to an audio CD on Wednesday, schedule your next review with your coach on Friday, and settle down with a good book over the weekend.

The second commitment I want you to make is tactical: Keep this book as a lifelong learning resource. Similar to a training workshop, just because you have read it once does not mean you have internalized all the value.

Here are some hints to help you continue on the path to lifelong learning:

- Refer frequently to the ideas you have read about here;
- Review the three keys at the beginning of each chapter to refresh your knowledge;
- Sign up for my free *Personal Trainer* e-zine when you visit www.barkscomm.com;
- Watch other speakers with a critical eye;
- Channel surf over to C-SPAN to monitor high-profile speakers;
- Take advantage of the publications and audio CDs in the Barks Learning Network at www.barkscomm.com/products.

The bottom line is there are plenty of ways to follow through on your commitment to lifelong learning if you want to become a better presenter.

I began by emphasizing that if you aspire to anything beyond ordinary in your professional or personal life, you need solid presentation skills.

My hope is that I have formed a foundation upon which you can build the platform to capture that promotion at work, win that new client, and gain respect in the eyes of your peers.

Unlock the truth about public speaking. Make it your goal to seize possession of the Three Keys to Great Presentations.

APPENDIX A

PRESENTATION INFORMATION FORM

Today's date: _____

LOGISTICS

Name of organization: _____

Contact person and title: _____

Address: _____

Phone: _____ Fax: _____

E-mail: _____

Web site: _____

Name of meeting: _____

Date of speech: _____ Time (begin and end): _____

City: _____

Specific location: _____

_____

Dress code (Business attire? Casual?): _____

Will there be a social event beforehand to get to know audience members?

_____

Will the speech be open to the public and media? _____

If so, which reporters do you expect to attend? _____

_____

_____

_____

How is the event advertised and promoted? _____

_____

Will the host organization be doing any publicity? If so, give specifics:

_____

_____

_____

Do you object to me doing publicity for my purposes? _____

Fee or Honoraria? _____ Amount? _____

Will host organization direct bill airfare and hotel? _____

Name and address for billing purposes?

_____

_____

_____

Names and phones/e-mails for people to contact for background:

1) _____

2) _____

3) _____

4) _____

5) _____

Are there any other seminars running the same time as mine? _____

If so, who and on what topic(s)? _____

_____

_____

_____

Who spoke at your last meeting? _____

_____

_____

_____

Who will speak next time? _____

_____

_____

MESSAGE

Presentation topic: _____

Length of speech: _____ Q&A afterward? _____

Am I the main speaker? _____ Or part of a panel? _____

If panel, who are the other panelists (names, affiliations, titles, URLs)?

_____

_____

_____

What are the audience's basic concerns? _____

_____

_____

What benefits does the organization want audience members to take away?

_____

_____

Name and contact information of person introducing you (attach his/her bio):

_____

_____

Any key audience members you should acknowledge? _____

_____

_____

Will remarks be full text _____ Talking points _____

Outline _____ Extemporaneous _____

Overheads _____ Presentation software _____

AUDIENCE PROFILE

Who is the primary audience? Business_____ Association_____ Non-profit_____

C-level? VPs? Managers? PR officers? _____

What is the audience's level of sophistication? High___ Medium___ Low___

How many people are expected to attend? _____

Are spouses invited?_____ My spouse?_____

Who are the troublemakers in the audience? _____

_____

_____

Will organization fax you an agenda? _____

Will organization fax you an attendance list? _____

What type of training holds the most interest for them?

    Media _____ Presentation skills _____ Testimony _____

MISCELLANEOUS

Does site have all needed technical requirements?

Projector for software presentation _____ Overhead projector _____

Flip chart (blank paper and markers) _____ Wireless mic _____

Will organization copy any handouts or do I need to do? _____

Do they need photo? _____ E-mail photo to: _____

Special meal requirements? _____

Notes: _____

_____

_____

_____

_____

_____

APPENDIX B

Taking Inventory

WE ALL HOLD INHERENT STRENGTHS AND WEAKNESSES when it comes to communicating in public. That is the essence of Winning the Communications Trifecta through effective use of your Video Tools, Audio Tools, and Message Tools. The key to improving your abilities lies in utilizing strengths to the maximum and keeping vulnerabilities to a minimum. In other words, accentuate the positive.

This handy checklist serves as a guide to your nonverbal choices. It is designed to remind you which items in your Video group and your Audio group are strengths that you need to **maintain**, and which are challenges you may wish to **sharpen** over time.

You have two choices with the keys that you place on your **sharpen** list: 1) work to transform them from liabilities to assets or 2) minimize their use in favor of other keys when you communicate with your audiences.

Video Tools
⇨ **A**ction
⇨ **F**acial expression
⇨ **E**ye contact
⇨ **W**ardrobe
⇨ **P**rops

Audio Tools
⇨ **P**itch
⇨ **A**rticulation
⇨ **V**olume
⇨ **E**motion
⇨ **R**ate

APPENDIX C

SECURING EXPERT ADVICE

YOU HAVE LIKELY HEARD THE OLD PROVERB, "He that is his own lawyer has a fool for a client." It also holds true when you seek to sharpen your communications edge. Most people—even top-notch communicators—do not know what to look for without an expert's guidance.

When the stakes get high, you need to locate an experienced communications trainer who can chart a course for your continued improvement when you deliver presentations and deal with reporters. I suggest you use the following questions to select a trainer who is right for you:

1. *Do you focus exclusively on communications training?* Don't get stuck with a "trainer" who accepts any type of business that happens along.

2. *How much experience do you have as a trainer?* A quality training demands knowledge gained over time. Ask how long your coach has specialized in communications training specifically, and how many people he has taught.

3. *Will you custom tailor a workshop specifically to meet my needs?* Everyone claims they customize their trainings, but not all do, particularly some of the big "assembly line" firms. Don't be trapped by a cookie-cutter approach.

4. *Are you easy to work with, or are you overly demanding of your clients?* Find a professional who believes in service.

5. *Are you flexible enough to accommodate some eleventh hour fine-tuning?* Communicating in public is a dynamic endeavor. Your trainer needs to be able to accommodate a few last minute refinements.

6. *What is your web site address?* Be sure to look for signs indicating how often the site is updated.

7. *What type of clients do you work with?* If you work for a Fortune 500 company, you do not want to rely on someone whose experience revolves around local non-profits.

8. *Have you developed flexible training modules?* A media training for someone who is going to undertake a television satellite media tour, for example, should contain different learning exercises than one for an individual approaching the trade press.

9. *Have you worked in a newsroom?* Ask this question if you are seeking media training. Reporters think differently than other folks. Your trainer needs to know first-hand the pulse of a newsroom.

10. *Are you an accomplished speaker?* Ask this question if you are looking for presentation skills training. Those who can, do. Those who can't, teach. Find a pro who knows what it is like in the speaking trenches.

11. *Are you skilled at message development?* A message is much more complex than just stringing together a hodgepodge of facts.

12. *Who will lead my training?* Some big outfits try to substitute junior assistants for more experienced hands.

13. *Does your trainer have the ability to serve as a speaker for a separate session?* Ask this question if your training occurs in conjunction with a larger meeting. This saves you money you would otherwise need to spend paying other speakers and their additional travel expenses.

14. *What books and articles have you written?* Thought leaders in any field should be published regularly.

15. *What type of experiential exercises do you utilize?* Make sure he videotapes each exercise and gives you the videotape; it is a great learning tool.

16. *Do you offer a training guide for each participant?* Nearly every trainer has a guide, but many are little more than a few quick copy pages stapled together. Insist on a real publication that will extend your lifelong learning beyond the day of your workshop.

17. *Will I see you after my workshop is done, or are you here today, gone tomorrow?* Even the best training can only point you in the proper direction. I urge you to develop a relationship with your trainer that will lead to lifelong learning.

18. *Do you offer a reduced rate if I sign a contract for multiple trainings?* You deserve a reward when you buy in volume.

19. *Do you believe in integrating fun into your workshops?* A deadly dull lecture will not further your learning curve.

20. *To which professional societies do you belong?* This should give you some insights into whether your trainer is keeping up to date with the latest communications training advances.

This handful of questions should help you select the experienced communications trainer who is right for you.

APPENDIX D

HAVE YOU EVER WONDERED HOW A FEW SIMPLE key strokes could sharpen your presentation software performance? Try these mouse-free commands during your next presentation.

COMMAND	KEYSTROKE
Launch a new presentation	Ctrl + N
Open your presentation	Ctrl + O
Insert new slide	Ctrl + M
Save your current presentation	Ctrl + S
Save as a new file	F12
Spell check	F7
Print	Ctrl + P
Help	F1
Find text	Ctrl + F
Select all text in a text box	Ctrl + A
Copy text	Ctrl + C
Cut text	Ctrl + X
Paste text	Ctrl + V
Bold	Ctrl + B
Italic	Ctrl + I
Underline	Ctrl + U
Create a larger font	Ctrl + Shift + >
Create a smaller font	Ctrl + Shift + <
Undo your last command	Ctrl + Z
Begin your slide show	F5

The following commands work only when your slide show is running:

Next slide	Enter or PgDn or down arrow or right arrow
Previous slide	Backspace or PgUp or up arrow or left arrow
Go to a particular slide	Slide number followed by Enter
Black screen	B
White screen	W
End your slide show	Esc

Mac users can make use of many of the same shortcuts by using the Apple key instead of Ctrl.

APPENDIX E

SPEAKER EVALUATION FORM

YOUR PARTICIPATION WILL ALLOW ME TO DO an even better job next time. Please take a few moments to complete your evaluation, making your comments as specific as possible. Thank you!

Organization: _____

Today's date: _____

1. Tell us about two or three important benefits you gained:

   _____

   _____

   _____

2. Did Ed have command of the necessary background information about your organization and its issues? _____

   _____

3. What did you think about the effectiveness of Ed's delivery? (Please add your comments below.)

   ____ He developed a real rapport; I feel like I could talk to him any time.

   ____ He kept me mentally engaged and on topic most of the time.

   ____ My mind wandered on occasion.

   ____ What a cold fish.

4. What portions of the workshop were most useful?

   _____

   _____

   _____

5. Which portions can Ed leave out next time?

_____

_____

_____

6. If time had allowed, what other areas would you like Ed to have covered?

_____

_____

7. I would consider bringing Ed back to speak to us:

____ Tomorrow ____ Maybe next month ____ Don't call us; we'll call you

Additional comments: _____

_____

_____

_____

____ Yes! I want to continue to learn from Ed. Sign me up as a subscriber to his free *Personal Trainer* e-zine. I understand that you will not share my e-mail address with anyone, anywhere, anytime. Please print clearly.

Name: _____

E-mail address: _____

Do we have your permission to share your comments with others in our marketing materials and on our Barkscomm.com web site? ____ Yes ____ No

APPENDIX F

RECOMMENDED RESOURCES

BABER, ANNE AND LYNNE WAYMON. *Make Your Contacts Count.* New York: AMACOM, 2002. *Sound advice specific to putting your best foot forward when networking.*

DAVIDSON, JEFF. *The Complete Guide to Public Speaking.* Hoboken, New Jersey: John Wiley & Sons, Inc., 2003. *If your goal is to become a professional speaker, this comprehensive manual deals with everything from marketing to contracts.*

EKMAN, PAUL. *Emotions Revealed.* New York: Times Books, 2003. *Ekman is one of the world's leading researchers into facial expressions.*

EKMAN, PAUL. *Telling Lies: Clues to Deceit in the Marketplace, Politics, and Marriage.* New York: W.W. Norton, 1992. *An earlier Ekman work offering insights into nonverbal communication.*

KISER, A. GLENN. *Masterful Facilitation: Becoming a Catalyst for Meaningful Change.* New York: AMACOM, 1998. *Packed with techniques for those who lead messaging discussions.*

KNAPP, MARK L., AND JUDITH A. HALL. *Nonverbal Communication in Human Interaction.* Thomson Learning, Inc., 2002. *A thoroughly sourced review of writings on nonverbal topics, tending toward a psychological and academic tone.*

LIPMAN, DOUG. *Improving Your Storytelling.* Little Rock, Arkansas: August House, Inc., 1999. *A concise "how to" guide that helps you build and deliver your stories.*

MACKAY, HARVEY. *Dig Your Well Before You're Thirsty.* New York: Doubleday, 1997. *Networker extraordinaire Mackay shares tips and stories gleaned from a lifetime of meeting, greeting, and selling.*

MEHRABIAN, ALBERT. *Nonverbal Communication.* Chicago: Aldine-Atherton, 1972. *The seminal research on how people receive your nonverbal signals.*

MEHRABIAN, ALBERT. *Silent Messages.* Belmont, California: Wadsworth Publishing Company, Inc., 1981, 1971. *This scholar's first book on nonverbal signals contains some interesting findings, but has nowhere near the systematic research as his 1972 work listed above.*

MONTOYA, PETER. *The Brand Called You.* Personal Branding Press, 2002. *Some of Montoya's ideas about consistency can prove handy when you consider how to develop a consistent message.*

MORRISON, TERRI. *Kiss, Bow, or Shake Hands: How to Do Business in Sixty Countries.* Holbrook, Mass.: B. Adams, 1994. *Excellent views into the customs and nonverbal styles of business people in other nations.*

SAFIRE, WILLIAM. *Lend Me Your Ears: Great Speeches in History.* New York: W.W. Norton & Company, Inc., 1997. *An indispensable compendium of debates, political speeches, patriotic addresses, lectures, sermons, and more.*

SMITH, BENSON AND TONY RUTIGLIANO. *Discover Your Sales Strengths.* New York: Warner Books, Inc., 2003. *The authors challenge much of the conventional wisdom about sales presentations and about boosting your talents, then back up their contentions with solid research from the Gallup organization.*

WILLIAMS, PAT. *The Paradox of Power.* New York: Warner Books, 2002. *Drawing on his personal experiences and historical figures, Williams offers lessons in leadership.*

ARTICLES AND NEWSLETTERS

ANTION, TOM. "Great Speaking E-zine." Sign up for your free subscription at www.antion.com/index.html.

BYRNE, DONN AND JEFFREY FISHER, JD. (1975). "Too Close for Comfort: Sex Differences in Response to Invasions of Personal Space." *Journal of Personality and Social Psychology*, 32, 15–20.]

CONNOLLY, REG. "The NLP Eye Accessing Cues," *The Pegasus NLP Newsletter*, Issue 09–4, January 2002.

HOTT, RACHEL, PHD. "Let Me Look Into Your Eyes: Eye-Accessing Cues," *Anchor Point Magazine*, Vol. 4, No. 1, January 1990.

KONOPACKI, ALLEN. "Making Eye Contact." www.tradeshowresearch.com/mec.pdf.

MORGAN, NICK. "The Truth Behind the Smile and Other Myths," *Harvard Management Communication Letter*, Vol. 5, No. 8, August 2002.

OESTREICH, HERB. "Let's Dump the 55%, 38%, 7% Rule," *Transitions*, (National Transit Institute), Vol. 7, No. 2, 1999, pp. 11–14.

PRESENTATIONS MAGAZINE. www.presentations.com.

ORGANIZATIONS

AMERICAN SOCIETY FOR TRAINING AND DEVELOPMENT
1640 King Street
Box 1443
Alexandria, Virginia 22313
(703) 683-8100
www.astd.org

C-SPAN
400 North Capitol Street, NW
Suite 650
Washington, D.C. 20001
(202) 737-3220
www.c-span.org

INTERNATIONAL ASSOCIATION
OF BUSINESS COMMUNICATORS
One Hallidie Plaza
Suite 600
San Francisco, California 94102
(415) 544-4700
www.iabc.com

MEETING PROFESSIONALS
INTERNATIONAL
4455 LBJ Freeway
Suite 1200
Dallas, Texas 75244
(972) 702-3000
www.mpiweb.org

NATIONAL PRESS CLUB
529 14th Street NW
13th Floor
Washington, D.C. 20045
(202) 662-7500
http://npc.press.org

NATIONAL SPEAKERS
ASSOCIATION
1500 S. Priest Drive
Tempe, Arizona 85281
(480) 968-2552
www.nsaspeaker.org

PUBLIC RELATIONS SOCIETY
OF AMERICA
33 Maiden Lane
11th Floor
New York, New York 10038
(212) 460-1400
www.prsa.org

WEB SITES

BARTLEBY. WWW.BARTLEBY.COM. *The long-time web gold standard for famous quotations.*

BIOGRAPHICAL DICTIONARY. WWW.S9.COM/BIOGRAPHY. *When you need the lowdown on a famous individual, this is your source.*

C-SPAN. WWW.C-SPAN.ORG. *A rich treasury of speeches, news conferences, Congressional hearings, and other forums. This is one of the best methods for observing how other speakers practice their craft.*

PAUL EKMAN'S WEB SITE. WWW.PAULEKMAN.COM. *One of the leading researchers into facial expressions offers articles and other resources.*

FEDERAL AVIATION ADMINISTRATION (FAA). WWW.FLY.FAA.GOV/FLY FAA/NEMAP.JSP. *Will that flight to your next speaking engagement be delayed? The FAA's Air Traffic Control System Command Center will tell you.*

GALLUP MANAGEMENT JOURNAL. HTTP://GMJ.GALLUP.COM. *This organization, well known for its Gallup Polls, leads the way in urging leaders to do first what they do best.*

HISTORY CHANNEL. WWW.HISTORYCHANNEL.COM. *Incorporate what happened on this day in history into your presentation.*

ALBERT MEHRABIAN'S WEB SITE. WWW.KAAJ.COM/PSYCH. *Mehrabian is widely credited with bringing "body language" into the realm of serious studies. His web presence includes links to books and articles by him and others.*

QUOTELAND.COM. WWW.QUOTELAND.COM. *This site arranges quotations neatly by topic.*

SPEECHBOT. HTTP://SPEECHBOT.RESEARCH.COMPAQ.COM. *A very cool site that uses voice recognition technology to allow you to locate audio from leading radio and TV talk shows.*

TOASTMASTERS INTERNATIONAL: WWW.TOASTMASTERS.ORG. *Click on the "Find a Club" link to locate a chapter in your area. Be aware that the information offered is scant. You will need to spend some time e-mailing or calling to determine which club is appropriate for your level of experience.*

INDEX

ABOUT THE AUTHOR

Eᴅ Bᴀʀᴋꜱ ɪꜱ ᴀ ᴛʀᴀɪɴᴇʀ, ᴀᴜᴛʜᴏʀ, ᴀɴᴅ ꜱᴘᴇᴀᴋᴇʀ who teaches today's leaders how to deliver dynamic, message-packed presentations.

More than 2000 business leaders, government officials, non-profit leaders, physicians, athletes, association executives, entertainers, and public relations staff have earned the benefits of a sharper message and enhanced communications skills thanks to participation in Ed's workshops.

His clients say he "knows how to elicit peak performance." They call him "a master at connecting with his audience" and "an effective educator," and give his public speaking workshops "two thumbs up!"

A dedicated writer, Ed has published numerous training guides, articles, and audio resources. He even offers a free subscription to his *Personal Trainer* e-newsletter at www.barkscomm.com.

He has served as President of Barks Communications since its inception in 1997. Prior to that, Ed gained his expertise in the nation's capital where, since 1986, he has directed public relations, speechwriting, and speakers bureaus for a number of organizations. He perfected his speaking talents during his 10-year tenure as a radio broadcaster.

Ed lives in the Washington, D.C., area with his wife, Celeste, and daughter, Polly.

You can contact ED BARKS directly at:

ED BARKS

Barks Communications
102 Blue Ridge Street
Berryville, Virginia 22611

(540) 955-0600
www.edbarks.com
www.barkscomm.com
ebarks@barkscomm.com

If you would like to arrange a speaking engagement for
Ed Barks, please contact Celeste Heath at (540) 955-0600 or
celeste@barkscomm.com, or fax your request to (540) 955-1038.

ORDER FORM

To order additional resources from the Barks Learning Network, fill out this form and mail to:

Ogmios Publishing, P.O. Box 132, Berryville, VA 22611.

You may also order on our secure online server at:

www.barkscomm.com/products.

PRODUCT	PRICE	QUANTITY	TOTAL PRICE
BOOK: *The Truth About Public Speaking: The Three Keys to Great Presentations*	$24.95	X _____	$ _____
Training Guide: *Keep the Audience on Your Side: The Public Speaking Companion*	$12.95	X _____	$ _____
Training Guide: *Face the Press with Confidence: The Media Interview Companion*	$12.95	X _____	$ _____
Audio CD: The Three Keys to Great Presentations	$19.95	X _____	$ _____
Audio CD: Do You Really Need Your Laptop for a Power Packed Presentation?	$19.95	X _____	$ _____
Booklet: Winning at the Witness Table: 60 Tips to Terrific Testimony	$15.95	X _____	$ _____

Product Total $ _____

Virginia residents add 4.5% VA Sales Tax $ _____

Shipping Method:

Priority Mail

    U.S.: $4.00 for first product and $2.00 for each additional product. $ _____

    International: $9.00 for first product; $5.00 for each additional product. $ _____

Fed Ex Overnight

    U.S.: $16.00 for first product and $4.00 for each additional product. $ _____

    International: Overnight shipping not available.

Grand Total $ _____

Full Name: _____

Company: _____

Day Phone: _____

E-mail: _____

Address 1: _____

Address 2: _____

City: _____

State/Province/County: _____

Postal/Zip Code: _____ Country: _____

Please enclose a check payable to Ogmios Publishing or provide credit card information below:

Name on Card: _____

Card Type: ❏ Visa ❏ MasterCard ❏ American Express ❏ Discover

Card Number: _____

Expire Date: Month: _____ Year: _____

I authorize Ogmios Publishing to charge my credit card for the above total.

I further affirm that the name and personal information provided on this form are true and correct.

Signature: _____